SHIMMERING SPOKES

ONE AUSTRALIAN'S 16 000KM ODYSSEY

D0229853

richard allen

NEW HOLLAND

First published in Australia in 1999 by
New Holland Publishers (Australia) Pty Ltd
Sydney • Auckland • London • Cape Town

14 Aquatic Drive Frenchs Forest NSW 2086 Australia

218 Lake Road Northcote Auckland New Zealand

24 Nutford Place London W1H 6DQ United Kingdom

80 McKenzie Street Cape Town 8001 South Africa

Copyright © 1999 in text: Richard Allen
Copyright © 1999 in maps: New Holland Publishers (Australia) Pty Ltd
Copyright © 1999 in photographs: Richard Allen

All rights reserved. No part of this publication may be reproduced, stored in
a retrieval system or transmitted, in any form or by any means, electronic,
mechanical, photocopying, recording or otherwise, without the prior written
permission of the publishers and copyright holders.

National Library of Australia Cataloguing-in-Publication Data:

Allen, Richard, 1963-
   Shimmering spokes.

ISBN 1 86436 521 8

1. Allen, Richard, 1963—Journeys—Australia. 2. Bicycle touring—Australia.
3. Fund raising—Australia. 4. Australia—Description and travel. I. Title

796.640994

Commissioning Editor: Anouska Good
Project Editor: Monica Ban
Designer: Roula Doulas
Artwork: Guy Holt
Reproduction: DNL Resources Pty Ltd
Typeset by: Midland Typesetters
Printer: Griffin Press

Acknowledgements

Sincerest thanks go to Cycle Against Cancer's principal sponsors: Coles Supermarkets, Macquarie Bank, GigaNet, Best Western Hotels & Inns, Custom Fleet and Lions Clubs.

Thanks also to other companies who provided goods and/ or services, including: Compaq, Avanti, Jayco, Groupe Sportif, K-Mart, Grey Advertising, Exhibitors Craft, Telstra, Kodak, Rosenbluth International, Echo Beach Resort and the many companies and entertainers that helped with launch parties in Melbourne and Sydney.

I am indebted to the core to the following people for accompanying me on the ride, either cycling or driving the support car. They are, in order of appearance: Jenny Allen, James Freemantle, Juliet Allen, Kurt van Wijck, Richard Fraser Allen, Steve Norris, Catherine Macmillan, Geordie Hall, Abbie Hall, Ian Louis, Roy Wiedemeyer, Rose Snell, Sandy Fairthorne, Emma Taylor, Rob Magnusson, Caroline Walford, Harriet Cameron, Eliza Cameron, Hugh Cameron, Andrew Mackinnon, Emma Eade, Nick Jones, Robert Joyce, John Joyce, Eric Graham, Margie Mort, Richard Stanley Allen, Jean Allen, Charlie Happell, Jen Rayment, Josephine Vanderweide, David Lowe, Kate Murray, Heather Le Roy, Tooey Morgan, Kurt Esser.

Thanks to the following for their help: Rob and Linda Brown, Caroline Ennels, Belinda Byrne, Chris Haslam, Michael Traill, Neil Watson, Rob Sitch, Jessica Rowe, Justin Miller, Petrina Lie, Michael Venus, Brooke McLachlan, Lucy Carruthers, Georgia Rasmussen, Kellie Holland, Lisa Smith, Roger Chomley, Anthony Castellaro, Marcella Pancia, Andrew and Vicky Rouse, Tessa Richards, Penny Richards, Susannah Gibson, Deb Nelson, Alex Warner, Huy Nguyen, Jonathan

Buckley, Anne Morrison, Nigel Onley, Pat Andrews, Jo Symonds, Diane Raymond, Susan Santella, Fiona McLachlan, Neil Melville, Bo Maslen, Beverley Geddes, Roger Geddes, Mervyn Lawson, Jan Hamilton, Narelle and Ross Gibson, Peter Crisp, Sandy Crisp, George and Georgie Reid, Richo and Lisa Allen, Elaine and Michael McKeon, Kevin Quirk, Mick Breen, Duncan Hall, Richard Smithers, Will Lester, Ian Darling, Tim Richardson and the staff at the state Cancer Councils.

A warm thankyou to: Fiona Inglis from literary agents Curtis Brown who demonstrated formidable resolve; Averill Chase, Anouska Good and Monica Ban from New Holland Publishers; Emma Eade for her determination, encouragement and companionship; and to Jane Cotter for her wise counsel and friendship. Any factual errors in this book are entirely mine.

Thankyou to the many schools who rode and raised funds for cancer research.

And finally, a special thanks to the companies and individuals who have donated so generously.

To Anne Elisabeth Syme Allen, my mother, a reader

Contents

Man's real home is not a house, but the Road . . .
Bruce Chatwin: *What Am I Doing Here*

RICHARD'S 16 000KM ODYSSEY

A Billion Chinese

'Twas Mulga Bill, from Eaglehawk, that caught the cycling craze;
He turned away the good old horse that served him many days;
He dressed himself in cycling clothes, resplendent to be seen;
He hurried off to town and bought a shining new machine,
And as he wheeled it through the door, with an air of lordly pride,
The grinning shop assistant said, 'Excuse me, can you ride?'

AB 'Banjo' Paterson

Pain, some long-distance athletes are fond of saying, is an opinion. The theory says that if, when completing an endurance event, you can somehow convince yourself that you are lying on a Phuket beach peeling prawns then your quest becomes easy. If you *cannot* convince yourself of this, then you will probably suffer a lot. Sports psychologists call it mind over matter. Others call it a lie.

As an Australian male brought up on simple values, I have never been much good at convincing myself of anything other than what is immediately apparent. Pain, for me, is as much a reality as, say, KFC or dandruff. You can't wish it away, just like you can't convince yourself that the sky is green or that Elle Macpherson is a close personal friend. If my stomach hurts while I am running and I feel like collapsing on the road and throwing up then I will, more than likely, do just that. The Phuket-and-prawns option is, quite simply, laughable.

I enjoy sport. In my twenties I was a handy-though-not-excellent long-distance runner. I twice broke three hours for the Marathon but neither run was easy, nor particularly enjoyable. I am not a natural endurance athlete by any means, relying mostly on bloody-mindedness and a thick skin. Time has taken its toll even on this; the girth has expanded and the pain threshold has slipped gently downwards as befits a 33-year-old who spends most of his time in a suit, catching the train to work and spending an inordinate amount of time sitting behind that bane of the twentieth century, a desk. Weekends are hardly more arduous, made up mostly of eating, beer and, in moments of enthusiasm, a quiet workout on the tennis court against a person of gentle disposition.

Given these obvious mental and physical frailties why would I willingly toss in a well-paid job and cycle 16 000km around Australia, especially when I know that long-distance cycling in Australia is akin to doing ten rounds with Mike Tyson, with teeth? A friend has done some of the more obscure parts—the Barkly Highway in Western Queensland, the endless North West Coastal Highway in Western Australia, the ghost-towned wilderness of South Australia—and tells me of the loneliness, the head-winds, days of pain and frustration, a bum the colour of a baboon's, and weeks of severe, infuriating jock-itch.

The answer is cancer. My mother, Elisabeth, was diagnosed with cancer in 1979 and died of it 17 years later, at two-thirty on a chilly November morning in 1996. My father, who was sitting up with her at the time, came into my room and said he thought the end was near. I arrived at her bedside as she took, literally, her last breath.

She was, many said, something of a conundrum, my mother. She lived in the well-heeled Melbourne suburb of Toorak, read a lot, and loved the theatre. She was also a keen punter and owned, with other equally enthusiastic purveyors of horse-flesh, a succession of average steeds which produced more pleasure than money. She traipsed around Victoria with verve—to Warragul, Sale and Ballarat—to watch her charges. Occasionally a horse finished in the top three but most of the time they came in respectable mid-field. She won once at

Melbourne's racing headquarters, Flemington, which gave her great joy. She died on All Saints' Day, two days after the Melbourne Cup, when Saintly won going away.

She bore her cancer with stoicism and humour. The best part of two decades living with the twentieth century's most insidious disease would test the patience of Job and the strength of Hercules. If you can be good at having cancer then *she* was; she was good at most things she did. Until two months before she died she insisted she would beat the disease. During the latter years of her life she waged a constant battle with her weight and, in her last days, she looked down at her stick legs and remarked, 'I've always wanted legs like this.'

My mother had an unusual upbringing. She grew up in Melbourne and her father and mother, my grandparents, divorced when she was very young. She saw her father, the Mayor of Kew and a larger-than-life character by all accounts, seldom before he died when she was still young. My grandmother, Annabel, was crippled with arthritis by the time I arrived on the scene, and my memories centre around her dishing out sweets to her grandchildren from her sitting-room armchair. The youngest of my three sisters, Juliet, would keep these sweets in her underpants—a habit I never understood and one which, I presume, she has since kicked.

My mother spoke little of her childhood—divorce was not common those days, and frowned on—and I guess it led to an introversion of sorts. If something was not worth saying, she said nothing. Even if something *was* worth saying she often opted for silence. Above all she detested the telephone. 'Actions speak louder than words,' she would say.

Perhaps this was why I decided on something physical to raise money for cancer research. And what could be more physical than a circumnavigation of Australia? By bike.

The bicycle, like my mother, is something of a conundrum. Humans have yet to invent a more efficient self-powered machine, and yet cycling is not necessarily easy. Certainly on a beautiful day with a tail-wind there are few things more enjoyable than cycling through a eucalypt forest or along some river flats. Conversely, when the temperature is 35 degrees and you have to cover 160km into a head-wind like a brick wall it is an existence little short of tortuous. However, I reasoned, when doing a weekend cycle in the Blue Mountains outside Sydney—and deciding that to cycle around Australia would be a Good Thing—a billion Chinese can't be wrong.

TWO WEEKS BEFORE DEPARTURE

I have been organising this bloody trip for two months now and all I want to do is get moving. One of my father's favourite sayings rings in my ear: 'Time Spent in Reconnaissance is Rarely Wasted'. It is an attitude from the war and half a century later it lives on. With him anyway. I would love to ignore it but deep down I know he is right.

It is the fifth of May 1997 and I leave in two weeks. It is, to use part of the sporting lexicon favoured by sporting coaches these days, crunch time. I feel I have already done enough single-handedly to organise the next three Olympic Games, but there are still people to contact and equipment to beg, borrow or steal: camping supplies, cycling clothes and books, spare tyres, accessories, a support car and people to drive it. Sponsors to sign up, insurance to organise, 400 schools to write to. Debtors to chase and creditors to avoid. On top of that, com-mittees in Melbourne and Sydney are organising two launch parties, hoping to get 300 people to each. There is, of course, not enough time to achieve all this. I wonder whether the time-management theory—that a job will always expand to fill the time available to complete it—has an inverse: that numerous jobs will compress to fill a limited time. I have a feeling there is no such law.

It is two weeks of plans and promises, cajoling and coaxing, phoning and faxing. My spirits oscillate like a third-world currency. Each bit of good news is a tonic, while bad news sends me into despair. Like a shoddy investment adviser I fly by the seat of my pants and eat meals on the run. I live on beef vindaloo and naan bread from the Indian home diner in Oxford Street, Paddington. Or chicken teriyaki in a white plastic container from Queen Street or curry laksa in a green plastic container from William Street. At one stage, to my amazement, I find myself eating at McDonald's. It is not, I realise, the sort of diet I should be pursuing before a seven-month endurance cycle. I wonder what endurance runner Cliff Young, the septuagenarian *running* around Australia at the moment, is eating.

I am organising the trip, which I have called Cycle Against Cancer, out of the NSW Cancer Council's office in the Sydney suburb of Woolloomooloo. They have been helpful, even though they tell me they are wary of people who want to raise money for cancer research via endurance events. They have heard them all: pogo sticking from Adelaide to Darwin; caber-tossing from Sydney to Wollongong; one man with a strong disposition wanted to swallow 1000 gold fish, promising $1,000 a fish. The vast majority of these ideas, they tell me, never happen, the proponents unable for a variety of reasons to translate their obvious enthusiasm into the real thing. The events that *do* happen invariably raise less money than planned. One woman, a few tell me with tut-tutting tones, cycled from Sydney to Perth, handed over less than $100 at completion, and ruined a high-profile marriage in the process. Although no-one says it I sense that many feel my venture will be similarly disastrous. People whisper to each other when I pass in the corridor. The state cancer councils, grouped together in a loose affiliation, give me 'in principle' support. Their implied scepticism goads me more than my father's war-time aphorism.

I seem to spend most of each day on the phone. I ring friends—asking them to support the ride or, better still, come along for a week or two—relations, existing sponsors and potential sponsors. I fax hundreds of pages to, it seems, thousands of people. I have written to 300 companies asking for support, including the 200 largest companies in the land. People express doubt that the ride is possible. I assure them that it is, though each conversation chips away at my reserve of positivism. Many people have nothing but enthusiasm for the ride, and *that* is wonderful. The most unusual response of all is people saying, 'What a wonderful idea. I wish *I* could do that.' My response is always the same: 'But you *can*!' I wonder whether my answer is a safety net of sorts; that the more people who do this, the more likely it is that I am doing something worthwhile and, more to the point, something *possible*.

The first team—my sister Jenny, a friend James Freemantle and I—are due to leave the Sydney Opera House on Monday May 19, and I plan to be back in Sydney on December 23. That means covering 16 000km in seven months. There is precious little information about endurance cycling in Australia. A friend and bike expert, Will Lester, recently cycled from Melbourne to Queensland and I pick his brains for days. Most of our phone conversations start with, 'Er, it's me again Will.'

We speak of water intake—up to eight litres a day in hot climes—and pedal spin, known in the cycling circles, pun noted, as cadence. Both, he says, are crucial to successful, long-distance cycling. 'Too many people don't drink enough water, which leads to dehydration, while too low a cadence [not spinning the pedals fast enough] can lead to knee problems and exhaustion,' he says ominously. We speak of stretching, high-carbohydrate food, sleep and laughter. A surfeit of all is important for a successful trip, he says. With only eight days to go and so much to do, the last of the list is not easy to drum up at the moment. No talk, I notice, of nervous breakdowns.

The choice of bike, too, is crucial. He recommends a hybrid bike: a cross between a racer and a mountain bike. What these bikes lose in speed they make up for in comfort and reliability. And when you are sitting on a bike seat for seven months, comfort is God. The route, we decide, should be anti-clockwise from Sydney, via Brisbane, Townsville, Tennant Creek, Darwin, Katherine, Broome, Perth, Albany, Esperance, Adelaide, Melbourne and Canberra. He suggests this route for two reasons: to get over the hot Top End during the dry season (June–September); and to get as many tail-winds as possible.

Australia is a windy continent. To a cyclist the wind is nature's manifestation of Fagan: often charming, occasionally helpful, but never to be trusted. From behind it is an ally but it is, at best, a fair-weather friend. A cross-wind can be annoying, while a head-wind can be anything between pest and executioner. The research I have done tells me that there is no way of cycling around Australia and having tail-winds the whole way. Generally, tail-winds heading west will mean head-winds cycling east, and vice versa. I have been told that if I have tail-winds for 60 per cent of the time then I will have done OK. It is not a statistic I am comfortable with; I was hoping for at least 80 per cent.

The itinerary requires more thought. A day-by-day plan is crucial so people can join the ride en route and fund-raising functions can be planned. Equally, I want to set distances within my capability, but do not want to hang around twid-dling my thumbs. Never having done anything like this before leaves me guessing—I have no idea what my body will cope with. I decide to break the ride into two halves: the first two months, between Sydney and Tennant Creek in the Northern Territory, covering 100km per day, five days a week; and then covering 130km per day for the remaining five months. If I travel at an average speed of 25km an hour, 130km will mean less than six hours on the bike each day. Two hundred and twenty days of, say, five hours' cycling each, means 1100 hours in the saddle. It seems an awfully large number: equivalent, I work out in a moment of self-doubt, to 370 three-hour exams, or 2200 sessions at the dentist.

I draw up the itinerary and send it, heart in mouth, to many people, aware that I am painting myself into a corner. What happens if someone flies to a town to meet me and I am simply unable physically to get there? What happens if I get the flu and am laid up for two weeks? Do I assume good health?

The response is heartening: people ring and volunteer to drive the support car for certain stretches. There are still some yawning gaps, which I hope will be filled as I go. Someone sends me a newspaper cutting about the perils of long-distance cycling. The sport can, it seems, do irreparable damage to knees, hips and lower back. Gravel rash is an ever-present danger, and road trains can reduce the unlucky cyclist to tagliatelle. Most disturbing of all is that long-distance cycling can dramatically reduce the sperm count.

ONE WEEK BEFORE DEPARTURE

Corporate Australia has been generous. Although I receive many letters from companies telling me their sponsorship budgets are already allocated, enough make sizeable donations to raise my spirits: Macquarie Bank, Amcor, Baulderstone Hornibrook, North, Visyboard and others.

Custom Fleet has lent a four-wheel drive, a Nissan Pathfinder, and Jayco a wind-down, off-road caravan. Avanti Bicycles has donated two hybrid bikes, Illusions, and Groupe Sportif cycling clothes, Telstra both a mobile and satellite phone, and K-Mart has given camping equipment. Coles Supermarkets has agreed to provide food for the entire trip. Grey Advertising has designed a logo and Exhibitors Craft in Sydney has put that logo onto a large sign. Donation brochures have been printed and countless companies have donated prizes for the two launch parties. I feel indebted to them all and write pitifully inadequate letters.

Largesse has its limits. I have been unable to persuade a company to donate either fuel or phone costs and I am resigned to paying for both from my own pocket, in line with the rule that participants on the ride will personally pay all expenses, so every cent we raise goes to cancer research.

One major problem: I have been unable to train as much as planned due to organisational commitments. I wanted to cycle at least 60km a day in the weeks before leaving, but weekdays have been a write-off. Weekends are a little more relaxed and I am able to cycle 70km each day, predominantly in Ku-ring-gai Chase National Park north of Sydney. Each ride leaves me shattered, and I wonder whether 100km a day is too much to expect for the first two months. It is, of course, too late to change the itinerary.

The launch parties in Melbourne and Sydney go well. A stoic friend, Catherine Macmillan, organises the Melbourne launch almost single-handedly and close to 300 people turn up. In Melbourne $30,000 is raised, $15,000 in Sydney. Cheques arrive at the Cancer Council with pleasing regularity, mostly from people I have never heard of. Three days to go and

$120,000 is already in the bank. I am aiming for $1 million, a figure that rolls neatly off the tongue but which is enormously large. There is no turning back.

DAY MINUS ONE. SYDNEY: PREPARATION

The narrow Dickensian streets of Paddington in Sydney are not the ideal place to prepare for a seven-month trip around the world's biggest island, especially when a caravan is involved. I make the mistake of driving our caravan, gleaming new and fresh from the manufacturers, down a dead-end street and I get some nasty looks; the beautiful people of Sydney's eastern suburbs have never seen a caravan in these parts before and I am taking up three car spaces in a suburb where people will garrotte each other for one. Backing the caravan out the next day takes the best part of an hour and, if nothing else, provides the first big lesson for the trip's support drivers: never drive into something without first determining you can drive out.

It is a day of frenetic activity: picking up the car, loading it with gear, saying goodbye to friends, paying bills, packing the rest of my life away in boxes and storing it in the attic of the house. Although it is winter in Sydney, and far from warm, I spend the day sweating profusely.

Dad has flown up from Melbourne to see us off and insists on taking six of us to dinner. Jenny and James have duly arrived from their respective haunts—Jenny from Maleny in Queensland and James from Melbourne—and are ready to go. I am not surprised that either volunteered to be in the first group, when things will go wrong with regularity I feel sure. Both have undertaken plenty of unusual schemes of their own in years past; Jen has lived both in Calcutta and a small village on the Kavango River in northern Namibia, while James has spent the best part of a year organising a round-Australia trip to make furniture from recycled timber. We eat at the revolving restaurant at the Centerpoint Tower in the city, looking down on the buildings and the matchbox cars. The clouds skirt around below us—an appropriately ethereal place for the last supper.

During dinner conversation is edgy, with lots of nervous laughter, as if someone is facing the firing squad at first light. I almost mention my will to Dad, but think better of it. I have butterflies not experienced since walking out to bat for the Under-13 cricket team. I am afraid of the pain and the loneliness. Most of all, I guess, I am afraid of failure. When chasing sponsors, mention of failure is taboo. Everything is upbeat and enthusiastic. Now, on the eve of departure, I am forced to think of the other, unpalatable side of the coin. What happens if I don't make it? What happens to the sponsors' money? What will supporters think? How will I look them in the eye? Where will I go to live? Is giving it your best shot considered enough?

At home there is last-minute packing to do. It is one-thirty before I get to bed and I have to get up in four hours. I wonder how long I can survive on no sleep.

CHAPTER ONE

Northern New South Wales *Mad as a Cut Snake*

Do you know, Mr Hopper, dear Agatha and I are so much interested in Australia. It must be so pretty with all the dear little kangaroos flying about.

Oscar Wilde: *Lady Windemere's Fan*

Day 1: Monday 19 May,
Sydney to Budgewoi
Distance: 115km
Distance so far: 115km

It is a mongrel Sydney day. Australia's most famous, beautiful and hedonistic city has been bathed in glorious sunshine for weeks, but today it is putting on its ugliest, most scheming, conniving face. It is pissing with rain. Fat dollops that wet through. The Harbour Bridge, which can be seen from outer space, is only 500 metres away as we huddle in a small group outside the Opera House, and it appears faintly from the gloom like a ghostly Kraken in a B-grade American thriller. Great brolly weather, bad bike weather.

Bikes and wet roads are not good partners and I try not to think about the possibility of falling off, as I did on a damp road at Ku-ring-gai a couple of weeks ago, clattering against the bitumen in a tangle of legs and spokes, wounding an elbow, both knees and plenty of pride. A broken arm on the first day would be a bad start.

13

The early morning has been confusing, disjointed, dream-like. The phone rang 24 times: well-wishers, journalists and a wrong number. I am careful to be nice to them all, although I have become thoroughly sick of the phone.

There were, of course, last-minute tensions. Somehow Jenny, James and I got out of the house without strangling each other. Jenny drove the car through Paddington's narrow streets, past the pimps and hookers of Kings Cross, here to the Opera House. It is a big ask for her, not the best of drivers, but, as ever, she seems unfazed.

Hard to believe that after two months of dreaming and another two months of frantic organisation we are an hour from leaving. The vast, red interior of Australia beckons and I can't wait, looking forward to leaving behind civilisation's sky-scrapers and smog, and embracing the outback Australia and the bush.

A bunch of hardy folk turn out to see us leave, including Dad, my youngest sister Juliet, her boyfriend Kurt and Cath-erine Macmillan and her kids. I try to see the bright side of the weather; their brollies make the occasion colourful. There are jokes about lycra, media interviews, and Japanese tourists wondering what's going on. A quick leg massage from Jen for the cameras, hugs all around, and then on the saddle. I feel like I am leaving for the first day at school. The bike seat feels strangely comfortable, but I'm sure this feeling is unlikely to last long. 'Come on, it's just a ride,' I say to myself.

'You're as mad as a cut snake, mate,' mutters an onlooker, looking at our route on the map. I think of myself on a bike, in the rain, about to tackle Sydney's notorious Pacific Highway, the first leg of seven months on a bike, and manage a weak, unconvincing smile knowing, deep down, he's probably right.

As the white sails of the Opera House disappear behind the columns of the Cahill Expressway I feel myself hyperventilating on a heady concoction of excitement and fear of the unknown. James and I cycle down Bridge Street, over George and into Grosvenor Street. We play Russian roulette crossing the busy Western Distributor and take the bike track across the Harbour Bridge. Below us the ferries chug like headstrong beetles into the elements between Balmain and Manly. Still it rains.

Sending Jenny, now a native of Queensland's peaceful Glass House Mountains—where cars and pedestrians go the same speed—over the Harbour Bridge, where drivers are like rottweilers, is asking for trouble. Sure enough, we fail to meet up on the north side. James and I cycle about frantically looking for her, but no sign. My former work colleagues in North Sydney yell encouragement. 'We've lost Jenny,' I yell back. They look dumbfounded. An hour passes. We are freezing.

A car drives up. It is Jim Chrystal, a Channel Nine cameraman who was at the Opera House, and he's spotted Jenny, sitting on the edge of the highway 5km from where we are, reading a book, feet on the dashboard. I curse Queenslanders and their relaxed attitude; Cycle Against Cancer has got off to an inauspicious start.

We are reunited and, in rain that seems somehow to have got worse, cycle up through Crows Nest and Artarmon. I feel all at sea, knowing there could not have been a worse start, weather-wise, for the ride. Cycling in the rain is not only dangerous but hard work. The temptation is to put on layers of wet-weather gear, which become sweaty and water-logged. Far better, as long as it is not too cold, to ride in normal cycling clothes and get wet. The rain thrums on my helmet like thousands of ball bearings. It is like cycling down a river.

Rain notwithstanding, it takes only one hour's cycling through Sydney's residential north, Pymble and Wahroonga, to reinforce why I look forward to leaving all this behind. Cars and trucks roar past, delivering goods or rushing to seemingly important meetings. After being in the thick of this lifestyle for years I yearn for the simple open spaces, some uncluttered miles and downtime. Getting caught in bustling city living is disturbingly easy and you don't even notice half the time. Before long, like a frog on the stove, you are bubbling away.

As always, cycling on a major road, I feel vulnerable. Cyclists are but simple souls on simple machines undertaking simple journeys, yet we are forced to battle for a ribbon of roadspace against smog-belching leviathans, the drivers of which take little pity on their self-propelled, two-wheeled cousins. As the busy Pacific Highway tracks out in front of me, I wonder why cars have become so feted by modern society and the bicycle a second-class citizen.

It is two o'clock and the outer limits of Sydney have disappeared, thankfully, into the watery haze. We have made slow progress; on a bike rhythm is everything, but the constant traffic lights and the pounding rain have made rhythm impossible. Jenny drives close behind, protecting us as much as she can. As a cyclist you have a choice: either take up a lane and get abused by motorists for holding up the world—*their* world—or stick to the gutter and risk being squashed as they squeeze past. Bikes *do* have a right to be on the road; convincing drivers of that is the hard part.

We take refuge in a café near Berowra, having travelled a pitiful 40km. Although we have covered only a short distance I am glad simply to be on the road at last, despite my mind being a collision of concerns and uncertainties about the future. Weeks of planning have come to something, even if that is only a wet and windy Pacific Highway and burning quadriceps.

Drivers heading north from Sydney can take either the Old Pacific Highway, which winds its way through the hills surrounding the mouth of the Hawkesbury River, or the spanking new six-lane highway between Sydney and Newcastle, designed to take many thousands of cars an hour. Not surprisingly, the Old Pacific Highway is now largely unused. Why take an old single-lane road when you can take a highly charged motorway and get somewhere in half the time? Of course this means that people who are prepared to take a little longer and travel a little slower—like us—have the road practically to themselves. It meanders through pristine bushland and has breathtaking views of Broken Bay to the east and the lakes around the seaside towns of Gosford and Terrigal. In keeping with one of my aims—to eschew things modern where possible—we take the road less travelled. It still rains.

James packs it in, deciding to drive the rest of the way with Jenny. I set off alone, battling fatigue, cycling on adrenalin only. The clouds lick the surrounding valleys and, eventually, thankfully, the rain decides it has punished me enough. My new cycling high ends when my back tyre flattens with a sigh, per favour of a rogue nail. It is time we can ill afford to lose; the light is already beginning to fade.

I descend into Gosford, an undistinguished town on the shores of Brisbane Water. The drivers seem particularly aggressive, or perhaps that's the imagination of an overworked cyclist nearing the end of his tether. It gets dark and James joins me for the final 15km while Jenny drives behind, her headlights showing the way. Enid Blyton would have described her as a 'trooper'; six hours in the car following very average cyclists with flabby bottoms, and she responds with a smile.

James says he is impressed with the way I have stuck it out. I, too, am happy, though disturbed at how long today's ride has taken. I wonder silently whether the itinerary I have set is unrealistic. Time will tell. I have been told that the first five weeks will be the toughest. Eventually my body will harden to the task and my legs will gain strength. That's the theory at least.

Entering Budgewoi my body feels like it has been mauled by a pack of dogs. We have earned a night in a hotel. The local radio station wants a recorded interview for the morning show and the interviewer insists I pretend that it is *already* tomorrow—difficult when today hasn't even begun to sink in. I think of my aching thighs, protesting quadriceps and tender behind. All this is overshadowed by a formidable desire to sleep. I have vowed to approach this one day at a time and have, somehow, negotiated day one. Just 218 to go.

Day 2: Tuesday 20 May, Budgewoi to Nelson Bay
Distance: 105km
Distance so far: 220km

I have the heavy feeling in the pit of the stomach that you get when you know you are about to experience pain. I am sore following yesterday's ride, and again wonder whether 100km a day, day after day, is too lofty an aim. Already schools have signed up to meet us on the way, and we simply *have* to meet them. Should have trained more.

Good headway along the Pacific Highway through Catherine Hill Bay. James rides with purpose and says he is determined to cycle the entire day. Yesterday's weather seems a bad omen and the sky brims with ominous clouds. After 45km, pleased at our progress, we stop to stretch at a service station overlooking an escarpment. A giant yabbie overlooks the service station, threatening to pick us up in its giant claws. What's new? I feel like I have been caught in a set of pincers for the last month.

The heavens open and we are wet through. Nelson Bay, our destination, is still 60km away and it is already two-thirty. Again we are running short of time. The steel mills and smoke stacks of Newcastle, New South Wales' second-biggest city, cast dark, satanic shadows over the rest of the city. A Novocastrian, heading home at the end of his shift, cycles with us for several kilometres. He has two more years before his employer, BHP, closes the city's 83-year-old steelworks. 'It's a pity that the company took such a long time to make the decision,' he says. 'Most of the workers have been hanging out for their severance pay for years. Big companies move slowly.' Cyclists too.

We cross over the murky Hunter River and ride alongside the ports which ship steel and coal from the Hunter Valley, looming against thunderous black clouds. Although the steelworks are unpleasant to the eye, those who work there will have to make big adjustments when they close. The price of BHP shares has risen $2 in the month since the closure announcement, which indicates that the economic rationalists and superannuation funds like the idea.

The mill closure will be a big nail in the coffin for a city that has had more than its fair share of bad luck since it was created in 1804 for the most intractable of Sydney's convicts. Back then it was known as the Hell of New South Wales; the breakwater out to Nobbys Head, with its lighthouse, was built by convicts. In 1989 Australia's most destructive earthquake killed 12 people in Newcastle.

The wind springs up and our speed slows. Only the second day and already a head-wind. We take turns to lead and draft, sharing the load. I wonder whether my present pain is a function of not enough training or a body ill-equipped for the purpose. Hopefully the former.

James grunts behind. Although I have drunk four litres of water already this may not be enough, and I vow to drink more in the future. I also vow that tomorrow we will leave earlier. Getting into camp late puts pressure on everyone. I know

Jenny shares the thought. On the outskirts of Nelson Bay a man in a four-wheel drive gives me the finger. A bull mastiff looks meanly from the side window and plastered to the rear window is a sticker: 'Far Q 2!'.

My legs are shot with pain, and I am having trouble walking. Stretching helps. It can only get better. I crawl into my sleeping bag and fall asleep to the sound of the South Pacific surf. I am genuinely fearful I will be unable to keep up this pace.

Day 3: Wednesday 21 May, Nelson Bay to Forster
Distance: 95km
Distance so far: 315km

I feel rotten after a poor sleep and have the makings of a cold. Last night I was supposed, somehow, to convert the caravan's small sofa, the table and an odd-looking piece of wood into a double bed. I managed to convert it into not even a single bed. Around three o'clock the whole lot, including me, collapsed on the floor.

Packing up a caravan for the first time is frustrating, and a wind-down caravan, I imagine, is worst of all. Food, cooking equipment and clothes must be put away in special compartments, while items peculiar to our trip—fold-away chairs, a table, a gas-lantern, water bottles—must be stored on the floor so the roof can be lowered. None of us is particularly technically minded and it takes several goes to get it right.

Early afternoon we are supposed to meet 160 students from the Forster High School. Riding with schools, the students raising funds for our cause, is a big part of the trip. I have sent letters to hundreds of schools and Forster High School was the first to reply, saying it would cycle with us to honour the death last year of a student, David Summers, from cancer. I would love for the day to go without a hitch. After Bulahdelah, west of Myall Lakes, we hit several tough hills and force the pace to get to the meeting. 'Shit Dick, you'll have a dead body on your hands if you keep this up for long,' says James, puffing behind. I feel lousy, but better than yesterday.

At a lay-by on the Forster–Seal Rocks Road an army of kids and bikes mills about, with an assortment of teachers, parents, police and media. They cheer when we arrive. Feel like a bit of a fraud: we've only come 300km. A teacher, Kevin Quirk, says more than $2,700 has been raised and I am staggered. A quick chat to a local TV journalist about Mum, which is not easy, and about the student support, much easier. 'How are you finding the ride?' asks the journalist.

'Well, I'm only on day three so I guess I should feel OK.'

'Oh, I was told you were nearly finished.'

Kevin sends the students off in waves so we are not cycling in a big bunch. On a road under repair, with cars speeding in both directions, 160 kids is a big deal, particularly when most of the kids want to play up to the TV camera, which tracks us for several kilometres. I shudder as they career across the road and cut each other off. A kid doing a face-plant into the gravel would be bad karma at this stage of the ride. 'Welcome to Alcatraz,' mutters one of the kids when we arrive at the school. 'Has it really taken you three days to get here from Sydney?' asks another with surprise. 'Dad drives to Sydney in three hours.'

A full moon rises over Forster's One-Mile Beach and we sit on the balcony of the surf club and listen to the breaking waves. It has been a wonderful day, and the school fund-raising has been kick-started fabulously. Although my body again feels like it has been through a mangle, I am conscious that I am feeling a little *less* worse each day. I only hope that my body realises that it will be this way for several months. The sooner it does, the better for all concerned.

Day 4: Thursday 22 May, Forster to Comboyne
Distance: 90km
Distance so far: 405km

The surf club has been busy since dawn—many of Forster's
Old Buggers Club having been for a swim or a run along the
beach, returning in various states of physical distress. Kevin
Quirk, looking fit and keen in lurid cycling gear, says he is
'inspired' after yesterday's ride. He introduces John Summers,
the father of the boy who died. He is quiet. 'Good on you.
Keep it going,' he says. I mumble something inadequate about
the excellent feeling on yesterday's ride. He smiles and looks
at the ground.

Ready to go but the car's battery is flat. A local tradesman
starts our car with jumper leads, then *his* car won't start. We
eventually get away at nine-thirty. I wonder whether we will
ever leave before eight.

We join the rat-race for the last 9km into Taree, hitting the
highway after a pleasant cycle along the fertile Manning Valley
under a blazing sun. Many Taree locals wave, having seen last
night's story on the TV.

I am determined to spend as much time off highways as
possible, so we head inland, destination Comboyne, 700 metres
above sea-level on the Comboyne Plateau. No-one in Taree
seems to know how long it will take but the consensus is it's
a 'bloody long way'. James elects to drive with Jenny, and I
appreciate the time alone on a country lane, away from the
pre-fab homes, caravan parks and shopping malls of the coast.
I have had precious little time alone in recent weeks. It is an
opportunity to distil the events of the past week and prepare
for the months ahead. That I am on the road at all, and sticking
to an itinerary based as much on gut feel as good management,
seems a minor miracle in itself.

Through Wingham the road veers towards the mountain range and the bitumen turns to gravel. Before long the road begins to corrugate and I slow to a crawl. 'Winding Road 14km' says a sadistic sign. Jenny and James have obviously ignored the sign saying 'No Caravans Allowed'. The time goes quickly, although the steep ride is tough. Climbing hills on a dirt road is far harder than cycling on flat bitumen—in the steep sections my wheels slip on the gravel—and my quadriceps and lungs burn.

Comboyne is right out of the movie *Babe*—spotless jersey cows, paddocks of green grass, pristine buildings and gardens manicured within an inch of their lives. A car slows as I cycle in and two septuagenarians creak out. 'Hello Richard, we're Barbara and Eric and we saw you on TV last night. My niece cycled with you yesterday. We've taken Jenny and James to the showgrounds to set up camp—you're on a bit of a slope but it's not too bad—and we're expecting you for a shower and a beer when you're ready. Up the hill on the left.' With that they drive off.

Barbara and Eric are not married, but friends, their respective spouses having died in the past year. In a week they set off for an English holiday and plan to build a house together when they return. 'We are lucky to have found each other,' says Eric. 'When you get to our age and find yourselves alone, all you want is a companion.' Their shower is hot and their beers cold. It is a delight to have some home comforts.

Comboyne's rugby team, the Tigers, trains under lights near our caravan at the showground. 'We're not much of a team,' says the captain, lacing up his boots, fag defying gravity on his bottom lip. 'In fact we haven't won a bloody game all season. The day after tomorrow we play the team second from the bottom, so it's our best chance.' They train like a team with a sniff of salvation. The coach, the local cop, drives off with his siren blaring, to the cheers of the team.

Eric and Barbara have organised for us to talk to the local bingo troupe in the pub. They listen politely. All donate money. 'Most of us have either had cancer at some stage, or know someone who has it,' says a large lady in a floral dress fossicking through her bag. The hat is also passed around the bar, netting another $35. One fellow, Garry, describes himself as the 'local bum' and slaps money on the table, ordering us beers. 'I see you're camped at the showgrounds so I'll drop in for breakfast tomorrow morning,' he says through a mouthful of broken teeth. 'Seven-thirty?'

Comboyne may only be 400km from Sydney, but it feels much more; $130 has been donated, but it feels much more.

Day 5: Friday 23 May, Comboyne to Kempsey
Distance: 89km
Distance so far: 494km

Garry fails to show.

Again I slept fitfully, due to both the slope of the caravan and my persistent cough, which neither Jenny nor James complain about but it must be driving them crazy. It is certainly driving me crazy.

The last day of the cycling week with a weekend to look forward to, and not a moment too soon. I thought yesterday that I had this cycling caper licked; today I feel like I have been run over by a herd of Afghan camels in football boots.

At the Comboyne Primary School we are welcomed by the school's three teachers and 40 wide-eyed kids who listen attentively to a talk about cancer prevention: keep out of the sun and forget about fags. They then take turns boasting about their parents' cigarette intake. I wonder how effective the talk has been. One of them estimates I am cycling 300 000km and seems grossly disappointed at 16 000.

I feel a sadness leaving the Comboyne Plateau. It has been a special place and kind to us. We cycle through Wauchope to find a community struggling. There used to be 19 timber mills in the region and today there are none. I feel fatigued and discover three broken spokes and a wheel rubbing against the brake. Cycling is hard enough without extra resistance.

Ten students from Telegraph Point Primary School join us for 12km and I ride alongside a girl, Maggie, who is no bigger than her bike and certainly no cyclist, but who has determination written all over her little face. By the time we reach the school her expression is one that is normally reserved for people beating world records. At the front gate I get my wheel caught in a roadside grate and fall off in an ungainly heap. The kids witness the whole episode and look at each other doubtfully. 'How are you going to get around the country if you keep falling off your bike?' one asks later. Curly one.

The road between Telegraph Point and Kempsey is bad news and James almost gets cleaned up by a truck. Poor drivers are a major concern. Fish-eye rear-vision mirrors attached to handlebars are among the most crucial pieces of equipment for long-distance cyclists. Being aware of what is going on in front *and* behind ensures a safer ride. The best approach with big trucks is to simply move onto the gravel verge when they approach. Most drivers have been excellent so far, but a bad one can ruin your day.

At the end of the first week, at South West Rocks on the mouth of the Macleay River, my thoughts are a jangled mess. I have covered the best part of 500km, and they have not been easy ones. Certainly it took far longer than planned to complete each day's distance, averaging closer to 15km an hour than the expected 25. I have been tired at the end of each day, and have become distressed on more than one afternoon. I have struggled more than I hoped, or expected.

On the positive side I made my target each day and that's an achievement of sorts. Last year I went on a climbing expedition up the 23 000-foot (6960-metre) Aconcagua in Argentina. The guide was Australian mountaineer Brigitte Muir who would often say: 'If you keep putting one foot after the other you must, eventually, reach your target. And no matter how tired you are you can *always* take another step.' Muir is tackling Everest for the fifth time at the moment, having been thwarted 250 metres from the top last time she was there. I get the feeling her comforting truism will be applied often over the next seven months.

Thirty-two times this week's distance is barely comprehensible. Writing this journal is comforting; each day has a clear beginning and ending and can be ticked off like items on a shopping list. Only 214 ticks to go. 'Forget about the ride as a whole; divide it up into bite-size chunks,' Will Lester told me before I left. 'Those chunks might be a day, may be an hour, perhaps 10km, perhaps 1km . . . perhaps the next tree. Take it easy. Enjoy yourself.'

Days 6 and 7: Saturday 24 and Sunday 25 May
Rest days: South West Rocks

The best part of hitting your head against a wall is stopping. The best part of cycling for a week is the weekend. I read, write overdue letters to the organisers of the launch parties, sleep, and eat an absurd amount. James and I treat ourselves to a massage and I change my bike's spokes with the aid of the *Idiot's Guide to Bike Maintenance*, an operation the book swears will take half-an-hour but which takes three. The book is right about the swearing though.

Our neighbours in camp, a number of pensioners who spend six months a year in caravans, part of the growing group dubbed the 'grey nomads', take turns to drop past and chat. 'Keep it going,' they echo. 'You're raising money for people like *us*.' One calls around with a snapper he caught this morning, then lends us his barbeque. Can't work out whether they are being kind because they respect our quest, or because we are obviously such rotten campers. I burn the fish.

Day 8: Monday 26 May, Kempsey to Nambucca Heads
Distance: 80km
Distance so far: 574km

First stop the mechanic. Jenny noticed smoke appearing from the car's brakes when descending the Comboyne Plateau and wants them checked out. The mechanic can find nothing. 'Just slow down a bit,' he says. We attach a wide side-mirror to the car, for better viewing.

Two television stations and one newspaper ring to set up interviews tomorrow in Coffs Harbour. Mobile phones spell the end of privacy and Jenny, as the phone's guardian, bears the brunt of the calls. The phone rang this morning, much to her surprise, when she was on the toilet. 'I think the caller guessed where I was because of the echo,' she says.

James and I take back roads, through picturesque dairy country alongside the Macleay River. The reverie ends on the Pacific Highway, where traffic again is fast and furious. Every so often a white cross or, worse still, a cluster of crosses, appears on the verge. Anonymous crash victims: Doreen, Peter, Craig. Somewhere close to here two buses collided a few years ago, killing many. Today, between Kempsey and Nambucca Heads, the road authorities are, literally, moving mountains to upgrade the roads. Hillsides are being carved away as enormous earth-moving machines rip through man-icured paddocks. Perhaps, I think, a more efficient train system would be better.

Again we are joined for the final 15km by ten students from Nambucca Heads High School, and I am relieved to reach a campsite. Nambucca Heads overlooks the mouth of the Nambucca River, the name meaning 'many bends' in the language of the local Gumbaingeri Aboriginal people. At the campground we are approached by a permanent park resident, Elaine. 'I have a melanoma and many of my friends here also have cancer,' she says. 'I'd like to do some collecting for you. Pity I didn't know you were coming earlier.'

Jenny cooks dinner, medium-rare steak that is excellently well-done. 'All it requires is some imagination,' she says. Mid-way through the meal the caravan's overhead cupboard comes off its runners and plunges to the floor. No-one is hurt, but it requires major surgery. I cannot believe we are having such trouble with this machine. Other caravan-dwellers seem to get by beautifully.

Day 9: Tuesday 27 May, Nambucca Heads to Coffs Harbour
Distance: 75km
Distance so far: 649km

I wake to the sight of three dolphins playing in the ocean. *They* travel so easily.

James and I do it hard, heading west into the hills towards Bowraville and up to Bellingen, an old hippy community where tie-dye shirts, sandals and counterculture are still the rage, although today's beards and dreadlocks are dusted with grey. I am disturbed to see another four broken spokes on my rear wheel. Bugger the *Idiot's Guide*; tonight I will visit a proper repair shop. I now have a name for my bike. As I cycle uphill, hunched over its warped frame, the name hits me like the 8.15 from Paddington: *Quasimodo*.

The cycle to Bellingen, rubbing rim notwithstanding, is not as hard as I feared, and I feel myself gaining strength by the day. We descend, endure another 20km along the Pacific Highway, and reach Toormina School outside Coffs Harbour, where a TV crew and two newspaper journalists have come along to hear us talk to 200 school kids. Where yesterday's kids showed all the enthusiasm of limpets, today's fire questions like a machine gun. 'How many times have you pranged your bike?' ('None,' I reply, convincing myself that Telegraph Point wasn't a 'prang' per se), 'How many animals have you hit?' (none also, touch wood), 'How's your bum?' ('Sore'). We are thanked by the two school captains, who can be no older than nine but who show the confidence of professionals. Schools are charged from the top. If the teachers are enthusiastic, the kids follow. You can feel the electricity as soon as you walk through the gates.

I do a physical stocktake. Sore bum, tender legs, aching shoulders. Head hurts too, but an inner glow from an itinerary stuck to. I'll bet even dolphins do it hard some days.

Day 10: Wednesday 28 May, Coffs Harbour to Grafton
Distance: 97km
Distance so far: 746km

Quasimodo looks refreshed and keen when I collect him from the repair shop, back wheel gleaming. The mechanic scratches his forehead. 'What'd you do mate, come cross–country from Alice?' he says. 'Never seen such a mess.'

'Just come up from Sydney actually. It's a lovely bike, but the spokes kept snapping.'

'How far are you riding?'

'Er, around Australia,' said with false bravado.

'Hmmm, better you than me.'

James and I cycle towards Grafton, Jen following, and are clearly approaching the tropics: banana trees are becoming common, as is the fertile green of sugar plantations near the Clarence River. On our left, to the west, are the mountains of the Guy Fawkes River National Park and beyond them, high on the Great Dividing Range 150km away, is the town of Glenn Innes. An election poster tacked onto a tree carries the picture of a man with a country smile and a trustworthy face. 'Bob Woods: Your Local Bloke'. No snappy advertising campaigns in the NSW hinterland; just honest, folksy electioneering. A sharp twang signals another broken spoke. *Blast it.*

The road is heavenly—no traffic and a smooth surface—and I realise my feelings have become hugely determined by the traffic. Battling cars and trucks on the highway is a constant drain and perhaps that's why I feel so good today. We have the road to ourselves, spinning through Nana Glen and Glenreagh. The 100km go tolerably quickly.

Grafton is a comfortable old town of 15 000 on the bubbling Clarence River, its streets lined with the sparkling purple of jacaranda trees, the result of council by-laws late last century which encouraged their planting. A photographer from the *Grafton Examiner* is keen to get the perfect picture and asks James and me to cycle *back* out of town 5km. 'Be patient,' I tell myself. 'You can't *buy* this publicity.'

I read that Brigitte Muir reached the top of Everest yesterday and ring her husband, Jon, at Natimuk in Victoria, to congratulate him. Suddenly *my* task, undertaken in an easy climate with good food, seems so much easier. *She* has just spent two months between seven and 10km above sea-level, in sub-zero temperatures, without a shower, eating lentils.

Day 11: **Thursday 29 May, Grafton to Casino**
Distance: 99km
Distance so far: 845km

James and I cover the first 40km in good time to Whiporie, where we see ourselves on the front page of the *Grafton Examiner*. The shopkeeper shuffles over and grunts. 'So *you're* the blokes doing the ride eh? Here.' He peels off $10. 'If you can find a cure for cancer, you've got my vote.' It flies in the face of what the Cancer Council has told me; that there is little direct benefit from newspaper stories.

We struggle into a head-wind, speed down to 13km an hour. It is not a pleasant experience and my energy is sapped, despite our taking turns to lead and draft. It is not a big wind—the leaves in the tree-tops look still—yet it *feels* like cycling into a brick wall. For the first time in two weeks I don't enjoy the afternoon's ride, a bad sign. I don't want the cycling to turn into a chore but more winds like this will make it hard. Forty per cent head-winds someone said. Hell.

Casino is beef country and we have arrived at the right time. It is Beef Week and the front page of the *Richmond River Examiner* shows a photo of a beaming Belinda Dockrill, recently crowned Miss Beef Week.

The Casino campground receives the thumbs up from long-time resident Bill Burt, who comes over for a yarn as soon as we arrive. Bill used to be a cane cutter near Mackay, then worked as a slaughterman along the NSW coast but mostly at Tenterfield, west of here. He is 71 but looks 80. 'In the 1970s my hands gave up the ghost and surgeons operated,' he says, rolling up his sleeve and showing me two long scars with a mixture of pride and sadness. 'The op didn't work and I haven't worked a day since.'

Bill's wife died in 1987 and that's when he came to Casino

'probably for good' to live in his box caravan. His son died a few years later in Newcastle then his daughter was murdered in Coffs Harbour. He reels off these tragedies like a shopping list. The hand that life has dealt him. Bill's neighbour has gone north to Townsville for the winter and he misses her. 'Love to go to Townsville one day,' he says wistfully. He spends the late afternoon sitting in a chair in the sun, outside his caravan, eyes closed.

There's a hoedown tonight—a country singing festival to celebrate Beef Week—at the showgrounds, including the ample Cosby Sisters and a diminutive local girl with a voice as large as the outback. Miss Beef Week prances about like a poddy calf. We are hoed-out after two hours and return to the campground. Tomorrow is a long ride into Queensland. A fluorescent glow flickers from behind a caravan's drawn curtains. Bill Burt is watching TV.

CHAPTER TWO

Eastern Queensland *Shimmering Spokes*

The trouble is that Queensland gets branded as being part of Australia.
Former Queensland Premier Joh Bjelke-Petersen

Day 12: **Friday 30 May,**
Casino to Rathdowney
Distance: 120km
Distance so far: 965km

On the road at dawn, aiming for the Sunshine State over the Great Dividing Range along a 140km squiggly road on the map. It will be a milestone of sorts to cross the first state border after a fortnight of cycling. It is also the longest day of the ride so far, and I leave Casino with a feeling of apprehension. Quasimodo moves sluggishly early on and I discover another four broken spokes. Why am I having so much trouble with the infernal things? I have not broken a spoke in ten years of cycling, and have accounted for 12 in a fortnight. James says my back wheel is 'wobblier than Pauline Hanson's policies' and I stop after 30km to tighten the back cluster and release some pressure on the surrounding spokes. Above me the faded lettering of a sign, tacked jauntily above the doorway of a lean-to shed, reads: 'Alan Grice Drilling Supplies. My Job is Boring'.

We sweat hard uphill through Kyogle, Roseberry and Grevillia towards the mountains which make up the Border Ranges

National Park, stopping after 60km to stretch. 'I can't believe you've got another six months of this,' says James, who returns to Melbourne in two days. With that he calls it a day and climbs into the car with Jenny.

I push on alone through the Richmond River Valley, dead calm with a blanket of fog hanging over the river. The road climbs and dips and on the rises I see the tops of the poplar trees peeking through the mist, small islands of glowing leaves.

I have always thought that Victoria's and New South Wales' mountains were the largest of the Great Dividing Range, which wends its way from the middle of Queensland down the spine of eastern Australia to just north of Melbourne. But sticking out from the Great Divide south of Brisbane, like a broken arm, is the McPherson Range, which boasts Mounts Barney, Clunie and Lindesay, all of which are more than 1000 metres high. Normally I would view this as a geographical statistic only, but today I must go over it.

Twenty-five kilometres west of Grevillia, short of Wood-enbong, the road tracks the lower reaches of Mount Lindesay. Jenny and James shout encouragement from the car as I churn the pedals like a coffee grinder, lungs set to explode. My legs are shot. I reach the border sign and we stop for a photo, me holding onto the sign more to stop collapsing than through any sense of achievement. One border down, seven to go. At the moment elation is a long way away; I feel more like curling up in the foetal position and sleeping. I hope other border crossings are not this difficult. 'Well done Dicko,' says Jenny. 'That didn't look easy.'

The truism about cycling uphill is that it cannot last. It is an exhilarating ride down the north side of the McPherson Range, freewheeling for the best part of an hour. We are supposed to be in Beaudesert for a lunch put on by the local branch of the Queensland Cancer Fund and despite the early start I do not make it. At midday, still 30km to ride, we stop at Rathdowney, put my bike on the car and drive the rest of the way. It means an extra 30km on Monday to make up today's shortfall, but I am pleased with 120km including a serious mountain range. Perhaps this ride *is* possible after all.

The Beaudesert cancer volunteers ply us with food as I stand there with shaking legs. Media commitments in the afternoon, including a 'celebrity hair cut', a photo of which, the barber promises, will appear in the local paper. Must be short of celebrities. I ring Avanti about Quasimodo's recalcitrant back wheel. They say they will organise for it to be remade in Brisbane. 'How much *do* you weigh?' asks the man on the phone.

We drive to Kooralbyn Valley south of Beaudesert for a well-earned weekend. Two weeks gone and almost 1000km under the belt. Although I feel I have bitten off a large slab of the world's biggest island, a study of the map indicates otherwise. I am less than one-measly-sixteenth of the way.

Days 13 and 14: Saturday 31 May and Sunday 1 June
Rest days: Kooralbyn Valley

Jenny's boyfriend Dean, manufacturer of environmentally sensitive toilets, arrives with his seven-year-old daughter from Maleny in his rumbling, Russian-made ute and the three of them go to a nearby rainforest on Saturday, while James and I put our feet up, trying to give our bodies some rest after the past fortnight.

I have put it off for several nights but decide today is the time to e-mail sponsors, supporters and schools. Compaq has provided a computer with e-mail-sending capability, but despite some rudimentary lessons I am still a luddite. The computer makes all sorts of buzzing noises but I am not convinced they are the buzzing noises it *should* be making.

On Sunday I drive James to Brisbane to catch a train to Sydney. It is sad to see him go: he has been a fine companion and sterling cyclist during the past fortnight when things have not been easy. His ready smile and easy-going nature has made the difficult bearable ... and he was a formidable cook.

Day 15: Monday 2 June, Rathdowney to Brisbane
Distance: 130km
Distance so far: 1095km

It is frustrating backtracking to Rathdowney to start today's ride. Travelling backwards in order to go forward seems a large part of this event. A southerly wind blows, the first real tail-wind of the ride, and I belt along like a steamtrain. Would that tail-winds could be ordered, like pizzas. My creative juices produce:

O, Lord give me a tail-wind
To blow me out of sight,
I don't mind the odd head-wind
So long as it's at night.

Brisbane journalists are interested in the ride and the phone, which I carry with me on the bike, rings all morning. One announcer is determined to find a place for us to stay and produces an offer of accommodation in Redcliffe, 30km north of the city. I wonder whether I would do the same—putting up an unknown traveller and his support team—if the boot were on the other foot.

Short of Beaudesert a local cyclist, Peter Sullivan, joins me and we cycle into town together. He had plans to come all the way to Brisbane, another 70km, but received bad news on the weekend: his father-in-law died of cancer. 'I understand completely why you are doing this,' he says, giving me two bottles from his soft-drink factory and waving me off from the out-skirts of town.

I reach Brisbane in two hours flat. It is an unforgettable ride, partly because I love the tropical sights and smells of southern Queensland, more so because of the wind. Cycling with a tail-wind is one of life's simple joys; a turning of the pedals can push you along at up to 60km an hour and the countryside passes in a blur. Not that the countryside today is particularly special: Brisbane has become a Mecca for people searching for a tropical paradise lifestyle and housing develop-ments and shopping malls have spread like an untreated rash. The city is now one of the biggest, by area, in the world and cycling through its concrete outskirts is sobering after two weeks in the country.

I negotiate Victoria Bridge, over the Brisbane River, and meet Jenny, youngest sister Juliet, and her boyfriend Kurt, in the city's Queen Street Mall. Juliet, a hypnotherapist, met Kurt, a Dutch dairy farmer, four years ago on the escalator of the Moscow underground. He followed her to Australia and they now share a house in the hills east of Melbourne. Both flew up from Mel-bourne this morning and are joining the ride for three weeks. Two members of the Queensland Cancer Fund arrive too, as do people who heard radio interviews this morning. Upon departure we are presented with a $50 parking fine for parking in the mall without a permit. Back in the Big Smoke.

Through the suburbs of Geebung, Bracken Ridge and Brighton. The southerly blows me up Sandgate Road, the Deagon Deviation Gateway and across Moreton Bay, where Moreton and North Stradbroke islands loom across the grey waters. I have covered 130km and step off my bike feeling fresh as a daisy. Love those tail-winds.

Gordon and Gill Bust say they regularly take in visitors and serve gallons of tea and cakes from a busy kitchen. Their son, legs like tree trunks, is a keen cyclist, and regularly rides 100km before work, rising at four. I feel most inadequate. The Busts are expecting us for dinner but we have planned it with one of Mum's cousins, Bruce Gutteridge, and his family, back in the city. Bruce seems to understand why I would want to cycle around the country, and has nothing but encouragement. 'Your Mum was my favourite cousin,' he tells me.

Day 16: Tuesday 3 June, Brisbane to Maleny
Distance: 90km
Distance so far: 1185km

The radio station rings at dawn. Did we have a good night? I give Hotel Bust a five-star rating and Gordon's chest swells noticeably as he serves up the third round of eggs. 'Got to keep that weight on,' Gill yells from the kitchen.

The new team will take some getting used to. My fitness has built up during the past two weeks and I will ease the pace to cycle with Juliet and Kurt, who plan to share driving and cycling duties. At last we have seen the end of the Pacific Highway and I am not sad to leave it. The road, as far as I can work out, is nothing more than a conduit between large seaside towns, where people travel as fast as possible, protecting jealously their patch of bitumen.

It is a case of frying pans and fires. Queensland, more sparsely populated than New South Wales, has few secondary roads heading north, which means our main option is the Bruce Highway, the Pacific Highway's equally fearsome—by reputation at least—northern brother.

Juliet at the wheel, Kurt and I negotiate busy Anzac Avenue through the suburbs of Kippa Ring, Rothwell and Deception Bay where low-slung houses battle for space with shopping centres and service stations. It is not a pleasant ride. 'Get off the road,' yells a truck driver from the inside lane, and more barbs follow as we join the Bruce Highway. Initially we stick up for our rights as cyclists, but it is a losing battle. Easier pretending to be demented, and wave outlandishly at everyone.

We leave the highway, not a moment too soon, at Landsborough, diverting west to Maleny, high on the eastern edge of the Jimna Range. Heartbreak Hill is 5km of steepness and I do it hard. Kurt does it harder. In a country where mountain ranges are ancient, weather-beaten and mostly, flattish, the Glass House Mountains, sacred to the Aboriginal people, stick out proudly like gothic sentinels to the west. In Maleny—with its I'm-too-old-to-live-in-Nimbin-but-still-want-something-different feel—we are welcomed in the main street by a group of local business-people, members of Apex, Rotary and Lions clubs, who hand over $400 they have collected on our behalf. At dinner, where 20 people join us including two kids from the local high school and my uncle and his wife from Noosa Heads, the proceeds of another collection, $350, are presented. What a town.

Day 17: Wednesday 4 June, Maleny to Gympie
Distance: 97km
Distance so far: 1282km

Some places in the world you feel sad leaving and Maleny is such a place. There is a feeling of genuine care here. As Kurt and I cycle down the main street, making for Gympie, many townsfolk come to wave us off and wish us luck. 'Give my regards to the UFOs on the Nullarbor,' yells one. One passes over a copy of the *Sunshine Coast Daily*; I am on the front page, clearly still suffering the effects of Heartbreak Hill.

Earlier, I say my farewells to Jenny, a difficult task after two-and-a-half weeks of living in each other's pockets. Being support crew for the first leg was always going to be difficult as we found our way, literally and metaphorically, up the New South Wales coast. She has been stoic under adversity and I love her for that. Supporting someone undertaking an endurance event is not easy, particularly when it involves packing and setting up camp, day in and day out.

Kurt and I cycle the dirt road through Kenilworth. The clouds covering the surrounding hills gradually disappear, revealing green, patchwork fields and content cattle. The secondary road saves us 10km but I'm not sure how much time we save; dirt roads are not conducive to speed. The corrugations slow us down and at one stage my water bottle dislodges and tumbles over the edge of the roadside embankment.

It takes more than Dutch courage to cycle 70km on no breakfast. Kurt complains of light-headedness and says he is seeing stars. I tell him that no breakfast, no stretching, no water and no training is no recipe for long-distance cycling. He eats a banana. He is tenacious, but even tenacity has its limits.

We are due in Gympie in two hours and I leave Kurt behind, pressing on to Imbil, where Juliet waits. Kurt eventually arrives and collapses under a tree holding his head, happy to swap duties with Juliet. Rushing, we take the wrong road and have to backtrack. I have to leave Juliet behind in order to make our one o'clock meeting. The road twists and turns like a snake in death throes and I am ten minutes late. Volunteers from the Gympie Cancer Fund have erected a banner and the Mayor presents me with a king protea flower which, she says, 'will keep for ever'. The only thing I can think of, standing there on wobbly feet, is where we will store it.

Three hundred kids clap in the forecourt of the local school and hand over $100. The further I travel the easier it is speaking to students about the ride. In the first week, having travelled less than 500km, they seemed to wonder what the big deal was. Thirteen hundred kilometres sounds more formidable.

Gympie, an old goldmining town, has a reputation for being a stronghold for the gun lobby, which became a political force when the Federal Government banned semi-automatic weapons after the Port Arthur massacre. The centre of town is not full of gun-toting rednecks, but friendly, helpful folk and the Cancer Fund volunteers bend over backwards for us. This afternoon's dash against time has left me drained and I cook mashed potatoes to replace lost energy. Potato and pasta, high in carbohydrate, have become my staple diet. Kurt cracks his head, already sensitive after today's exertions, twice on the caravan's overhead cupboard, and decides bed is the only safe place.

Day 18: Thursday 5 June, Gympie to Biggenden
Distance: 130km
Distance so far: 1412km

A knock on the caravan door reveals the portly campground owner with $20 to donate. Last night he would not hear of us paying for a campsite. We have been shown astounding generosity by so many people already. We make the *Gympie Times*, page three, two pages behind Pauline Hanson, the founder of the One Nation party. Wacky political policies beat a wacky idea any day.

Around the country today cancer organisations are serving tea, part of the Australia's Biggest Morning Tea annual fundraising drive, and I have been asked to speak at the Gympie Golf Club alongside Bob Ansett, the former rent-a-car king, who hums in from Noosa Heads in a huge four-wheel drive. It is midday before I start cycling, with 130km to negotiate, and I have nagging doubts. Juliet and Kurt drive on ahead and say they will see me in two hours. I feel like a condemned man deserted.

Should have stayed in bed. A head-wind acts like a brake and two trucks force me into the gutter in the first half hour. I curse them, feeling both angry and embarrassed at my lack of composure. Can find neither rhythm nor speed and wonder if both have disappeared forever. If it was a training ride I would simply turn around and go home, but this is not an option today. Or any day. I remind myself to increase cadence and drink water.

I miss a turn-off and cycle 15km in the wrong direction. A pedestrian points towards a pencil-thin dirt track disappearing weakly into the scrub. 'Haven't been down there for several years, but I reckon that's the way,' she says. A sign on the side of the road points to Devils Mountain, an appropriate landmark under the circumstances. After the best part of an hour on the corrugated road I reach Kurt, standing next to the car as if waiting for a train. 'Juliet started cycling ages ago,' he says. It is already three-thirty and I'm 80km short of Biggenden. I stretch for ten minutes and climb wearily back on the saddle.

I battle the head-wind, alone. Were I not so tired it could be an enjoyable cycle. The road is surrounded by sparse eucalypts and it dips and turns alongside Munna Creek like a small roller-coaster. Through the trees to the east I can make out the low-slung Urah Range. There are few cars and no trucks, which is welcome after the Bruce Highway. Those who pass wave and toot their horns but little short of a magic carpet would pep me up today. I am tired, my legs chafe and my patience deserted me long ago.

I have also committed the unpardonable sin of not drinking enough water. During my marathon-running days the hydration mantra was 'If You're Thirsty It's Too Late'. The theory is that once your body starts to crave water it has got to the point of no return, and a dehydrated body functions far less effectively. Those who dehydrate too much can collapse, or lose consciousness. Still 50km to go and I guzzle water, angry at my dumb, elementary mistake.

I pass a memorial bridge erected by local farmers for victims of the Great War, another good excuse to stop and stretch. Doubt accompanies my fatigue and for the first time I wonder whether this whole thing is such a good idea after all. There are still 200 days of this, day after day, and perhaps I have not allowed enough recovery time. My legs hurt like hell.

Snap out of it Dick.

I think of Mum and the suffering she went through, which fortifies me. There is a reason for this ride. I put my head down and turn the pedals.

Can always do one more turn. Make for the next tree, then the next one . . . Keep looking ahead, only 40km to go . . . a snip.

I wonder whether others who have done similar things had such doubts. What about Nobby Young of Gladesville in New South Wales, who walked around Australia between February 1993 and February 1994? Did *he* have problems? What about Bob Hanley, who did the same thing between 1975 and 1978 but pushing a wheelbarrow? In my frazzled state of mind I cannot even comprehend how anyone would want to do this. A *wheelbarrow*?!

The gloom descends and Biggenden, according to a crooked distance post on the road, is still 27km away. I yearn for an injury to justify a lift, then curse my feeble will. I follow the faded white road line in the darkness, petrified that cattle will be on the road. A pair of headlights cuts through the gloom and Kurt arrives. He follows me for the final 10km, lighting the road ahead. I arrive and collapse on the ground. Juliet looks concerned. 'Water?'

'Yes please, and lots of it, but after a beer!' Biggenden campground is like an oasis and merely to stop is a luxury. I offer a prayer to the cycling gods for my safe deliverance.

Over dinner, more spaghetti than I ever thought it would be possible to eat, Kurt tells me he came across a fire on the side of the road this afternoon and began hitting it with an old blanket from the car. A ute pulled up and a wizened farmer drawled: 'Hey mate, watcha doin'?'

'Putting out the fire,' Kurt replied.

'Well I wish you wouldn't,' he replied. 'I've just spent half an hour trying to light the bastard.' Queensland: Beautiful one day, most odd the next.

The phone rings. It is Richard Wadley, secretary at Biota Holdings. His company wishes to donate $2,000. *Now* the day makes a little more sense.

Day 19: Friday 6 June, Biggenden to Mundubbera
Distance: 118km
Distance so far: 1530km

'Where ya' ridin' to?' asks a kid on a hotted-up BMX when I emerge stiffly from the caravan.

'Around Australia actually.'

'Then why do you look so sick?' he asks, steaming off in a cloud of Biggenden campground dust. I would give a lot for his energy, if only to catch him and give him a clip over the ear. I feel like Methuselah after a heavy night on the turps.

After yesterday's tribulations I approach today's ride with trepidation. On reflection lack of water *had* to be the cause of my listlessness. I drink two litres of water with breakfast and urinate four times in the first half hour. 'Piss Often, Piss Clear' is an old cycling adage. I am certainly pissing often.

In order to keep off the Bruce Highway, the memories of which north of Brisbane still rankle, we will head inland, then track north towards Rockhampton.

It is impressive how the body can recover from a mauling.

The first 60km—through rolling green hills on the Isis and Burnett highways—are not as hard as I feared, although my arse feels like someone has taken to it with a cricket bat. Kurt is improving with time and we cycle together to Gayndah, where the service station owner gives us two bags of oranges. This is citrus country, and even the Gayndah information booth is in the shape of a Giant Orange. 'Pity you're not staying here tonight,' says the man in the booth. 'Tomorrow's the start of the Queen's Birthday weekend, which means it's the first day of the Citrus Festival!'

The grass turns from green to brown as we push west, into the Queensland rural heartland 200km from the coast. The houses become ramshackle, surrounded by bits of rusty machinery and whippet-thin dogs straining on leashes next to upturned 44-gallon drums. Some of the villages are bordering on ghost-towns and the ground could do with a good feed. Fat cumulus clouds gather overhead but no sign of rain.

I am delighted to reach our destination, Mundubbera, only mildly wrecked, but definitely confused. Why do I feel so much better than yesterday despite having cycled only 12km less? I decide that water is the key, and today we had no head-wind. I experienced this unexplained polarity of feelings when training for marathons. Some training runs would be a joy, powered by seemingly boundless energy—the runner's high—and limitless *joie de vivre*. Other days, for no apparent reason, would be a chore; bones aching, muscles creaking and everything muzzled by a general feeling of listlessness and apathy.

Gayndah had the Big Orange, Mundubbera has the Big Mandarin. And a history to crow about. Former Queensland premier Wayne Goss was born here, boasts an information sheet in the main street. The sheet is full of other facts: Henry Zipf planted the first citrus plant in 1933 and the local rivers are home to the amphibious lungfish. Next door, at Dodgey Brothers second-hand mart, business is slow. The CES advises, categorically, that there are 'No Job Vacancies Available'. Another noticeboard displays an open invitation to Thelma Young's sixtieth birthday at the showgrounds, 'to celebrate Thel's birthday and miraculous recovery'. Sounds intriguing, and too good to miss. Sadly, we'll never know—we will be 1000km to the north on the said day.

Day 20: Saturday 7 June, Mundubbera to Monto
Distance: 110km
Distance so far: 1640km

The brown soil of Mundubbera turns to rust-red and citrus country to land supporting beef, dairy and lucerne. Huge sprinklers spray Niagara-like in the distance. Brahman bulls loll around in the sun, swishing their tails about. The Brahman's Indian heritage stands it in good stead in the hot Queensland climes because it is resistant to ticks, which burrow into the flesh of less hardy cattle.

The patchwork of the orange plantations becomes scrub and the cockatoos screech overhead. I stop to help a tortoise cross the road. The most common roadside sight, however, is Forex cans and bottles, Queensland's most popular beer. I count 35 over a 3km stretch. To the left are thin, dusty tracks leading to cattle stations with names as evocatively Australian as the tuckerbox: *Coonambula*, *Cockatoo*, *Quaggy*. Along the road is Dead Bullock Gully and Suicide Corner. 'It was a bitch of a road before we improved it,' says a roadworker.

After 60km I reach the tiny hamlet of Abercorn, where dogs pant on the boiling asphalt and humans are conspicuously absent. Kurt astounds me by saying he has been here before, on his Australian wanderings three years ago. Juliet and I follow

Three Moon Creek Valley and enjoy the time together cycling and talking, with no deadlines. We have lived in the same city for many years, but this is precious time together. The map says 35km to Monto. We cycle 35 and a sign says we have 10km remaining. Bloody maps. Perhaps I wobble a lot.

We are met by Jenny Forsyth, the Monto Cancer Fund representative and her two daughters, Kelly-Anne and Melissa. Jenny, though petite, is clearly a human dynamo and carries the reputation of saving Monto's railway station several years ago when the Queensland Government had it earmarked for closure. Her campaign involved hanging an effigy of the transport minister in Monto's main street. Clearly not someone to tangle with.

The Forsyths seem an all-too-common Queensland family. Jenny does the talking while Kelly, her husband, might well have had his voice-box removed. He is a truckie, and the family's front lawn is obscured by three two-storey semi-trailers and pieces of machinery. It also explains his penchant for coffee, which he consumes by the gallon during the evening. Kelly has seen every inch of Queensland—Charleville, Roma, Chinchilla, Longreach—and provides valuable information about the best route north. 'The Bruce Highway north of Rocky is as bad as it gets, so you'd do better going inland, through Dingo and up the Fitzroy Developmental,' he says. Sounds *far* more interesting anyway.

Thunderstorms are predicted.

Day 21: Sunday 8 June
Rest day: Monto

It doesn't rain.

We join the Forsyths on a day off at the nearby Cania Gorge National Park, where I severely stub my toe playing soccer with Melissa and Kelly-Anne. By the end of the afternoon I can hardly walk.

I limp around town in the afternoon and see evidence that the pro-gun lobby is more vocal here than in Gympie. In the window of the general store is a yellowing piece of paper: 'This year will go down in history. For the first time a civilised nation has full gun registration. Our streets will be safer, our police more efficient and the world will follow our lead into the future. Adolf Hitler, 1935.'

Supplies of PVC pipe have run out as farmers bury their semi-automatic guns. 'Anything to stop the bloody politicians gettin' their hands on them,' one tells me in Monto's main street. 'They know jack-shit about life on the land, and anyway, I reckon they'll change the laws back again soon. Besides, why should *we* pay for the actions of an idiot from Tassie?'

Day 22: Monday 9 June, Monto to Biloela
Distance: 100km
Distance so far: 1740km

My toe is swollen and throbs like a rock concert. Last night I slept fitfully. I gingerly cycle a few hundred metres and am surprised: most of my weight is on the ball of my foot and the toe takes little weight.

The cycling gods are smiling. A long hill to negotiate, up the side of Mount Margaret, and then glorious downhill, with a tail-wind. Cycling nirvana. Juliet and I speed along at 40km an hour. *This* is the way to ride. Like a good Protestant I almost feel guilty enjoying it. A tail-wind is like a holiday; it cannot last. I am delighted to see Juliet and Kurt enjoying their cycling. Although they share the driving duties, and therefore cycle roughly half my distance each day, it is no pushover for them.

To date in Queensland we have been hemmed in by hills

and scrub. The views have been restricted and, I have found, my thoughts insular. Today is like the drawing back of a veil. The scrub disappears and the views open up under a blazing sun. Despite my toe I cycle on a high with a feeling of euphoria and freedom, and can't wipe the smile from my face.

Fifteen kilometres from Biloela, two brothers, Daniel and James, wait for us at a lay-by for the cycle into town. Daniel, who cycled out into the head-wind, looks wrecked. James got a lift with his Mum. I ask where Dad is. 'He was killed recently, when a water tank rolled on him,' Daniel says matter-of-factly.

We cycle into town together chatting. Biloela is 150km from the coast on the west side of the Kroombit Tops National Park, and the boys tell us we are 'now in Banana Shire', named not after the fruit but an old yellow bull. It is also, Daniel and James tell us with wide eyes, the 'Shire of Opportunity'.

Dr Richard Tan and his wife Dominique have us to stay in their house made from parts of the old Biloela Hospital. Originally from Malaysia, Richard has worked with cancer patients in Biloela for years and volunteered to help us when hearing we were coming through. The couple used to breed race-horses, with some success judging by the photos on the walls, but have now downgraded to pigeons. Dominique loves yoga and meditation and is fascinated by Juliet's hypnotherapy. 'I'd love to experience a past-life regression,' she says. Richard barbeques squab rissoles at a fund-raising dinner for us. Juliet, a strict vegetarian, passes.

Day 23: Tuesday 10 June, Biloela to Westwood
Distance: 105km
Distance so far: 1845km

Although in a comfortable bed, and inside, I sleep fitfully. Perhaps camping becomes habitual. At the Biloela Primary

School the kids listen attentively and ask questions, including the usual ones about 'stacking the bike' and hitting kangaroos. 'Do you ever think of quitting?' Laughter. Saved from having to answer.

Thirty kilometres north-west of Biloela, again with a welcome tail-wind, is the Jambin Pre-School. Parents attend and many of the kids make donations, holding onto their tax-deductible receipts like gold leaf. One donates $5. 'Thanks,' I tell his mother afterwards. 'Actually it's his birthday money from last week,' she says with pride. 'He really wanted to donate it.' I am floored.

Earlier this year the Jambin region received its first good rain for seven years, says one of the parents. Everything still looks parched, but people remain hopeful. Someone mentions El Niño and everyone laughs. Country people have long realised they can do nothing to influence the weather; far better to roll with the meteorological punches. Short of Dululu, 50km south-west of Mount Morgan, we cross Alma Creek, the bed of which is as dry as a bush-rat's belly. A recently painted depth indicator marks a height three metres above the top of the road.

The wind has changed, now a cross-wind. Perversely, I have found I get more tired when I force myself to cycle slower than my normal speed. I draw away from Juliet and reach the Capricorn Highway, heading west from Rockhampton towards Emerald and Longreach and marking the Tropic of Capricorn. A photographer from the *Rockhampton Bulletin* arrives and takes some shots. 'Get to the Criterion Hotel tonight,' he says. 'It's owned by my girlfriend's parents. Best steaks in town.'

'Rocky', population 61 000, is Australia's beef capital, and the administrative and commercial hub of central Queensland. It is also a beautiful town, with generous streets and a setting on the attractive and substantial Fitzroy River. I am indisputably in the tropics now, and making headway. Our next-door neighbours at the Rockhampton campground, Tom and Nat, are from Dubbo in New South Wales, heading north like thousands of others to escape the winter. Five years ago he had treatment for bowel cancer and lymphoma and hands Kurt $5. 'I'm taking life one day at a time,' he says, which we agree is a good way to go.

Constant pains in my shoulders and neck prompt me to buy a set of aero bars. Aero bars, consisting of two pads for the elbows and a steering bar for the hands, are attached to a bike's handlebars, and long-distance cyclists swear by them, for aiding aerodynamics and reducing strain. I'll be interested to see if they make a difference.

Day 24: Wednesday 11 June, Westwood to Dingo
Distance: 103km
Distance so far: 1948km

A phone call from the Cancer Council in Woolloomooloo brings pleasing news: donations have continued to arrive during the past three weeks and the total stands at $147,000. We have been distributing leaflets on the road which must be generating income, in addition to donations and the money raised by schools. The *Rockhampton Bulletin* has described me as the 'Million Dollar Cyclist'; we are a long way short of that figure and I remain hopeful that a company will come in as a Naming Rights Sponsor in the near future. Several companies are sitting on proposals; getting answers from them is the hard part.

Cycling west on the Capricorn Highway, along the tropical line of latitude, represents a milestone; with nearly 2000km covered I feel for the first time I have made real progress. I spend much of the morning hunched over my aero bars, delighted. Although the crouched position makes breathing harder, there is markedly less wind resistance. Should have bought them weeks ago.

My 58-year-old second cousin, another Richard Allen, joined the team in Rockhampton. He is heading to Princess Charlotte Bay north of Cooktown in Far North Queensland to see where an ancestor survived a cyclone at the turn of the century, sailing south. Thirty others didn't. 'If he had died, I wouldn't be here today,' Richard says. I hope he retains these positive thoughts towards existence at the end of the week.

He is certainly prepared for the week to come, a compass around the neck, a Foreign Legion hat and a pair of modern sunglasses bought for him by his daughters because of the expected 'searing heat' (it is a pleasant 20 degrees today). He looks like a cross between Lawrence of Arabia and Darth Vader, cycling with purpose and precision on his 30-year-old Lawrencia bike.

Beyond Gogango is a large rock bearing a plaque: 'The Westwood section of the Capricorn Highway was opened by the Hon. Russ Hinze, Minister for Local Government, Main Roads and Racing'. Russ Hinze was one of Queensland's largest, and more colourful political personalities, a product of the period that produced more than its fair share of such. I am reminded of some graffiti I saw on a headstone-shaped rock near Queensland's Port Douglas several years ago. 'Here lies our local MP. He's not dead yet, but he sure can lie.'

Like the politician who opened it, the Capricorn Highway has a generous middle section, wide shoulders and veers slightly to the right. We make good time through Grantleigh and Edungalba. It is a disturbing moment when, in the early after-noon, we encounter our first road train, a double-carriage semi-trailer careering down the middle of the road, cattle packed to the rafters. It passes perilously close and I wobble in its wake. I have heard that road train drivers swerve for nothing, ploughing through kangaroos, and even cattle and camels. And I already know that cyclists are at the bottom of the transport food chain.

Richard, lagging behind on his first day, calls it quits after 45km and hitches a ride to the car. He is picked up by Harry, all sinew and bone from Texas ('That's Texas on the Queensland/New South Wales border. I'm no bloody septic.') on his way to Weipa, still 27 hours away, to fish with friends. 'Do it every year, mate,' he says. 'I'm glad to give the wife some peace and quiet and she's glad to get rid of me.' Richard's Lawrencia shares the back of the ute with a large esky of bait.

Juliet and I cycle together for much of the afternoon and, approaching Duaringa, are kept company by a 100-carriage coal train heading for the collieries south of Blackwater. We pass a dead kangaroo, bloated, flyblown, smelling like the plague. The side of the road is littered with broken glass and giant shavings of rubber, a Pro Hart painting on bitumen.

Since the drastic day between Gympie and Biggenden I have felt stronger by the day, though mindful I have not attempted 130km since that rock-bottom day. Tomorrow is a similar distance, and will be a litmus test. As we ride into a sunset of purple, orange and ochre, the 600-metre-high sandstone plateau of the Blackdown Tableland National Park rising out of the nearby plains, I conclude that I am still having bad days, but they are getting less common.

When you arrive at a town with a name like Dingo there's only one thing to do: head for the pub. The four of us double the numbers. The locals—angular types covered in layers of dust, battered Akubras perched on thinning thatches—eye us suspiciously. A game of snooker is in progress in a long and thin room not designed for the purpose. Players play with cues angled sharply downwards, explaining both the number of rips in the tablecloth and the number of holes in the wall.

Juliet gets talking to Mal, who has a head twitch like he's trying to shake something from his ear and whose family have lived near Dingo 'since the ark'. 'I've done everything—had a crack at farming, coal mining, now I'm a truckie. I've been all around Australia: Sydney's too brash, Adelaide's too boring, and The Isa's too bloody far away. The best place in the country is right here ... Dingo. I'm glad you came through. You couldn't say you'd seen Australia if you hadn't.'

Day 25: Thursday 12 June, Dingo to Middlemount
Distance: 130km
Distance so far: 2078km

Dingo's campground is a paddock and a noisy one at that. Coal trains clank throughout the night and an endless cacophony of road trains steam past, honking their horns at nothing in particular. The shrill cry of galahs cuts the night. The most noise, however, is made by the campground's permanent resident who returns after pub closing time and objects to the proximity of Richard's tent. After five minutes of cursing and swearing Richard emerges to request some silence. After a brief, animated conversation they become firm friends. 'Well, seeing that you're my neighbour you'd better come in for a nightcap,' he says.

One of the benefits of mining in Australia, in addition to jobs, are the roads that mining companies put through otherwise uncharted regions. They are, by and large, straight and true, and not used by cars other than mining vehicles largely because they do not, by and large, lead to places other than mines. The Fitzroy Developmental Road tracks north from Dingo, via Middlemount, to Nebo in the heart of beef and sugar country.

Richard and Juliet drive the support car while Kurt and I make good time for 70km, during which I pass through the 2000km mark of the ride. The countryside flattens out, strewn with saplings, while herds of Brahman take a quizzical interest in our progress. We emerge from the bush and the horizon opens up to the coal-bearing eastern edge of the Denham and Harrow ranges. A line of decrepit timber telegraph poles follows the road, its wires long since disintegrated. By contrast, an army of giant aluminium poles marches in formation towards the coalfields. We pass a bullet-riddled roadsign on which someone has painted 'Space Madness'. Further along a marijuana plant has been painstakingly drawn on the road.

Although the ride is not easy, I pull into Middlemount with something left in the energy tank, even if it is just sloshing around the bottom.

Middlemount is a surgically clean town servicing the Norwich Park open cut coalmine. People drive Holden Jackaroos and live in pre-fab houses surrounded by superbly manicured lawns. Even the shopping centre looks like it has been scrubbed with Pine-O-Clean. The kind reception we have received in other towns—we have paid camping fees only once—is not replicated here. 'You'll have to ring my boss at the mine if you want free accommodation,' says the campground manager.

'You'll have to ring the manager in Melbourne,' says the boss when we get through. We give up and pay the $7.

Day 26: Friday 13 June, Middlemount to Nebo
Distance: 143km
Distance so far: 2221km

Because most of the traffic from Middlemount goes south, the Fitzroy Developmental Road deteriorates north of the town.

An evil north wind has sprung up, a head-wind. Kurt and I struggle from the start, taking turns to lead and draft to spread the load but the morning passes slowly.

Sod's law that we get a head-wind during a 140km day, the longest day of the ride to date. Yesterday my mind wandered and time passed in a reverie. Today there is no such luxury. Each turn of the pedals requires a concerted effort and the pain is real, here and now. We try talking but the conversation is forced, eventually cycling only to the sound of our heavy breathing and the whirr of our wheels. Searching for something to do to pass the time, I calculate I will pedal three million revolutions to complete the ride, which does little for my state of mind.

On either side of the road, 20km apart, are the entrances to cattle stations. The letterboxes to *Bombandy*, *Leichhardt Downs* and *Saltbush Park* are either fridges or 44-gallon drums on stilts, which could take delivery of a herd of cows. We cycle for an hour alongside a paddock that has been cleared, trees and saplings lying in piles on the ground, waiting to be burned. I have witnessed such clearing and there is nothing delicate about it: take two graders, put a hundred-metre chain between them, and drive back and forth.

The road narrows to one lane lined by rich, blood-red earth. There are now new road rules: small vehicles give way to larger ones, we give way to everyone, and everyone gives way to road trains. The few drivers that pass wave and toot. Kurt yells and I look down to see a black snake sliding across the road ahead. It's too late and I'm not sure who is more surprised, me or the snake, when I hear the *ker-thump*.

At the Valkyrie State School, 100km north of Middlemount, one teacher and 25 students travel up to 50km each day to get to school. Actually, the school should not be here at all. 'When the school started, the classroom was delivered as a pre-fab box,' says the teacher. 'It was *supposed* to be delivered 20km to the south, but it was raining on delivery day and the Department of Education plonked it here.' The kids are a delight, in spanking blue and yellow outfits with wide-brimmed Akubra hats covering angelic faces.

After two peaceful days, we are back in the action on the Peak Downs Highway, the main conduit between the Clermont cattle stations and the coastal towns of Sarina and Mackay. The traffic is especially busy today in preparation for next week's Mackay Show. Three coal trains rumble past, taking their precious cargo to the Hay Point Coal Terminal south-east of Mackay.

I feel delicate on arrival in the small cattle town of Nebo. I know I could not have accomplished today's distance a month ago, which is a comfort of sorts. At least I am getting fitter.

We are guests for the weekend of 35-year-old cattleman Nigel Onley, who runs a station at Nebo and consults to a number of southerners—Collins Street farmers—who own plots in the region. Nigel is preparing cattle for the show which, he says, has changed much over the years. 'I remember it used to have a freak display, including a person with two heads,' he says. At dinner he looks with disdain at the leg of lamb we produce. 'This is cattle country, guys, I'd hide that if I were you.'

At night we hear dingo howls and Nigel looks unconcerned. 'The odd dingo keeps the 'roo and pig numbers down but as soon as they start attacking the cattle you have to get rid of them.' Richard, who leaves tomorrow for Princess Charlotte Bay, tells of former Victorian Premier Joan Kirner, who spoke to a crowd of disgruntled farmers in Gippsland some years back when their sheep were being attacked by dingoes. Kirner told them the Government favoured castrating the dingoes. 'Listen lady,' yelled a cocky from the back of the room. 'The dingoes are eatin' the sheep, not rootin' 'em.'

Days 27 and 28: Saturday 14 and Sunday 15 June
Rest days: Nebo

Nigel's parents live at *Hamilton Park*, 40km south of Nebo. Jill and John Onley are a rustic Queensland couple who have lived in the region for 30 years, recently selling their station to BHP, which paid good money to get access to the valuable artesian water supply.

The value of land around here oscillates on mining gossip. A rumour circulating recently that a mining company was considering Nebo as a residential base for a mine sent land prices soaring. The selection of another town saw prices fall just as quickly. Today land sells for $100 an acre, though carrying capacities are not large. Bigness is the key; there are not too many viable small farms.

John, all leathery skin and pursed lips, has lived on two eggs a day all his life. 'You don't need to eat anything else,' he says. 'Eggs have everything.' He runs a successful Brahman stud and is hoping for a good result at tomorrow's show. His prize entry, a grain-fed bull the size of a small truck although only nine months old, already weighs a tonne. The Onleys make a generous donation and fill our fuel tank.

Nebo is victim to Queensland's fickle weather. Being on the west side of the Connors Range the rainfall is not predictable, and the region is in drought more than farmers would care for. Every now and then the rain belts on the corrugated iron roofs like a jackhammer for days, especially when cyclones are about. On the way back home Nigel points out the railway bridge near Mount White. Although seven metres above Nebo Creek even it, occasionally, is submerged.

Day 29: Monday 16 June, Nebo to Mackay
Distance: 79km
Distance so far: 2300km

Up at six and it is freezing. Students of the Nebo Primary School gather on the tennis court, huddling together for warmth as the wind whistles through the chicken wire. I feel like an ice-cube. The students are excited to hear about Friday's snake though disappointed that no-one has hit, or perhaps *been* hit by, a kangaroo. When I mention that our route takes us through Charters Towers on the Flinders Highway, one announces proudly: 'I chundered in Charters Towers.'

The cold has a nice side effect: a gutsy tail-wind blowing up from the wintry southern states. Kurt and I are propelled 70km over the Balaclava Mountains to Mackay. We reach 50km an hour on the way down, through clean and green sugar fields. Sugar mills belch smoke, and the sweet smell of refined sugar fills the air. The whitewashed stilted houses—Queenslanders—and their pristine gardens indicate the industry has provided good returns, although sugar is a classic cyclical industry: when prices are good everyone plants cane, then oversupply drives prices down.

In Mackay, preparations for the show are in progress. Ferris wheels crank over and cattle trucks disgorge hopeful bovines. The local paper, the *Mackay Mercury*, carries an editorial warning local girls not to get caught in the excitement of the show and fall in love with a 'showy'. The showmen have a reputation of dumping their new girlfriends further up the coast. A photographer from the same paper fails to meet us in town. I ring the chief-of-staff. 'Sorry mate, there's been a four-car pile-up outside Alligator Creek,' he says breathlessly.

Day 30: Tuesday 17 June, Mackay to Proserpine
Distance: 85km
Distance so far: 2385km

The Mackay Show has clowns and coconut shies, dancing girls and dodgem cars. But while agricultural shows in big cities seem to have lost their original purpose to gaudy commercialism and showbags, the Mackay Show remains cattle-driven. We run into John Onley and his prize bull, being shampooed lovingly, its eyes closed in ecstasy.

Dugall and Kerry McDougall, originally from Charters Towers where he drove trucks for a goldmine and she worked in the company office, have entered cattle from a station 60km south of Mackay: two steers in the Coastal Pasture Division. The judge's decision goes against them and they don't register a place. Dugall laughs, but is clearly disappointed. 'Just wait for the Sarina Show,' he mutters. 'We'll show 'em there.'

The only way between Mackay and Townsville is the Bruce Highway which has the dubious reputation, as far as the locals are concerned, of being the worst section of road in Australia. We share the road with farm machinery and cattle trucks, and I am cheered. The drivers do not have the no-speed-except-top-speed attitude of those down south.

Again Kurt and I have the assistance of a tail-wind and cycle at 30km an hour through Aminungo, Kuttabul, Mount Ossa and Bloomsbury. The sugar country is flat and beautiful, flanked by the Eungella National Park and the Dicks Tableland in the west. This tail-wind cannot last forever.

Day 31: Wednesday 18 June, Proserpine to Bowen
Distance: 90km
Distance so far: 2475km

Today's tail-wind is stronger still. 'With any luck, so long as these high pressure systems keep coming through, you may get them right across the Top End,' says a local.

It is sugar harvesting season and the early-morning sun glows orange on the horizon, through a mist of ash from the burning of the cane. Evenings produce violent sunsets of reds, oranges and purples. Around Proserpine, paddocks of cane, ready for harvesting, sit alongside fields of delicate, green shoots.

The turn-off to Shute Harbour is an unlikely juxtaposition. Two of Australia's greatest revenue earners, sugar and tourism, existing side by side. Mini-buses take Japanese to ferries leaving for the Whitsunday Islands, passing cane farmers tirelessly working their harvesters. The impression is that the Whitsundays, once one of Australia's premier holiday destinations, may be on the decline. Their billboards look tatty and tired while others advertise the bold and new: 'Come And Pig Out Where It All Began—The Original Hog's Breath Café'. 'Fanta Sea Whale Watching'. 'Magnetic Island—Be Attracted'.

It is stunning country for cycling. Bougainvillea and banana trees outdo each other in colour while, out at sea, the saw-toothed mountains of Gloucester Island could well be the setting for a romantic South Pacific blockbuster. It is all a blur as Kurt and I speed on, flying in the wind.

At Bowen there are more campgrounds than houses, catering for the travellers heading north in search of the winter sun from Melbourne, Adelaide and Hobart. Every year an Adelaide couple, Stan and Kitty, drive their campervan to Queensland by a different route: Broken Hill, Bourke, Cunnamulla, Barcaldine. 'It's the only way to see Godzone,' says

Stan with a piano-key smile, his legs, in long white socks and Hush Puppies, propped on a wine cooler.

Day 32: Thursday 19 June, Bowen to Ayr
Distance: 120km
Distance so far: 2595km

An atmospheric anomaly has rendered Bowen significantly drier than regions to the north or south. In particular, the Don River is as dry as the Sinai. Later in the day we cross the Burdekin River, one of Australia's great river systems. The bridge is 500 metres long and often inadequate during wet seasons.

Again, cycling is easy with a tail-wind, which eases a 120km day. The highway, while nothing like the fearsome road we were promised, gets busier and we have to pay more attention to those we share it with, heavily laden cars beetling north, packed to the gunwales with fishing rods and mountain bikes, towing boats more often than not, a trail of sun-seeking ants giving credence to the Victorian Government's slogan, 'Victoria—On The Move'. We get occasional glimpses of the ocean, Abbott Bay and Upstart Bay, the latter framed by the formidable 700-metre-high Station Hill in Cape Upstart National Park. Around us are sugar plantations, sitting under rocky outcrops and majestic mountains. Again I cycle on a euphoric high, captivated by the colours and smells.

The road deteriorates markedly approaching Ayr. The shoulder disappears and deep potholes threaten to tip me up. Roadworks indicate the road is on the improve. Everything's relative. 'Jeez, mate, you should have seen this 25 years ago,' says a roadworker. 'It had one lane and there were as many dead motorists about as dead 'roos.' Later we meet a truckie who cut his teeth driving cattle from Brisbane to Cairns, 2000km, a trip which took a week. Today it takes two days.

'The road was just two tracks through the grass,' he chuckles.

Two friends of Juliet—Sarah and Michael—have us to stay. They recently moved north from Melbourne, she to pursue a career in medicine and he to complete a PhD in Biology. Property prices are competitive; they have a house in Townsville and rent another in Ayr. 'We can't do much but offer you a room,' they say. 'We have plenty of those.'

Day 33: Friday 20 June, Ayr to Townsville
Distance: 94km
Distance so far: 2689km

The Bruce Highway north of Ayr, part of Australia's national highway, is described by locals as a 'national disgrace'. Narrower than yesterday, the potholes are wider and deeper. And the trucks faster. Twice I am run off the road by semi-trailers—pulling up in thick dirt on the side of the road, heart pumping. Kurt suffers similarly. It is like a giant game of chicken: hold your nerve as long as possible, but every so often discretion is the best course.

Townsville, overlooking picturesque Magnetic Island, is a big landmark for me. Not only is it as far north as I will go on the east coast—on Monday I head inland through Charters Towers towards Mount Isa—but it marks the end of the first five weeks of the ride. I have been told often that this would be the toughest, and will determine if I will be able to cope with the next six months. It has not been an easy time, especially when head-winds got up, but I am still in one piece, with moving parts still moving, albeit with a few creaks.

Enthusiasm is infectious at a reception at a supermarket in the city. A group of Cancer Fund volunteers collect money, while the supermarket sells sausages and donates the proceeds.

Again Michael and Sarah look after us. Michael tells us of

his PhD research, which shatters a few Queensland myths. Although this area has the reputation for being a pristine tropical wilderness, commercial development is threatening its delicate ecosystems. Developers are felling 400 000 hectares of trees a year in Queensland, more than four times the rest of Australia, at one stage clearing land by spreading herbicides from the air.

While the Queensland Government plans to import endangered rhinoceroses to start a game park, conservationists say Australian mammals are being neglected. 'Twenty Australian mammals have become extinct since the 1770s,' Michael says, 'and others are threatened.' South of Cardwell, 150km north of Townsville, is a colony of endangered mahogany gliders living in a patch of woodland that farmers are illegally tearing up for sugar cane. Nearby, developer Keith Williams continues to plan a 2000-berth marina opposite the pristine Hinchinbrook Island. Motor boats spell death to mermaids of the deep, dugongs, which feed close to the water's surface.

But, concedes Michael, the biggest threat to native animals is the cane toad, introduced from South America, which has no known predators and whose toxicity can kill animals that eat it. The cane toad is moving inexorably southwards, closing in on the Victoria–New South Wales border. Of even more concern is its movement west, taking it closer to the delicate wetlands of Kakadu National Park near Darwin. It is a journey of more than 2000km through furnace-like conditions. Nothing stops the *Bufo marinus*.

Days 34 and 35: Saturday 21 and Sunday 22 June
Rest days: Townsville

We are given the royal treatment: lunch at the town's cancer hospital, a mayoral reception in the Townsville Mall, and tickets to a rugby game.

Juliet and Kurt leave on Saturday. They have been a dazzling support and strong travellers. Kurt's enthusiasm for fund-raising embarrassed even me at times—setting off with bucket in hand to raise money in campgrounds—and surely no-one has ever asked for a free campsite more convincingly. He hit his head on the caravan's overhead cupboard 14 times, setting a standard for others to chase.

The next team, friends Stephen Norris and Catherine Macmillan—and Catherine's two young children, Geordie and Abbie—arrive Sunday. Catherine, who lost her mother to cancer and who organised the hugely successful launch in Melbourne two months ago, raising $30,000, will drive the support car to Tennant Creek. Steve, an Ulsterman who moved to Australia ten years ago to teach, will cycle as far as his ageing legs will carry him, aiming for Mount Isa, 1000km away. He does, he reminds me as we discuss tomorrow's plans, have a dicky knee. 'My physio doesn't know I'm here,' he says. 'Be gentle.'

CHAPTER THREE

Western Queensland *Dinosaurs and Drovers' Dogs*

Clancy's gone to Queensland droving and we don't know where he are.

AB 'Banjo' Paterson: *Clancy of the Overflow*

Day 36: Monday 23 June,
Townsville to Mingela
Distance: 94km
Distance so far: 2783km

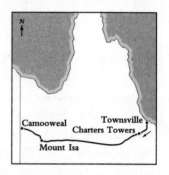

The part of Queensland I am cycling towards has its roots in the gold rush, the route originally opened up for the Cobb & Co. coaches which cut through the North Coast Hinterland and the boundless Barkly Tableland. The first gold was discovered at Charters Towers, 140km from Townsville, in 1871, by an Aboriginal boy, Jupiter Mosman. In its heyday at the turn of the century, Charters Towers boasted 100 mines and a population of 30 000. Mosman Street, the main thoroughfare, had 25 pubs, and the town had its own stock exchange. Locals called Charters Towers, simply, The World.

A new team requires some adjustment and we do not leave Townsville until late morning. Catherine bravely offers to do the shopping for the next fortnight so Steve and I can get moving. She also banks the money collected up the coast, about $3,000. As we cycle out of Townsville the Cancer Fund volunteers wave us off from street corners.

Steve has decided to come for a number of reasons: one of his parents died of cancer and, more recently, a teaching colleague was killed when a car she was in hit an elephant near Victoria Falls in Zimbabwe. 'It made me realise that you never know what's around the corner,' he says as we cycle through the outskirts of Townsville.

We cycle around the western edge of Mount Elliot, passing Ross River Reservoir—origin of the mosquitoes which carry Ross River virus—and travel through farming land on the east side of the Leichhardt Range. Steve cycles strongly and by day's end is surprised he coped so well after only one training ride. It has been a good day for him to start, cool weather and a slight tail-wind. At Mingela, Catherine arrives with a horror story of banking and shopping; buying provisions for five people for a fortnight is not easy.

Mingela is a one-horse town, with three horses. A lodger at the hotel, Brian, is having a week off from *his* journey, riding three Arabs along old stock routes from Cape York to Melbourne, a trip that will take him two years. He looks like he's been going ten years.

There is no campground in Mingela and the hotel owner lets us camp in his backyard, which we share with piles of rusting machinery, a flock of geese, seven turkeys and a goat. His hotel is full of cobwebs, dust and ants. Most importantly, it sells beer. We deserve a few, especially Catherine.

After dinner, as we sit under a canopy of stars, another lodger, Stan, appears clutching a beer. 'Mind if I join you? The evening's beautiful,' he says quietly, one eye focusing on me, the other on something over my left shoulder. 'I've just come out of an alcoholic clinic in Townsville and love being outside under the night sky. When I left the clinic I grabbed my motorbike and now I'm on the move. Only problem is,' he says with a nervous chuckle, pulling up an old tin to sit on,

'I'm not sure where I'm moving to.' In the morning Stan, and his motorbike, are gone.

Day 37: Tuesday 24 June, Mingela to Charters Towers
Distance: 47km
Distance so far: 2830km

The Flinders Highway tracks south-west and shimmers in the rising heat as I bid farewell to Mingela. The soil *seems* hotter, a deep, scorching shade of red. The scrub is lower, as if trying to shrink from the burning sun. There will not be an easier day than today, less than 50km, achieved with the aid of another tail-wind. Traffic is light—unhurried country life—as we pass through Macrossan, on the east bank of the dusty Burdekin River. A railway track keeps us company, heading with confidence into the interior, to Mount Isa. It gives *me* confidence too, as if there is something worth cycling towards.

With new mining techniques Charters Towers is undergoing a mini-gold rush. Even old tailings, mine cast-offs, are being put through the mills again, and the gold extracted. There remain the vestiges from last century's gold rush: wide streets, imposing houses with classic verandahs and lace-work, and grand public buildings. In the campground I speak to a boilermaker, Vern, from one of the mines. 'I work four weeks then have two weeks off; it's a great arrangement,' he says.

In a country with a strong union history, Charters Towers seems an exception. 'There are no such things as unions at our mine these days,' Vern says. 'If I have a problem I go straight to the boss. Things happen faster than going to the union representative and stirring up trouble.'

A journalist from the local paper, the *Northern Miner*, tracks us down and takes photos with a small instamatic. As with most papers in country towns there have been cutbacks, and multi-skilling is now all the rage. 'I'm the reporter, photographer and sub-editor,' she says. 'Pretty soon I could be the editor too, which would be good, but there'll be no-one to order around. I'll be the only one.'

Charters Towers has a feeling of the interior about it. I am not disappointed to have left the east coast, home for two-thirds of Australians, with its motels, fast food outlets and shopping malls. I crave the desert and want to see camels, spinifex, saltbush and tumbleweeds. Most of all I crave the open spaces, the horizon, with no people and no cars. I have travelled little through Australia's interior and have never even made a pilgrimage to that most Australian of icons, Uluru. It is good to be here.

Day 38: Wednesday 25 June, Charters Towers to Pentland
Distance: 109km
Distance so far: 2939km

The locals call last night's rain 'snog rain'—gives you a good feeling but it would be better if it went further. Alistair McDougall, father of Dugall McDougall who I met in Mackay, drops by to make a donation. Like all people around here he moves with assuredness, speaking slowly and with thought, oozing common sense.

The country is as flat as four-day-old Coke—nothing but low-lying scrub grasping at survival in the waterless plain. The horizon is an interminable distance and there is a screaming silence in the still air, broken only by the occasional demented screeches of galahs. Steve's breathing is raspy and I slow the pace down. No point in killing ourselves.

It is hard to believe people live out here. A peeling sunburnt sign points down a dusty track to faraway cattle stations: *Powla-thanga*, *Broadleigh Downs*, *Corea Plains*, the furthest 210km away. Tacked below is a warning to those intending to travel the route, 'Sixty-Five Kilometres of Gullies and River Crossings'. Written in the unsteady hand of someone who may have just survived the drive.

Mid-morning we pass another sign, tacked onto a tree at eye level. 'Richmond Laundromat Now Open'. Richmond is still 300km away. I love that Queensland sense of humour, making fun of their lot. I think of some lines from *We of the Never-Never*, by Jeannie Gunn, about life on a cattle station near Darwin at the turn of the century. An old bushman said to her when she arrived from Melbourne:

'I've been forty years out-bush, and I've known eight or ten women in that time, so I ought to know something about it. Anyway, the ones that could see jokes suited best. There was Mrs Bob out Victoria way. She'd see a joke a mile off; sighted 'em as soon as they got within cooee. Never knew her miss one, and never knew anyone suit the bush like she did.' And as we packed up and set out for the last lap of our journey, he was still ambling about his theory. 'Yes,' he said, 'you can dodge most things out-bush; but you can't dodge jokes for long. They'll run you down sooner or later.'

A town, Homestead, is marked on the map but is nothing more than a roadhouse. Roadhouses, and the people who run them, are the lifeblood of outback Australia, providing fuel, food, grog, accommodation, news and gossip. A man sits in the shade outside, leaning on a suitcase that has seen better days. He slides a foot in and out of a once-polished shoe, now lacking a lace. He looks like he is waiting for a lift, but makes no effort to hail passing motorists. He disappears into the roadhouse and does not reappear, leaving his suitcase in the dust.

I have seen many two-carriage road trains in southern Queensland, but this morning I witness its uglier brother, the three-carriage road train, 50 metres long and full of cattle. I see it ten minutes before it reaches us, throbbing and shimmering in the rising heat, and hear it ten minutes before seeing it. When it passes the road shakes and the wind hits me like a wall. Ten minutes later, near the dry Campaspe River, is an old abattoir, now closed, looking like an abandoned city. More economic rationalism. Another kick in the guts for the bush.

In Pentland, Steve cooks dinner in the caravan, cracking his head twice on the overhead cupboard. Says he feels confident he will beat Kurt's record.

Day 39: Thursday 26 June, Pentland to Hughenden
Distance: 147km
Distance so far: 3086km

The Flinders Highway stretches to the Never-Never like a bad court case. One-hundred-and-fifty kilometres to cycle today, another record. *This* will test the work of Steve's physio.

We work hard through the red expanse, home only to stunted ironbarks and bloodwoods, resembling bonsais in the waterless earth. I clock up 3000km this morning; day 39 and not yet one-fifth of the way. Christ, this is a big country. Steve and I make the most of this seemingly unlimited time together and talk about all manner of subjects, interspersed with long periods of silence. We know each other's families and, in addition to teaching together many years ago, have other things in common, including an interest in sport.

The top of the Great Dividing Range is more a small bump than the mighty location its lordly name would suggest. The range not only determines which way Australian rivers flow—to the east mainly into Lake Dalrymple and the Burdekin, to the south-west into the Diamantina River or Cooper Creek and, in wet seasons, to Lake Eyre—but also the temperatures. From here the heat will be more intense, the light brighter. Our tyres stick to the bitumen and flies hang in the air.

Although buses pass occasionally—heading across the country from Darwin, Townsville or The Alice—we see only one train. The passenger train travels only twice a week these days. The track is being improved though and thousands of concrete sleepers sit in piles, like ancient Aztec monuments, waiting to replace the ironbark sleepers. Around the hamlets of Torrens Creek and Prairie, decaying kangaroos line the road, the smell overpowering. Just as suddenly, as we enter the Jardine Valley where there are signs of grazing, the kangaroos disappear.

At Torrens Creek, Catherine and the kids catch up in the car and we stop for lunch. Geordie is upset and Catherine, I can see, is beginning to lose patience. I am impressed with her fortitude. I am impressed with Geordie's too; he has coped well with life on the move. Steve, with three daughters, is good backup. I am as useful as tits on a bull.

The final 35km are tough on us both and after lunch we grunt and groan for the best part of two hours along a burning road. Our 147km for the day is a new record for the ride, and again I am impressed with the way Steve has performed. Seven hours on a bike is no easy task *and* he manages a smile at the end. I do the final 20km hard: my legs ache, my arse is sorer still, and I can feel a cold coming on.

Hughenden, population 2000, sits on the Flinders River which cuts up north through the Gulf Savannah country, reaching the Gulf of Carpentaria near Normanton. Rain falling 50km south of here flows south. During the dry season river beds become playgrounds; the Flinders shows skid marks from late-night motoring revellers.

The town is a large railway junction and a crossroad for routes to Longreach and Barcaldine to the south and Cairns to the north-east, 600km away on the Kennedy Developmental Road. There is a sandalwood industry here too, exporting to, of all places, China. It is a noisy town: trains shunt in throughout the afternoon, and galahs and cockatoos take off and settle in flocks, screeching like the devil.

There is a more ancient life form for which the town is noted: years ago, according to the locals, dinosaurs roamed these parts, and the town now boasts a life-size replica of a *Muttaburrasaurus*, Hughie. Even the rubbish bins are shaped like dinosaur feet.

Catherine and the kids go to bed, feeling unwell, while Steve and I feel we deserve a beer at the end of a big day. As a city boy I have long held the belief that Aboriginal and white Australians mix freely and without prejudice in Australian bars. Nothing at the Hughenden Hotel makes me think otherwise until 20 minutes after arriving, when the barman sidles up to us and tells us we are welcome in the 'Special Bar' out the back. 'We're happy here,' we echo each other.

Days 40 and 41: Friday 27 and Saturday 28 June
Rest days: Hughenden

A welcome early weekend. The locals refer to the Porcupine Gorge National Park 60km north of Hughenden as the Mini-Grand Canyon. By the side of the road, a pile of white rocks marks the grave of mailman Corbett, speared on his mail delivery in 1861. It is starkly beautiful country, mostly basalt rock with red and black soils which came from inside Mount Desolation, a volcano—now extinct—20km to the west. In all directions is grazing country: Mitchell and Blue grasses swaying in the wind sweeping off the Barkly Tableland.

We pluck up courage to swim at the Hughenden pool, which is freezing. A gardener, working on a nearby flower bed, leans on his rake and studies us. 'You're from Victoria, aren't ya,' he says, more statement than question.

Nods from us.

'You can always tell the Victorians,' he replies, coolly. 'They swim up here in the winter time and they pinch all the avocado out of the salads.'

In the evening I visit Ian Lettice, the head of the Hughenden Lions Club, who donates $100. He has a yellowing beard and a lived-in face, and tells me this is his third stint in Hughenden in a 40-year career with the railways. 'That's the equivalent of two life sentences,' he growls. His wife, tinkering in the kitchen, yells, 'Give us a break Darl', you love it here.'

'Hmmph,' he says.

Day 42: Sunday 29 June, Hughenden to Richmond
Distance: 117km
Distance so far: 3203km

The day gets off on the wrong foot when I announce I want to run dry the caravan's gas bottle, which we use for cooking and to power the fridge. I want to know the bottle's capacity before I reach the Northern Territory where gas will be in short supply. My statement starts a tense discussion that continues for half an hour and simmers for the rest of the day. Catherine says not having gas could be dangerous and that I have a 'cavalier attitude' towards safety. I argue the contrary; that wanting to know how much gas the bottle holds is planning for the future and therefore an attempt to *improve* safety. We agree to disagree, which does not resolve the tension.

The disagreement crystallises for me the difficulties involved in leading a team of people in demanding circumstances. I am sure

Catherine feels the same way, but from the other side. A team of five people trying to live together harmoniously while undertaking demanding physical activity is not easy. For my part, I find it difficult to locate that elusive line between making decisions to ensure things go smoothly and being pushy. In particular, how much should I ask for suggestions from the present group when the most workable solution to a problem has been determined painstakingly by a previous group? Why re-invent the wheel? Some people are happy to rely on a previous group's findings, while others need decisions to be made afresh, and need to be intimately involved in the decision-making process. Of course, what is good for one group might not necessarily be good for another. Organising an event and cycling up to eight hours a day is not easy; driving a car for someone cycling up to eight hours a day is probably harder.

Another blessed tail-wind and Steve and I cover 60km in two hours, seeing not a car. The saltbush of the past two days has been replaced by brown knee-high pasture in all directions. Again the verge is littered with decaying kangaroos, one of which, in the middle of the road, is prodigious in size. Steve heaves it to the side, blood trickling from its nose.

Just when you think you have discovered true wilderness, civilisation has a habit of rearing its head. Mid-morning we pull over at Marathon, aptly named for a dusty, wind-swept lay-by. There, under the corrugated iron lean-to, is a group of contented Germans enjoying a bacchanalian feast—bread, wine and all manner of sausage and cheese—laid out on a crisp damask tablecloth. Next to them a Japanese couple create intricate pancakes on a gas-fired wok. It is a surreal sight. The Germans toast us with crystal glasses, gewurztraminer and contented smiles. 'Good cycling? Ya? Ya?'

A familiar twang indicates another broken spoke, this time for Steve, and five minutes later he gets a flat tyre. It is only the second flat tyre during the trip, following mine on the first day, and, as we change it wallowing in the Flinders Highway roadside dust, I reason that only two punctures in a combined 6000km is no cause for complaint. I have been told that they will become more common near Broome, where bindy-eyes—spiked seed pods (*Emex australis* or *Soliva pterosperma*)—make mincemeat of inner tubes and drive cyclists to madness.

While Hughenden was parched, the township of Richmond is, quite literally, blooming. Bougainvillea lines the main street and the town's gardens cascade with colours, women in floral aprons tending proudly to their patches. Richmond sits above the Great Artesian Basin, so water is plentiful here.

In the main street we meet former Mayor Jack Brown, now a committed member of the local Lions Club. Jack was stationed here during World War II, in charge of the poisonous gas dump. 'I married a local girl and stayed on,' he says. 'Richmond's the best town in Western Queensland.'

When the war finished Jack's job was to dispose of the gas. 'It sounds pretty technical, but it wasn't really,' he tells us. 'We shot bullets into the barrels, after making sure we were upwind. We also had the OK from the local weatherman that the town wouldn't be vaporised.'

Outside the Richmond Marine Fossil Museum (we are at least 500km from the coast) a plaque commemorates the opening of a section of the Flinders Highway. Cutting the ribbon was none other than Russ Hinze, the Sunshine State's Minister for Local Government, Main Roads and Racing. Russ got about.

I fill the gas bottle.

Day 43: Monday 30 June, Richmond to Julia Creek
Distance: 157km
Distance so far: 3360km

Should have stayed in bed. While driving the caravan out from camp I hit a telegraph pole and bend its steps. A mechanic belts them back into shape with a sledgehammer and slices bits off with a fearsome angle grinder. There is now no longer a bottom step, which will especially tax Geordie and Abbie, who already have trouble getting into the caravan. Steve and I visit the local Dalgety store for provisions, where the locals are rugged up like Michelin Men in the cold. 'Do you always dress like that?' says the shopkeeper, looking at us suspiciously. Men in lycra are not common in Richmond.

Another record day, 160km and, inexplicably, another tail-wind. Someone up there is watching over us. We cover 75km in two hours while Catherine drives on ahead. Despite the gruelling week I feel stronger than ever. The human body is remarkably adaptable, I muse as we fang down the Flinders Highway. Some days I feel I could cycle forever.

The chill leaves the air when the sun rises and before long the temperature nudges 30 degrees. I regale Steve with the horror of the Gympie-to-Biggenden day and remind him to keep up the fluids. There is now a firm rule; two litres of water to be drunk before cycling in the morning, and another two during the morning, with top-ups where needed. We spend a lot of time stopping to leak, but it's a small price to pay for good health.

In addition to water I have found that an hour's stretching a day, half an hour after 60km and half an hour at the end of the day, is good for the health, speeding recovery and allowing a succession of long days. I struggled to touch my toes before the start of the ride; now I can touch them with only mildly excruciating pain.

The road looks like someone dropped a typewriter ribbon on a yellow shag pile. On either side of our ten feet of bitumen the fields are full of wispy, head-high grass with the occasional gnarled eucalypt. Mostly there is nothing between us and the very distant horizon. I have never seen a sky so blue. Vast sections of the Flinders Highway are being remade and throughout the morning we are passed by hulking machines carting gravel and tar from some distant source, belching acrid smoke. Twice we are stopped by orange-coated roadworkers, sunburnt faces and farmer's arms, swivelling stop signs at us on the single-lane road, even though we have seen no car for hours. 'Sorry boys, them's the rules,' says one as we stand beside him for the best part of ten minutes. He regales us with the problems of working in the wilderness. 'No women, that's the main problem.'

'What about Mount Isa?' I ask.

He gives a despairing look.

Steve and I agree that the old road, despite its cracks, is better to cycle on than the stretches of new bitumen. At least the old road has a smooth surface, worn down by decades of road trains and countless generations of Holdens, while the new road is made from rough gravel, which adds friction.

Fifty kilometres short of Julia Creek a sign points to Nelia. We take a detour to the old railway town and find a community on its last legs, three houses each more dilapidated than the last. No-one answers our calls at the post office; old leather-bound ledgers gather dust on the shelves and a handful of ancient postcards sit dog-eared on a rusting revolving rack. The only water, warm and salty, comes from a bore.

Across the road a tennis court is a reminder of better days, now all weeds and cracked asphalt. Inside the tilting shelter, which protected yesterday's spectators from the piercing afternoon sun, is a coiled tennis net, five cricket stumps, a rat-eaten batting glove and a heavily tarnished cup—'Nelia Cricket Club, Town Versus Country Match'—showing the winners over the years. Beyond is an oval, recognisable only by a ring of trees, now covered in long brown grass and memories. What faceless bureaucrat decided trains would no longer stop here, sealing this town's fate? No more tea and scones by the tennis court. No more Cuff and Collar cricket matches at Nelia.

The tail-wind disappears and we feel cheated, spoiled by a dream run. The final 20km to Julia Creek is hard work, and I call on all reserves of energy and commitment. Again I am amazed at Steve's capacity for endurance; 160km is no trifling distance. Short of Julia Creek, as if I needed a reminder of the distances of Western Queensland, we pass the entrance to the Wills Developmental Road. A shiny sign reads, 'Dalgonolly 73, Spoonbill 108, Normanton 420, Burketown 467, Karumba 500'. The last is a town on the coastal flats at the mouth of the Norman River, not an expression of disbelief; in Australia everything is a long way away.

We have deserved a night in a pub and are welcomed at Gannon's Pub by friends of my cousin. Julia and Peter Hayden moved to Julia Creek from Roma two years ago and will stay here 'as long as we enjoy it'. The hotel is a hive of activity and I share a beer with two cooks who follow the Queensland rodeo circuit. Today they have driven down from the Saxby roundup at *Taldora* station, 170km to the north. Tomorrow they return to Townsville, a trip close to 700km. 'Ah, it's nothin' at all,' one says when I remark at the distance. 'Do it on our ears.'

They are unshaven, unkempt and spend the evening ribbing each other mercilessly. Such is pub life in Australia; anyone's fair game, and if you don't like it, you're fairer game still. At the epicentre of the banter is Jim, who used to run *Arizona* station. 'He drinks a lot these days,' Julia says to me later on.

'He still cops a fearful ribbing from the boys for being rescued by helicopter from the top of his chicken shed during the floods of '74 when the Gulf moved 50km to the south.'

Day 44: Tuesday 1 July
Rest day: Julia Creek

Catherine drops a bombshell. They will return home from Mount Isa, in four days' time, a week early. She gives a number of reasons for the decision: misses her boyfriend in Melbourne; they all have colds; and she is not comfortable taking Abbie and Geordie into the Australian outback. We have had our differences this week regarding organisation, and I wonder whether this is a factor. I try to persuade her to change her mind, but nothing doing. Steve, too, is leaving from Mount Isa as planned and I wonder who will drive the car the 600km between Mount Isa and Tennant Creek. I still don't have a driver between Darwin and Broome. I can sense things unravelling.

I venture with some trepidation to the hairdresser. 'So, mate, what brings you to Julia Creek?' asks the proprietor, snipping her oversized scissors in the air with what I consider to be a little too much carefree abandon. Before I finish my explanation, a period no more than four minutes, I have short back and sides to die for.

Day 45: Wednesday 2 July, Julia Creek to Cloncurry
Distance: 140km
Distance so far: 3500km

Outside, last night's temperature fell to three degrees. Among the furphies about the Australian outback is that it is always like a cauldron. 'Cold as a nun's tit,' mutters a fellow, breathing fog under the pub's verandah, waiting for opening.

Steve and I leave at eight, primed for another big day and fearing another head-wind. Sure enough it scythes off the fields and creek beds to the south-west, the only saving grace being the road, which oscillates like Foucault's Pendulum, occasionally providing a side-wind. The wind is cold and we each wear three layers of clothes. My newly revealed ears feel like they have been slapped in ice.

The horizon seems a million miles away. The thick grass has disappeared but the cattle seem surprisingly well-fed. Steve and I speak little, content to dream intermittently of arrival in Cloncurry, and tail-winds. It is the comfortable silence of a team; I feel an empathy towards him as we work together to complete a difficult task, volunteering in turn to lead and take the resistance, respecting, trusting.

A dusty track leads off to the north, pointing to *Caleewa Downs*, *Haddington* and, most appropriately, *Lands End*. No-one speaks of hectares in these parts; stations sell for $30 an acre, often less. Not for the first time I wonder how the owners handle the tyranny of distance. What are their escapes? What do they do for a good time? How, especially, do the farmers' wives feel when they marry and arrive for the first time to live out here? It is one thing to pass through this place, another to live here.

The saplings of the past fortnight become proud eucalypts short of Cloncurry and the colours have gained new degrees of brilliance: the earth is redder, the leaves greener and we see the first signs of yellow wattle. Gum trunks are a sparkling white against a blue sky. I am undeniably now in the real outback, and among hard-nosed miners. Plumes of smoke emerge from corrugated iron sheds and the chugging of generators breaks the monotonous gusting of the wind. The region is home to mines with captivating and romantic names like Duchess, Gunpowder and Phosphate Hill.

Into the wind, 140km is the equivalent of close to 200km

without wind and Steve and I are of delicate disposition when we reach Cloncurry—despite drinking enough water to float the *QE II*, stretching and eating copiously. We have ridden more than seven hours with only two stops, the longest day of the past six weeks, and we ease ourselves to the ground, groaning. We once ran a marathon together, around Lake Windermere in England's Cumbria, having heard about it the night before. Tonight we revisit the pain.

Cloncurry, in the Gulf Savannah region, is home to more than 3000 Queenslanders, though they are perhaps closer to being Territorians. Everything about the town points to generousness. The hotels are large, the streets wide, and people wear big, hearty smiles. Early this century Cloncurry was the largest copper producer in the British Empire after John McKinlay, leading an expedition to search for Burke and Wills, discovered the metal. Today it is a pastoral centre and known universally as the birthplace of the Royal Flying Doctor Service, started in 1928, providing medical services to the outlying stations.

My camera's state-of-the-art battery has run flat and I fear there will be no replacement here. I find, to my astonishment, a camera shop, and am equally amazed when the owner, fossicking under the counter, emerges with a replacement. Never underestimate the bush.

A public noticeboard carries the advertisement:

For Sale: Rotty/Bully cross. Ideal pig-hunting dog.
Not recommended for family with small children.

Day 46: Thursday 3 July, Cloncurry to Mount Isa
Distance: 122km
Distance so far: 3622km

The 120km stretch of bitumen between Cloncurry and Mount Isa is a little plot of Australian history. There is a memorial cairn to the Burke and Wills expedition, which passed by on 22 January 1861. At the time, the explorers' spirits must have been high as they neared the Gulf of Carpentaria, despite having endured Australia's inhospitable centre. They would have witnessed the same scene that we see today, save for the Forex cans scattered around the base of a 44-gallon-drum rubbish bin. Next to the cairn the Corella River bubbles contentedly, the first running water I have seen in a fortnight.

The disaster of the Burke and Wills expedition occurred some five months later, in the wilderness of Cooper Creek near what is now Innamincka. Wills' final diary entry was:

Friday, 29th of June, 1861—Clear cold night, slight breeze from the east, day beautifully warm and pleasant. Mr Burke suffers greatly from the cold and getting extremely weak; he and King start tomorrow up the creek to look for the blacks; it is the only chance we have of being saved from starvation.

Wills' body was discovered by Alfred Howitt in September 1861, and his letters and journal were subsequently edited by his father and published in 1863 under the surprising title: *A Successful Exploration through the Interior.*

A kilometre beyond the cairn is a memorial to the Kalkadoon and Mitakoodi Aboriginal tribes. In 1884 the authorities dispatched a sub-inspector of police, Frederick Urquhart, to quell the resistance of the Kalkadoon. In September, Urquhart's men gathered at a rocky hill north of Kajabbi, later known as Battle Mountain. The massacre was swift and merciless and the

Kalkadoon, armed only with spears and shields, were all but wiped out by the guns. The memorial carries the words:

You who pass by are now entering the ancient tribal lands of the Kalkadoon/Mitakoodi, dispossessed by the European. Honour their name, be brother and sister to their descendants.

A further 9km on is the former site of Mary Kathleen, a uranium mining town from the 1950s to 1982, now demolished.

Steve and I cycle strongly through jagged hills, the steep gullies revealing clumps of scrub and bush, birds flitting through the trees. Kangaroos disappear shyly into gorges and the suicidal cry of galahs bounces off the ochre cliff-faces. I flew over here two years ago and it seemed different from the air; dull, featureless and far from life-supporting. Today it pulses with colour and movement. It is comforting, after two weeks of flat country, to be back on a gradient, re-acquainting ourselves with forgotten muscles. I have been cycling on gear five (of 21) for days and am happy to explore its neglected colleagues.

The towering smoke stacks of Mount Isa appear on the horizon and we are met by a journalist and a photographer from the *North West Star*. Minutes later a phalanx of parents and kids, the latter on bikes and clad in lurid cycling outfits, appear on the side of the road, and cheer as we approach. We cycle into town together, accompanied by two policemen on motorbikes, lights flashing. It is a fabulous moment.

'The Isa', 900km from the east coast and 1900km from Brisbane, is one of the most remote cities in Australia, but the 24 000 people who live here are among the best serviced in the land. The city has swimming pools, ovals, tennis courts (producing Australian tennis champion Pat Rafter, among others) and a busy business district. The town is one of the most diverse in Australia, boasting 60 ethnic groups. Typically, people come to Mount Isa for a year or two, and stay 20.

The Mayor, Don, welcomes us at the Civic Centre in his mayoral robes and medallions, and tea and scones are served. Mount Isa is renowned worldwide for its palliative care work and fund-raising for cancer research, and Don tells us that, being on the only east-west road in Western Queensland, fund-raising groups often pass through. The response is always positive.

It has been a tough ride along the Flinders Highway, and Steve and I celebrate his last night with a Guinness at Mount Isa's Irish Club. Catherine, still stricken with a head cold and an ear infection, is in bed early. The club is a fun one, an eclectic collection of races and nationalities mixing freely and happily. We trade yarns with two men from Brisbane who have just returned from a fishing expedition at Karumba. At closing time an Aboriginal woman, Barbara, invites us to join her partying in town. Steve's bus leaves in seven hours and, though tempted, we decline.

Days 47–49: Friday 4–Sunday 6 July
Rest days: Mount Isa

Mount Isa owes its existence to a rich copper, silver, lead and zinc mine—5000km of tunnels—and at one stage its owner, Mount Isa Mines, was the largest company in Australia. The smelter's 300-metre exhaust stack dominates the skyline, casting smoke into the atmosphere 24 hours a day.

The thought of having three days in the one spot with no cycling is a luxury. Packing up and moving camp each day becomes difficult and I plan plenty of sleep and housekeeping chores: washing clothes, servicing the car, and overhauling the bikes which are beginning to show wear and tear having been on the road seven weeks. Quasimodo's chain is stretched and his tyres are worn to the bone. People have spoken about puncture problems in the Northern Territory, and I follow an old cyclist's trick—cut the wire rims from the old tyres and put them inside the new ones, giving extra protection from bindy-eyes and glass shards.

The next stage of the ride will be different, through the sparsely populated Northern Territory where shops are as common as surfboards and water a scarce resource. Provisions must be bought and stored. Now is also a time for mental preparation for the next stage of the ride, where I will cycle alone for the first time.

But first to say goodbye to the stalwarts of the past two weeks. Steve leaves on a bus for Townsville, retracing our steps of the past fortnight, while Catherine, Geordie and Abbie fly to Darwin, then Melbourne. Catherine has organised a replacement driver for the next week, Ian Louis from Townsville. Again, I have that floating, out-of-control feeling of a team breaking up. Alone for the first time on the trip I am too tired to cook dinner and opt for a hamburger, then escape to the theatre, where *Jurassic Park* seems an appropriate flick. After the past four days my joints feel like they belong to a *Muttaburrasaurus*.

Cycling is a big deal in Mount Isa; every year the town hosts a 240km road race to Cloncurry and back, the Barkly Challenge, won this year by a 16-year-old from the Institute of Sport. On Saturday I meet members of the Copper City Cycle Club who donate the proceeds of a recent fund-raising ride, $300. They invite me to ride in tomorrow's 40km race to Lake Moondarra and back and I quickly concoct an excuse. Actually, I could think of nothing worse.

I drive to the Kalkadoon Pub at Kajabbi, scene of Urquhart's battle with the Kalkadoon, two hours north along a dusty, undulating road, for a party to raise money for the Queensland

Cancer Fund. The pub's owner has a beard which hangs to his belt buckle and the inside of the pub is covered in a layer of dust and cobwebs, giant yabbies, bras hanging ghoulishly from the ceiling, and graffiti. Above the door is written in scrawly print: 'Man, dem some weird shit happenin' here in Kajabbi.'

The party becomes a male-bonding ritual, largely because there are no women. Jackaroos never pass up a good party, and some have driven all day to get here. A band, Down to Earth, is the hottest thing from town and following its off-key cover songs there are cane toad races and horizontal bungee jumping. I stay long enough to take some photos for the local paper (the photographer is curled up under a bush somewhere) before driving back to Mount Isa under a bright midnight sky.

On Sunday I drive along the Waggaboonyah Range to Gunpowder, a mining community 120km north-west of The Isa, to lunch with friends of friends, and collect Ian Louis from the airport on my return. He is a former truckie who used to do the 5000km Townsville–Darwin–Townsville milk run in three days flat. These days he has a pig farm but says he is an entrepreneur 'in the broad sense of the word'. He is a hard-talking, meat-eating Queenslander with a flowing beard and a cultivated belly. He speaks like an ack-ack gun. Our first hour together is him talking and me saying 'pardon?'

Day 50: Monday 7 July, Mount Isa to Camooweal
Distance: 190km
Distance so far: 3812km

After three days' rest I feel recharged; good because today's distance is 190km, far longer than anything I have experienced to date. Despite this I am not nervous, more excited at the thought of completing it, and challenged by the concept of completing it alone.

I collect Quasimodo from Joe's Bicycles (no charge for over-haul). Sitting on a bench is a Swedish cyclist covered in scabs who, three days ago, mangled his front wheel when he fell into a cattle grid near Cloncurry. Ian and I do three weeks' shopping at Coles. I make a point of seeking out the manager and thanking him. 'Never heard of you,' he says. 'But if head office reckons it's OK for us to sponsor you, then it's OK.' Top of the shopping list is pasta and a sack of spuds, both of which Ian looks at warily. 'I'm happy eating anything so long as it once stood on four legs and, preferably, mooed,' he says. The fridge in the caravan is small and only runs when we are stationary. Experience says we can store meat for no more than a week, which should get us to Tennant Creek anyway.

At the start of my new road, the Barkly Highway, I am kept company by four kids from the cycling club. It is their last day of school holidays and they yabber excitedly about the new term. One of them tells me his father works for ATSIC, the Aboriginal and Torres Strait Islander Commission. 'Is he Aboriginal or from the Torres Strait?' I ask.

'Neither, he's Burmese,' replies the kid smiling, 'and my mother is Malaysian.'

As we cycle over a hill I glance back at Mount Isa's smoke stack, wobbling in the morning's heat. Queensland's melting pot. Ian has driven on 70km, and once the kids pile into a mother's car and turn for home, I have no choice but to concede that I am alone.

Edward Abbey, an American, wrote a book about life in the desert, *Desert Solitaire*, and contends there is no limit to the human capacity for experiencing a sense of home, whether that sense relates to a houseboat in Kashmir, a view down Atlantic Avenue in Brooklyn, or a cabin on the shore of a blue lake. Theologians, pilots, even astronauts have found that home can exist in their unusual surroundings. Abbey writes:

For myself I'll take Moab, Utah. I don't mean the town itself, of course, but the country which surrounds it—the canyonlands. The slickrock desert. The red dust and the burnt cliffs and the lonely sky—all that which lies beyond the end of the roads.

I understand him. Although I am undeniably in the Australian outback—only the small township of Camooweal exists in the 700km between Mount Isa and Tennant Creek—I feel quite at home here. I suppose it is a function of the nomadic existence; once you start travelling and get over the need to be with people and attached to a house, being in the wilderness seems the most natural thing in the world, to the extent that the thought of living within four walls is unsettling. 'Life itself is a journey to be walked on foot,' wrote British travel writer Bruce Chatwin when he travelled to Nepal in 1983 seeking the Yeti.

I have become accustomed to the open spaces, become attuned to these surroundings. These days the expanses are my friend. I feel a euphoria of sorts, and I cannot wipe a silly grin from my face. It is, quite simply, a thrilling moment to be alive, on an extraordinary expedition; no cars and no people, just the vast horizons of the Barkly Tableland, ant nests rising like sentinels, and no sound but the hum of the wheels and my own controlled breathing. I feel like I could take on the world. 'Look out Territory, here I come!'

Three hours and 85km later the euphoria has gone. Now, it's simply a case of me and the road. And doubts. The road is flat and straight, merciless and unwavering. Churn the pedals, increase cadence, keep up the water levels. Hard work. Hard, too, to find something to think about. In past weeks there has been mindless chit-chat, laughter, geographical discussion, word games and sporting trivia: Name all the Indian cricketers with surnames starting with 'P'. Is the Nawab of Pataudi worth a point or instant disqualification? Today I have no-one to talk to. Me and the road. Me and my mind.

I think of Mum. If she were still alive, I would not be here.

I have been drinking constantly and by the time I meet Ian for lunch, next to the road leading to *Old May Downs*, I am out of water. I wolf down three sandwiches and take another three litres of water. He sets off for Camooweal. 'See you there,' he says jocularly. Camooweal is still 80km away and only three hours of sunlight remain.

Although I have drunk five litres of water already today, it is clearly not enough and I have underestimated the effect of the heat. I finish the next three litres with 50km still to cycle. The cyclists' mantra rings in my ears; I have been pissing neither often nor clear. Haven't pissed at *all* during the past hour, actually. My mouth feels like the inside of a bird cage.

The first stages of panic have set in when a van appears on the left and a bloke *is* pissing, on a small plant on the side of the road. He is a Swiss, travelling with his girlfriend, and they have a water tank in their mini-van the size of a four-drawer filing cabinet. They fill my water bottles, giving me a choice of raspberry, lime or lemon cordial. I am ashamed I got to the point of having to rely on others—what would have happened if no-one was about?—and am lucky to have emerged unscathed. Perhaps carrying three litres of water on the bike is not enough. I must either carry more or fill up more often. There *are* water tanks along the Barkly Highway, but no-one can vouch for the water quality.

The couple has been travelling four months, camping in lay-bys and on river banks. 'We hope to find a waterhole at the Buckley River and stay there four days,' he says in spotless English. The front of their van shows a patchwork of dents, as if someone has taken to it with a machine gun, and I point to them. 'Rocks thrown up from passing cars,' she says. 'I get a shock every time we are hit.' I wonder what such a missile would do to me and remind myself to keep my head down.

Although hydrated the final 50km pass in a slow, painful blur, distress building. The devil sits on my left shoulder, tempting me. This ride's become unhealthy. An obsession. Ahab and the whale. Why not toss it in? Didn't Churchill say the only exercise he ever took was walking to funerals of friends who took exercise?

Roadworks prevent rhythm and earthmoving vehicles throw up gagging bulldust. I limp into Camooweal as the sun sinks over the Barkly Tableland, turning the sky a dusky purple, outlining the awkward shapes of the water towers. Ian says Camooweal has changed little since he drove trucks through 15 years ago. 'It's flat as buggery and nothing happens here,' he says disdainfully. 'If it wasn't for the truckies the town would have died years ago.' At the moment I wouldn't be impressed if Camooweal was the home of Versailles, the Sistine Chapel Ceiling and Disney-on-Ice. I am rooted and collapse in a heap.

Ian has set up camp behind a service station in a dusty campground. Next to the caravan is a sign on a gate: 'Beware of the dog—he's a bummer'. Steak, of course, for dinner, then bed. I consult the *Lonely Planet Guidebook* about what to expect west of here. I know from snatched conversations and folklore that the Barkly Highway holds dark secrets; travellers have disappeared on the road. The guidebook does not mention this, although the writer is emphatic in his contempt for the road: 'There's nothing much for the whole 460km to the Threeways Junction,' he says simply. Five hundred kilometres of nothing; has there ever been a more damning assessment of a piece of bitumen?

CHAPTER FOUR

The Northern Territory
Spinning Through the Never-Never

*He was a bushman of the old type, one of the men of the droving days;
full of old theories, old faith, and old prejudices, and clinging always to
old habits and methods. Year by year as the bush had receded and
shrunk before the railways, he had receded with it, keeping always just
behind the Back of Beyond, droving, bullock-punching, stock-keeping,
and unconsciously opening up the way for that very civilisation that was
driving him farther and farther back. In the forty years since his boyhood,
railways had driven him out of Victoria, New South Wales, and
Queensland, and were now threatening even the Never-Never, and Dan
was beginning to fear that they would not leave 'enough bush to bury a
man in'.*

Jeannie Gunn: *We of the Never-Never*

Day 51: **Tuesday 8 July,**
Camooweal to Soudan
Distance: 133km
Distance so far: 3945km

The Never-Never, if you believe the dictionary, is 'sparsely
inhabited desert country, a remote and isolated region'. Others
say it is an amalgam of Aboriginal folklore mixed with a healthy
dash of white settler Top End nervousness. One thing's for sure,
it is as much a concept as a place. It is the Aboriginal dreamtime

and their songlines. It is vast plains and yellowing, plunging cliffs, bow-legged stockmen and handsome Aboriginal ringers, camp-fire yarns about swirling serpents and giant echidnas. It is deep gorges and wild rivers, old man goannas and thrashing crocs, cracked saltpans and groaning wetlands. It is a place where a postman used to ride for hundreds of kilometres to deliver a letter, and where station owners would look after him like royalty when he arrived. It was a place where you lived life according to a simple rule: if you got sick you either got better, or you didn't. It is, as much as anything, a place of extremes—at the same spot in the Never-Never you could either die of thirst, or drown, depending on the time of year.

'The Territory', as the Northern Territory is simply called in the Top End, represents 20 per cent of Australia's area, about 1.3 million square kilometres. It is inhabited by only one per cent of the country's population, about 180 000 people, 50 per cent of whom live in the main city, Darwin, and 22 per cent of whom are Aboriginal. The gold rush in the 1870s put the Territory on the map, and throughout the twentieth century numbers swelled as the telegraph system was installed and roads and railways built, attracting graziers, farmhands, business tycoons and, more recently, tourists.

Perhaps it is the climate, or the frontier nature of the place, or even *because* it is so far away from mainstream Australian life, that the Territory has always attracted people of odd disposition. Miscreants and madmen, runaways and rebels seem to find their way there. Darwin, they say, is home to the Wanted and the unwanted. Many of them stay forever, attracted by the climate, a community of similar disposition and a legal system that seems to turn a blind eye to odd-balls. There is, notably, no speed limit on Territory highways; it also seems quite appropriate that Territorians are the only people in Australia who can bet on elections. For the Wanted, escape from Darwin is easy. Simply board a boat in the Darwin-to-Ambon yacht race and jump ship in Indonesia.

If you elect to stay in Darwin, be prepared for a vastly different place during the build-up and wet season when people can go 'troppo', driven mad by the heat and the incessant rain. During the wet season marriages end and domestic violence increases. People go to pubs to brawl as much as to drink.

Equally, the Territory has always been a place of opportunity. When pastoralists opened up the Top End early this century there was plenty of work about, droving or mustering, so long as you could sit on a horse. Those handy with a gun could shoot buffalo or crocs. The less talented went in for dog-stiffening (dingo poisoning), with scalps fetching five shillings each, traded in at police stations or general stores, where they were as good as hard currency.

Newcomers preferring less honourable pursuits and needing quick cash often turned to cattle-duffing, where fenceless tracts of land presented good opportunities to sneak off with a few, or a few hundred head. The Australian habit of barracking for the underdog and the notion of a fair go meant cattle duffers often received lenient sentences when caught, or got off entirely. This was a nationwide phenomenon, and not altogether surprising in a country that began its European settlement as a penal colony.

It was the same in Queensland. One of the most famous cattle rustlers was Harry Redford who, in 1870, stole a thousand head from Longreach and drove them 2400km to South Australia—through country that, a decade earlier, had defeated Burke and Wills—and sold them. Redford's drive opened up a new stock route and, when he was arrested three years later, he was found not guilty by an admiring public.

Cattle rustlers who found themselves in Darwin's Fannie

Bay Jail hardly had arduous lives. The jail was run by a sympathetic Mr Dempsey, who allowed cattle duffers to drink as much as they liked and leave jail for afternoons, so long as they were back by six o'clock. If they failed to make the curfew they were locked out! Once, an inmate, Jack Buscall, failed to return by curfew and scaled the walls in an attempt to climb back *into* jail so as not to offend Dempsey. He fell to the ground, broke his back and spent the rest of his life in a wheelchair. He was, of course, released immediately.

The Territory's reputation was built during the cattle droving days of the 1880s, when men made superhuman treks from the eastern states to stock local cattle stations, opening up new stock routes in the process. It built legends of toughness that continued into this century, and remain today. When Englishman Tom Cole, author of *Hell West and Crooked*, arrived in the Territory in 1925 he was impressed by a cattlehand who did his own dental work, pulling out his own teeth with a pair of fencing pliers, and seemingly enjoying the challenge.

I have these larger-than-life stories in mind as I set off from Camooweal, bound for the Territory border. They are struggling for landmarks here in Queensland's last town and someone came up with the buffaroo, a kangaroo with horns. A peeling statue sits next to the roadhouse, the accompanying sign explaining the derivation of the animal: 'A female kangaroo which went in search of something more exciting than male kangaroos and got more than she bargained for'.

I reach the border after 15km, and it is a monumental letdown. A large roadsign and a bent cattle grid in the middle of an arid plain. The sign is covered in graffiti, penned by Japanese, Canadians and Brits. One says, 'Annie, Yulan, Linden doin' it 6/6/97'. I stare at the date and realise it was only yesterday. 'Who needs a four-wheel drive when you've got a Torana?' says another. I take a self-timer photo—discover later that I have chopped off my head—and remount Quasimodo.

All passing cars are four-wheel drives, and most tow caravans. Many of the drivers slow down for a chat, driving along beside me. Others honk, wave and flash their hazard lights. There is a palpable feeling of togetherness. 'There were no caravans out here when I drove these parts 20 years ago,' says Ian at lunch. 'Can't understand why they would want to come out here anyway. What's wrong with the east coast?'

Ian's entrepreneurial spirit kicks in and, as we munch on sandwiches under the only tree for miles, he wonders aloud how he could convert the grey nomads into filthy lucre. 'A set of dinosaur tracks and a $10 charge would get 'em in I reckon, or perhaps a bowling rink at one of these wayside stops,' he muses. While I rest my limbs he chips away at rocks on the roadside with a prospector's hammer, searching for gems. 'Ah, bugger 'em,' he says after ten fruitless minutes, chucking the hammer into the back of the car.

Whoever invented the Barkly had poor imagination. To the north the Tableland is a vast tract of yellow, dotted with the occasional tree or windmill, and the odd cow searching for shade. The scene does not change for hours. Eighty kilometres west of Camooweal, on the edge of *Avon Downs*, is a police station, two fibro houses surrounded by impressively green lawns. Most of their work must be humdrum, helping tourists with water or fuel, reassuring the spatially spooked, occasionally looking for the geographically embarrassed.

The police had more gruesome tasks when the roads were poorer. In the 1930s a couple, the new doctor at Tennant Creek and his wife, set out across the Barkly Tableland to help a patient at *Rockhampton Downs* 160km away. The road was nothing but a dirt track which passed Number 3 bore. Beyond the bore the tracks of thousands of cattle blotted out the road and the couple got lost. Trying to find the road across country over tussocky Mitchell grass and gilgai holes their car broke down. They tried to walk back to the bore, which they could see shimmering in the distance, only 12km away. The temperature was 116 degrees and both died 4km from water. If they had looked closely before setting off they would have seen the top of the windmill marking Number 7 bore only 4km in the opposite direction.

At 100km I feel fatigued. The wind, which blew gently from the east in the morning, has switched to the north-west and increased in strength. I am careful not to curse it; it has been kind to me in recent weeks, and I may need it again. I hunch down over my aero bars and push ahead, convincing my legs not to desert me. The worst thing is to stop; not only is it hard to get back on the bike but a stationary person, at the risk of sounding trite, is not making ground. Better to keep pedalling, if only slowly.

Through the sweat dripping down my forehead I see a familiar van in my mirror: the Swiss couple. They could find no water at the Buckley River yesterday and decided to press on to Tennant Creek. I am jealous; they will be there this evening and it will take me another three days, two if I'm lucky. They drive alongside for 15 minutes. 'We are in awe of the space here,' says the woman. 'All we have at home are those silly mountains.'

Ian and I camp at a wayside stop and road trains rumble past all evening, lit up like Christmas trees. 'I pity the poor bastards driving those trucks,' Ian says, looking at the red tail-lights receding into the distance, clearly thinking about his own life behind the wheel. 'I reckon they're mad as blue-arsed flies, driving Darwin to Townsville and back again. They get home, have two days off and start all over again. All that cargo should be on a train. It's no way for a good young bloke to spend his life.'

The night sky is brilliant and the Barkly Tableland glows in the starlight. Even without Ian's binoculars we see three satellites beetling across the heavens. Low on the horizon Mars winks at us in reds and greens. NASA has just put a probe on Mars' surface. At the moment it is crawling around, examining rock samples and taking photographs, 70 million kilometres away.

Day 52: Wednesday 9 July, Soudan to Barkly Roadhouse
Distance: 128km
Distance so far: 4073km

Six months to go. After two hours' cycling, 4000km clicks over and I have mixed feelings: both pleasure and foreboding. Still so far.

Ian predicted a tail-wind today and he is right. It blows mightily and I make short work of the 130km. The rich fodder of the Barkly Tableland stretches to nothingness, broken only by the faint outline of the Mittiebah Range to the north, low-slung hills in ochre, speckled with green. The tableland covers 700 000 square kilometres and boasts 50 grasses. Mostly it is the perennial barley, Mitchell grass. In contrast to yesterday's paucity of cattle, I can see large herds of cattle from the road.

A hefty chunk of the Barkly Tableland is taken up by Australia's largest cattle run, *Brunette Downs*. The size of cattle runs in the Top End has reduced in recent decades—some runs used to be the size of England—but *Brunette Downs* remains impressive, measuring 12 000 square kilometres. Its southern boundary is only 80km from here and its northern boundary is midway between here and the Gulf. But for every successful cattle station there are plenty who have done it hard. I pass an old, disused café, its windows broken and surrounds littered with beer cans. You would have to be a raving optimist to think there was a quid to be made out here.

I have become accustomed to the sight of dead kangaroos, though could never become accustomed to the stink, which wrenches at the nostrils like smelling salts. Today I pass dead cattle; there are no fences here and cattle stray onto the roads. Road trains don't leave much of them. I am distressed to see two wedge-tail eagles, lying dead within ten metres of each other on the verge. Later, Ian tells me that he has heard of people shooting one—and the other, mourning the loss of its mate, becomes an easy target. It is a filthy story and I convince myself these two were hit by cars.

We camp at the Barkly Roadhouse, the only accommodation between Tennant Creek and Camooweal, where a generator throbs all night like a metronome and caravans dot the landscape. There are wayfarers to talk to, including a couple from Warrnambool in Victoria who have taken their three kids out of school for a month to show them the Top End. 'Wish we'd made it three months, there's so much to see,' says Dad.

'Or a year,' says his son, hopefully.

The Barkly Roadhouse is for sale, price $2.5 million, same as the turnover. Seems a lot until you see the price of petrol: 99 cents a litre. 'Daylight bloody robbery,' mutters Ian. You can charge what you like in the outback. Monopolies rule.

Day 53: Thursday 10 July, Barkly Roadhouse to Tennant Creek
Distance: 220km
Distance so far: 4293km

Dawn is an Armageddon sky, thick clouds skimming overhead and electricity in the air. The wind blew like the clappers all night and I prayed it was from the east. I am in luck.

A tail-wind like this is too good to pass up and I set out

with firm intentions to make it to Tennant Creek, 220km distant. It is bitterly cold and I put on three jumpers, feeling like a mummy. At lunch, alongside an enormous windmill which cranks away like an old politician, I have covered 140km. Again there has been nothing to see except a few cattle, bullet-riddled roadsigns and the turn-off to the Tablelands Highway, which tracks north past *Brunette Downs* and the Heartbreak Hotel to Borroloola, 400km away.

More dead animals. The usual 'roos and cattle, also birds and snakes. Even a dead ostrich, its head resting on the edge of the bitumen as if asleep. Each carcass swarms with maggots and flies and the stench rumbles around in my gut long after I have cycled past.

I ride in a daze for much of the afternoon—like an ant on a map—thighs burning and knees crying murder, trying to drum up enthusiasm but aching for the end of the day. The wind drops and the clouds sit low above me, a dull, grey blanket, a coating on the pain. My lungs feel like they are contracting with each breath. The fatigue and restricted view— the scrub has grown higher than eye-level—brings on a distress of sorts. My internal horizon becomes insular and I begin to get annoyed at passing cars, especially those who toot their horns. Can't they see I'm in no mood for humour.

After seven hours and 190km I emerge at Three Ways, where the westbound Barkly Highway meets the north–south Stuart Highway. My guidebook says the junction, 500km north of Alice Springs, 1000km south of Darwin and 640km west of Mount Isa, is 'basically a bloody long way away from any-where.' There is a roadhouse, a kitsch memorial to John Flynn the flying doctor, and a torpor in the air. Half a dozen hitch-hikers swish lethargically at flies. Some lie on their backpacks, hats over their eyes, while others stand, hoping to make a better impression on passing motorists. One, red beard and sunburnt face, holds the familiar hitcher's demand: 'Broome or Bust'. They look like they have been there a long time.

I think of an English friend who is adamant that the secret to successful hitching is to wear a tie. 'It gives you that slight air of respectability, that crucial edge over your competitors,' he used to say, 'even when worn over a T-shirt or, occasionally, no shirt at all.' He claimed he once hitched from Paris to Baghdad in three days—28 lifts in 3000km, waiting a total of only 37 minutes—and wore his tie the whole way. None of today's travellers, so far as I can make out, is cravatted.

Distress aside, reaching the end of the Barkly Highway is an enchanting moment and I yell with satisfaction when I see the sign, punching, as much as my fatigued arms will allow, the air. Nothing to hear me but three crows, picking at the bones of a dead Brahman on the side of the road.

Tennant Creek is 30km south of Three Ways on the Stuart Highway and my weary bones propel me there, knowing that I will have to retrace my steps after the weekend. I get a second wind knowing the longest day of the trip is almost over. Hills near the town are the first I have seen for 600km, and it is good to give the legs a change of routine. Tennant Creek, the watercourse, is dry, and I pass by the old Telegraph Station, its sandstone walls glowing orange in the setting sun. The hills, too, are almost luminous, and the screeches of cockatoos and galahs fill the evening air. It is as if nature has recognised my day of toil, and provided a calming end to a difficult day.

Tennant Creek, according to legend, was settled when a wagon load of beer broke down in the early 1930s, and by the time the drivers had consumed the freight they decided the site would be good for a town. A gold rush followed shortly thereafter, the first strike discovered by an unlikely partnership of the one-eyed Tom Noble and the blind prospector William Weaber. Nobles Nob became the richest open-cut goldmine of its size in the world and the town's future was assured. As I cycle into town people mill about on the nature strip, laughing. I later learn it is dole cheque day. It is also 'Thirsty Thursday'—no takeaway grog sold to give dole money, the authorities claim, the chance to filter down through the families before the pubs re-open.

Ian has waited patiently at the Tennant Creek campground. In the evening I take him to the bus station so he can return to Mount Isa then fly to Townsville. He has been a lifesaver for me, stepping into the breach, as well as being excellent, engaging company. His relaxed approach to life, his dry wit, and his knowledge of the region have been invaluable, and has made a potentially nerve-wracking week for a city boy in the Never-Never most enjoyable. 'It's the best place in the world, the outback,' he says as we discuss the past week waiting for the bus. 'The people here are a special breed. They all pull together. Don't be afraid to ask them to help you; they will do their best, you can be sure of that.'

I thank him with as much emotion as one Aussie bloke talking to another at an outback bus-stop will muster. 'No worries mate,' he replies as we shake hands. 'It's been bloody good fun. Travelling that prick of a road again has reminded me why I gave up trucking. You've done a good week's work. Good luck for the rest of the ride. Better you than me.' With that he boards the bus, and is gone.

Days 54–57: Friday 11–Monday 14 July
Rest days: Tennant Creek

On first impressions Tennant Creek is not a place for the faint of heart, all cowboy boots, faded denim jeans, leather jackets and people leaning against street lights, eyeing passers-by. For people with delicate sensibilities, it could be intimidating. My sensibilities, after 50 days dressed in yellow skin-tight lycra, must be dulled; I am intrigued and have four days to discover the place.

Clearly there is a grog problem. Rusting cans litter the sides of the road and empty wine cask bladders blow around in the wind. By lunchtime drunks loll about on the nature strips and park benches, occasionally holding out a money-seeking hand to passers-by. In the evening the Julalikari Night Patrol (sponsored by Normandy Mining) cruises the streets and returns many to their houses. It is hard to determine whether the night patrol is a taxi (why the locked cage?) or a paddy wagon (why the sponsorship?).

The town suffers from isolation. Different Federal governments have tossed around the idea of extending the Adelaide–Alice Springs railway to Darwin, which would open up towns like Tennant Creek and Katherine, but all such plans have foundered over funding. There are simply not enough people and not enough votes in the Top End for major infrastructure development, and the plan remains on the 'maybe' list. All travel is by road; the downside is the constant sound of road trains rumbling through town, heading for The Alice.

The disused Telegraph Station north of the town is a collection of handsome sandstone buildings that were part of the Overland Telegraph Line, opened in 1872. The purpose of the line was simple: connect Australia's southern states with Darwin, and then Europe via the submarine cable to Java. Until then mail took six weeks to reach England. Before it was opened, explorer John McDouall Stuart had been up here three times en route to the north coast, and the telegraph line's installers were disappointed they could glean little from his records, save for the obvious: it was inhospitable country, often with stretches of 300km without water. And yet they took only 18 months to construct the 3000km line.

Between Darwin and the South Australian border there were six telegraph stations 300km apart, serving as repeater stations to boost the power conveying the traffic. In addition to Tennant Creek they were Daly Waters, Powell Creek, Barrow Creek, Alice Springs and Charlotte Waters. Each station had an operator and a linesman and was completely self-contained, with 20 or 30 horses for transport and a herd of cattle for beef and milk. The linesman's job was to look after the stock, brand and break in the young horses, and kill a bullock for meat for the employees, and visitors, who were occasional at best. When a break occurred it was the linesman's job to ride out to repair it. With 300km between stations locating a break could sometimes take days.

Tom Cole, author of *Hell West and Crooked*, was the Tennant Creek linesman in 1929, and once had the task of finding a break when both lines to the south of Tennant Creek went dead. He set off in 110 degree heat with an Aboriginal boy called Joe, three camels, a camp oven, billy cans and a week's rations. Two days later they came upon the problem; an owl had flown into the wires and twisted them together. Cole writes:

Joe took an axe from a pack bag and cut a long stick. He got on his camel, rode over to the trapped bird and gave it a whack. It flew to pieces and communications were restored between Australia and the outside world. Joe and I laughed our heads off.

I attend a local Aussie Rules football game, a ferocious battle between two pub teams, the Sportsman's Spitfires and the Memorial Club. The teams are equally represented by Whites and Blacks alike, many of the Aboriginal players showing the sixth-sense skills and dexterity they have taken to the big leagues in the southern states. The Spitfires win on the last kick of the day and have to buy the meat for the after-match bar-beque. The losers buy the beer. At one stage during the match the full-back kicks straight to a member of the opposition who kicks a goal. It is an elementary football mistake but instead of jeers, which would be the response in the Big Smoke, the supporters are sympathetic. It says a lot, I muse, about the Top End, where honest triers are admired as much as those with the silky skills.

I collect money in the two pubs after the match, raising $500. The Lions Club sells sausages at the Sunday rodeo and donates the proceeds, another $700. I get a call from a Lions Club in Perth, which wants me to address a gathering when I come through. It is a fortifying weekend and I am confident the on-road fund-raising is gathering pace, adding to the donations arriving periodically at the Cancer Council. The total is now $170,000.

I am relieved to have received phone calls from two cousins—Caroline Walford and Andrew Mackinnon— volunteering to drive the car between Darwin and Broome. Roy Wiedemeyer, a Melbourne-based safety consultant and driver for the next week, arrives at three-thirty Sunday morning having, for reasons known only to himself, bused from Melbourne via Cairns and the Barkly Highway. He gives me a silver medallion of St Christopher, protector of travellers, made by his sister-in-law Ali. 'Gosh, I'm looking forward to getting away from Melbourne's winter,' he says upon arrival. Clearly he hasn't noticed I am rugged up like a Laplander. Yesterday it snowed at Uluru, a most uncommon occurrence. I don't have the heart to tell him.

Day 58: Tuesday 15 July, Tennant Creek to Renner Springs
Distance: 160km
Distance so far: 4453km

A new person in the team usually means a late start but Roy, an expert in things mechanical, quickly picks up the idiosyncrasies of the caravan. By the time we leave he knows more about it than me. After four days off I am, worryingly, looking forward to getting back in the saddle.

The wind is from the side and I make good progress through Three Ways. Many of the hitchers are still there. 'Would love to help guys, but these are only built for one,' I yell, hammering past. Some weird looks in return, and one finger. Don't think they appreciate my flippancy, especially the Broome-or-Bust man, who still holds his sign.

As far as bitumen goes, the Stuart Highway north of Tennant Creek is a dream, a cyclist's Yellow Brick Road. It is smooth, hard, pothole-free, with shoulders as wide as Greg Norman. Until World War II the road was nothing more than a dirt track connecting Darwin and The Alice but the Government decided that the Japanese bombing of Darwin called for an upgrade, and it has been maintained since.

The impressive escarpments of the Short and Whittington mountain ranges track the west side of the road. Beyond them, between here and Port Hedland on the Western Australian coast, is 1500km of the Great Sandy Desert. After weeks of table-top flatness, seeing the ranges is like stumbling into a long-lost debtor. Early indications, certainly, are that the road engineers had the sanity of drivers, possibly even cyclists, in mind when they built the road. It tracks the dry foothills of the ranges and gives impressive views, in a minimalist Territorian way anyway, of the countryside. Stunted scrub hangs low over tortured termite mounds, parting occasionally in the distance to reveal patches of scarlet earth. Overhead, wispy cirrus clouds skit across my bow. Again, I cycle on a high, feeling a love for this wild and uncompromising country.

Fifty-four kilometres north of Three Ways near the turn-off to *Rockhampton Downs* is a memorial to Stuart at Attack Creek. On 25 June 1860 Stuart and his mates, William Kenwick and

Benjamin Head—racing Burke and Wills to the Gulf—were attacked by natives and they turned for home. Camping next to the memorial are Pauline and Don, straight-talking folk from Ipswich in Queensland, who give me a cup of tea and some fruitcake. They travel six months a year and tell me they are heading home to 'find some bloody warmth'. 'We've just come from Broome where we were kicked off an Aboriginal reserve for not having a permit,' Don says. 'Why the hell should we need a permit? I am just as much Australian as them, and I should be allowed to see what I bloody well want. It makes my bloody blood boil.'

The final 60km fly by. Again I am pleased at how my body has adjusted to the demands of a 160km day. I could no more have cycled this distance two months ago than flown to the moon. It is partly due to conditioning—I must be fit as a mallee bull—but the change of direction too has given me a spark. I pass a sign twitched onto the side of a cattle grid—'Caution, Fresh Cows'—and I think of Camooweal's buffaroo.

Roy, keen to mix cycling and driving, rides to meet me from Renner Springs and we cycle the last 25km together. Renner Springs was named after Dr Frederick Renner, a doctor in the district during construction of the Overland Telegraph Line. It appears there was a lot of work for a doctor at the time. A fellow named Tom Nugent had taken up a lease, *Banka Banka*. Nugent was allegedly a member of the Ragged Thirteen, a group of petty criminals operating in the Kimberley and Victoria River districts. During the gang's time they were held responsible for killing Alan Giles, a former Tennant Creek postmaster, now buried outside the Renner Springs drafting yards. Nugent died of dropsy at Tennant Creek in August 1911, and is buried at the Tennant Creek Telegraph Station.

Stuck on the wall of the store in Renner Springs is a yellowing piece of paper with scrawly writing:

*Lost in Renner Springs area: blue heeler bitch with three legs,
broken tail, no teeth. Traces of canker and distemper. Blind in one
eye and partially deaf. Answers to the name of 'Lucky'.*

Day 59: Wednesday 16 July, Renner Springs to Elliott
Distance: 96km
Distance so far: 4549km

The wind comes gloriously from the south and I average 35km
an hour to Elliott. The views, especially out west where the
lancewood and bulwaddy trees stretch forever, are enchanting.
Many of the trees are coming into flower.

Elliott seems a tough place to live and, not for the first time,
I wonder what people *do* in these parts. Although the town
services the nearby *Newcastle Waters*, *Powell Creek* and *Tan-
dyidgee* stations there can be only limited business coming from
these. To the west, between here and the Western Australian
border, is 140 000 square kilometres of Aboriginal Land Trust,
largely unproductive desert. Many of the local Aboriginal
people have chosen to live in Elliott and sit out next to the
road, or lie on bed frames outside their crumbling, blackened
houses. It is a depressing sight.

Appearing at our camp is a man on a bike loaded to the
gunwales. Peter, from Salzburg in Austria, is cycling 'very, very
slowly' from Darwin to Adelaide. 'Man, this is tough,' he says
in broken English, managing a smile. 'I have had this head-
wind for two weeks and I've had enough of it. A guy told me
in Austria that I would have a *tail-wind* this time of year. When
I get home I'm going to punch him on the nose.'

Peter is struggling to make 60km a day, worried he will have
to resort to a bus in order to make his flight to New Zealand
in early August. Heading in opposite directions tomorrow we
are, of course, hoping for diametrically different wind

directions. For a moment I find myself hoping he gets his northerly wind—he is lugging 30kg of gear and I carry nothing—but it is only a brief moment. We cook him dinner and offer him a bed in the caravan but he opts to camp out, curling up in his sleeping bag on a paper-thin sleeping mat under a looping bulwaddy tree.

Day 60: Thursday 17 July, Elliott to Daly Waters
Distance: 166km
Distance so far: 4715km

I wake to the sound of sawing. Peter's pannier rack broke yesterday and he is fixing it with a fretsaw, an old coathanger and some electrical tape. I give him one of our cycling shirts and wish him luck. He gives us a large tin of energy powder which he has carried from Darwin and now realises he doesn't like. The wind, sadly for him, is from the south. We shake hands and he grimaces stoically before setting off, with the speed of a drugged tortoise, towards Renner Springs. I cannot see him making it by dark.

Twenty kilometres from Elliott, 3km from the highway, is the small township of Newcastle Waters, formerly a calling place for drovers taking cattle up the Birdum or Barkly Stock Routes or along the Murranji Stock Route to Top Springs. The town has been turned into a shrine to drovers, now an all-but-forgotten breed. On the Junction Hotel's wall is an extract from a poem by ex-drover Bruce Simpson:

Now the droving is done and no more from the scrub,
Come the drovers to camp by the Newcastle pub.
They are gone from the routes with their horses and packs
And the tall grasses blow o'er their deep-trodden tracks.
There is bitumen now where the big diesels roll

And the dead men grow lonely by Murranji Hole.
Now the sky curlews wail and the sad chorus swells
As though missing the music of the Condamine Bells.

A list of 400 drovers from years past includes names like 'Territory Jack' Scanlon, 'Wild Jimmy' Edwards, Joe 'Looking Glass' Dowling, Smiler Marsden, 'Splinter' and 'Slippery' Prendergast, and the brothers Archie, Charlie and Henry Farquharson. In 1909 the Farquharson brothers drove 1000 *Mistake Creek* bullocks from Top Springs to *Newcastle Waters*, along 180km of the drought-stricken Murranji Track, through lancewood and bulwaddy 'so bloody thick a dog couldn't bark in it' and lost only five beasts. Australian history, a town plaque says, records no equal droving feat.

The road north of Newcastle Waters has tangled scrub on both sides. Few cars pass, although those that do make full use of the Territory's no-speed-limit law. Another tail-wind makes cycling easier than it should be and I make Daly Waters by mid-afternoon, having covered 170km. Daly Waters, a one-horse town 3km off the highway, is famous for, of all things, its links with aviation. It was the first refuelling stop for Qantas in 1935 and British aviator Amy Johnson landed here in 1930 after failing to beat the England-to-Australia speed record by three days.

The town's hotel, built in 1893 from corrugated iron and wooden beams, is the oldest pub in the Territory and its walls are festooned with stubby holders, Lions Clubs' banners, notes, coins and old saddles. In recent years more contemporary items have been added: bras, jockettes and photos of tipsy locals flashing browneyes at unfortunate cameramen. A scrawled sign behind the bar announces: 'Credit given only to women over eighty, accompanied by their mothers'.

Bruce, the guitar-playing publican, entertains the visitors

outside with a collection of bawdy Aussie bush ballads. The locals, who have heard it all before, elect to stay inside and drink. Bruce is replaced by an elderly couple from Colac in Victoria, she on guitar and vocals and he on the accordion, who struggle to find the right key, but diners stay on respectfully. 'They're bloody awful, but at least they're up there having a go,' one whispers to another.

Throughout the evening a group of Vietnam Vets— including one missing a leg called, predictably, Stumpy—collects money for Kids with Cancer. Roy and I eat with Ron, from Coburg in Melbourne, whose wife died of cancer last year. He is travelling Australia, sleeping in the back of his car, 'while I have the chance.'

I wonder how Peter fared into the head-wind.

Day 61: Friday 18 July, Daly Waters to Mataranka
Distance: 178km
Distance so far: 4893km

Another long day, 180km. The road undulates and there are good views over *Nutwood Downs* and *Maryfield* towards the Gulf. The scrub has thinned out because of a recent fire. The wind comes from the south for the third day running and again I average more than 30km an hour. I can't believe the luck I am getting. Long may it continue. Ron passes, heading for Kakadu, honks, and gives me the thumbs up out the window. He has the road to himself.

Short of Larrimah, looking like a midget submarine, appears another cyclist, a Japanese called Ken, battling away. Like Peter two days ago, Ken's bike is loaded with gear, including six or seven two-litre plastic water bottles attached to various parts of his bike by pieces of bailing twine. He, too, is making for Adelaide and is also struggling. Sweat pours off his body. 'I enjoy ride,' he says. 'Is good fun. Is excellent country.' We exchange salutations and addresses and he wobbles off.

I call in at Larrimah, the only town between Daly Waters and Mataranka, to stretch and replenish my water bottles at the town tap. There was once a railway line between Darwin and here but it was abandoned after Cyclone Tracy on Christmas Day, 1974. Why the authorities chose Larrimah for the terminus is not clear; the town has nothing going for it except, oddly, a second-hand book shop.

Mataranka has thermal pools with fabled recuperative powers. For a cyclist who has covered 350km in two days, they are a godsend. The pools flow into the Roper River which is a deep azure-blue surrounded by palm trees and birds, a most unlikely sight in this barren country. It is also the first flowing water I have seen since Cloncurry 16 days ago.

Roy and I retire to the Mataranka pub, reputedly haunted, and meet an Aboriginal woman, Deirdre, who is completing a Diploma of Education at Batchelor, south of Darwin. Her aim is simple: to teach young Aboriginal children the local dialect, Magarryai, which is slowly dying. 'It is spoken only between *Hodgson River*, 100km south-east of here, and Jilkminggen,' she tells us. 'Television has wrecked our language, and I feel it is my responsibility to preserve it. We Aboriginals have lost so many things, but there's no way we are going to lose this.'

Day 62: Saturday 19 July
Rest day: Mataranka

Life in the Mataranka district has always been hard work, and dangerous. A visit to the local cemetery shows many died young, and in tragic ways. Jack Grant, in charge of the *Elsey* horse teams, drowned at the junction of Two Mile Creek and Katherine River in 1932. Edward Liddle was electrocuted at the Mataranka Hotel in 1947. Henry Ventlia Peckham, the Fizzer in *We of the Never-Never*, drowned crossing the flooded Dashwood Crossing at Campbell's Creek in 1911 while delivering a letter seeking urgent medical attention for a woman at *Victoria River Downs*. The Fizzer had replaced Fred Stribe on the thousand-mile mail run from Katherine to *Anthony Lagoon*. Stribe died of thirst on the Barkly Tableland. Aenneas Gunn, the Maluka in *We of the Never-Never*, the head of *Elsey*, died of malarial dysentery in 1903, having been in the Territory only one year. Jeannie Gunn returned to Melbourne almost immediately and never returned. It is hard to believe that all this happened less than 100 years ago.

Four team members arrive at Mataranka for a short period on the ride: Rose Snell, Sandy Fairthorne, Emma Taylor and Rob Magnusson. Importantly, they have brought food from Darwin, including fresh fruit and vegetables, ambrosia to Roy and me after the past week. Although we consider ourselves adequate cooks, our recipes have developed a sense of sameness, predominantly—in fact totally—based on tinned tuna. All have been dubbed Tuna Surprise. The only thing surprising about it now is how often we have eaten it. I think I am growing gills.

Day 63: Sunday 20 July, Mataranka to Katherine
Distance: 120km
Distance so far: 5013km

A late start as the new team members come to terms with the mobile accommodation. Roy decides to finish his week by cycling with me to Katherine, 120km, during which I clock up 5000km. He cycles strongly.

I have had a cold brewing for several days and today it hits with a vengeance. I hack and cough and Roy, wisely, keeps his distance. I am aware that the constant pushing of my body since Mount Isa, during which period I have covered 1500km, averaging close to 150km per day, could be taking its toll. The human body, adaptable to a point, will object if taken too far, and the immune system is often the first thing to go. I am looking forward to a rest in Kakadu.

The further I move north, and the closer I get to rivers of substance, the bigger the trees become. No more so than around the Daly and Katherine rivers, which have their beginnings on the escarpments of Kakadu National Park, feeding into the Timor Sea. The eucalypts near Katherine are especially majestic, and much grander than the feeble things 500km to the south.

The Katherine rodeo is on: one of the largest and most well-supported in the Top End. People come from hundreds of kilometres away—Camooweal, Kununurra and beyond—to buckjump, campdraft, drink and generally create trouble. Plenty of buckjumpers come off with bone-jarring thuds but, showing traditional Territory grit, pick themselves up, dust themselves off, collect their crumpled hats and trudge off with a smile. One rider slams into a fence and breaks his arm. There is no sexism at the rodeo and the women hit the ground just as hard. 'It's a place where men are men, and women are men,' chuckles Aiden, across from Burketown for the week. Today is Sunday and the atmosphere, on the last day of the rodeo, is noticeably relaxed. Perhaps it is always like this; after all the letters 'NT', according to the locals, stand for 'Not Today'.

I treat myself to a motel room for the night to watch the final round of the British Golf Open on TV, yearning for some escapism and possibly feeling a little sorry for myself on account of the cold. The British Open is not, I discover, broadcast in the Territory.

Day 64: Monday 21 July
Rest day: Katherine

Roy, a stalwart for the past week at both driving and cycling, boards a bus bound for The Alice, Adelaide and Melbourne. Again, I am sad that a team member is leaving after we have shared so much. By the time Roy gets home, in two days, he will have travelled 8000km by bus and 300km by bike.

Day 65: Tuesday 22 July, Katherine to Pine Creek
Distance: 110km
Distance so far: 5123km

The new team keeps me company in turns on the spare bike, with the aid of another tail-wind. Rob cycles 60km and swears he will give up the fags when he gets home. I enjoy cycling with them—the conversation drifts along easily and laughter fills the air—and doing it at their pace reminds me of the importance of taking things a little easier. I have been pushing limits in recent days.

Pine Creek, 250km south of Darwin, has a population of 400 and sits at the southern entrance to Kakadu National Park. The town was the scene of a gold rush in the 1870s, prospectors arriving from Victoria and South Australia, and creaking timber and corrugated iron buildings sit hunched in the main street. One of them, the bakery, started life in 1908 as a butcher's store in Mount Diamond on the Kakadu Highway. It was transported to Pine Creek, and ant-bed-mortar ovens still stand out the back of the crumbling building. A Chinese father-and-son team, Jimmy Ah You and Jimmy Ah Toy, baked bread in Pine Creek until the war, when the building was taken over by the army.

Today, Jimmy Ah You's grandson, 60-year-old Edward Ah

Toy—a third-generation Australian—runs the general store in Pine Creek, selling hats and sunscreen, fuel tanks and grog, fruit and vegetables. His office is piled high with invoices and cheque butts, seemingly with no order to them, but he has a sharp look in his eye that you associate with good business-people. He tells with relish the story of his family's history.

'Before my grandfather, Jimmy Ah You, arrived here he was a market gardener in Darwin and sold his cabbages door-to-door for three pence each. One day a guy offered him one penny for his cabbages and my grandfather he told him to get stuffed. He came to Pine Creek in 1920 and ran the bakery business here. Dad came down here from Darwin in 1935 to start this shop. I was born in 1937 in the old Pine Creek Museum and was delivered by Clyde Fenton, the famous flying doctor.'

Between 1942 and 1945 Jimmy Ah Toy took his family to Adelaide, moving back to Pine Creek in 1945 when the war had finished. 'Dad caught the train to Alice Springs and bought a five-tonne Maple Leaf truck made by General Motors. The family shipped up the drapery to start the shop again because the store had essentially been ransacked in the three years of the war. I did High School in Darwin between 1951 and 1954 and I came back here in 1955. By that time uranium mining had started on the South Alligator River at El Sherana and Coronation Hill, and that created lots of extra business. He asked me to come to Pine Creek while the uranium boom lasted and I am still here 40 years later. There was another gold rush between 1985 and 1993 and then the Union Reef Gold Mine started near here three years ago. We have been fortunate in that respect.

'My Dad was quite a guy. He set up a soup kitchen for the people who came here when Cyclone Tracy hit. He was president of the Pine Creek Progress Association and chairman of both the school committee and Trustee Association. He got an MBE in the late 1960s and was appointed a Justice of the Peace after that. His philosophy was that if you live somewhere you should help that community.

'Chinese-born Australians are a peaceful sort of race and they tend not to make trouble. I get a bit of abuse, though. Some locals call me slant eye when they have had a few beers. Some are resentful of the fact that Dad had the foresight to buy a few blocks of land for a good price many years ago. But I am happy here and I am proud of my family and its history in the Pine Creek and Kakadu region. I have four kids and three of them have university degrees.'

Edward Ah Toy's is only one of many Chinese families to make its mark in the Top End. In 1874 the first group of 187 Chinese arrived as bonded labourers from Singapore. Two years later the South Australian Government, anxious to revive mining in the area, decided to allow unrestricted entry and by 1880 the Chinese population in the region peaked at more than 6000. The numbers swelled further following the opening of the Darwin–Pine Creek railway, which employed 3000 Chinese labourers. At one stage the Chinese population in the region outnumbered Europeans by 20 to one.

Many, like entrepreneur Ping Que, became naturalised Australians and established profitable mining and business ventures. Ping Que became recognised as one of the most efficient and productive miners in the Top End and imported his own 'coolies' from Singapore to work his claims. When he died in 1885 the obituary in the *Territory Times* referred to him as 'far and away the smartest mining man we have yet met . . . and one of the pluckiest and straightest men.'

In camp a tall, elderly man wanders over, looking like he has just stepped from the battlegrounds at Culloden, complete with kilt, sporran and bagpipes. Eric Graham from Perth, but of proud Scottish descent, has seen our fund-raising sign and is adamant we should touch the locals at the pub. He will provide the entertainment. Clearly the bagpipes are not common in these parts and no sooner has he pumped out the first few bars of 'Scotland the Brave' under the pub's verandah than an Aboriginal lady puts her head out the door and screeches: 'Shut that bloody magpie up!'

We return triumphant, having raised $200. Someone finds Eric a whisky and he tells us his story. He is 71, a former builder and arrived in Australia from Scotland on New Year's Day, 1929. He is travelling Australia with his wife, June. His sister, he tells us, died of cancer, hence his interest. Perhaps inspired by the whisky, Eric says he is available to drive the car from Exmouth to Perth in two months, playing the bagpipes along the way, 'if you're looking for someone, that is, lad.' As chance would have it I do not have a driver for this section of the ride and accept gratefully. Never look a gift Scotsman in the mouth.

Days 66–77: Wednesday 23 July–Sunday 3 August
Rest days: Kakadu/Darwin

Twelve days off is a luxury I look forward to, and can afford, having made excellent time across Queensland and up the Stuart Highway. It is a good time to allow a little recovery too: my cough has got worse and I need sleep.

Emma, Rose, Sandy and Rob head for Darwin, while I drive up the Kakadu Highway into the depths of the national park. Kakadu, the dense and wild country off the East Alligator River bordering Arnhem Land, covers an area of more than one million hectares (about 20 000 square kilometres) and is owned by the Aboriginal people who lease it to the Australian Nature Conservation Agency. As a UNESCO World Heritage region it is now one of the most important places in Australia.

Even those who think that Australian culture is an oxy-moron become transfixed here, enchanted by the wetlands and the bird life, the Aboriginal paintings, the plunging escarpments and waterfalls. The region has, of course, been a home to Aboriginal Australians for thousands of years. Explorer Ludwig Leichhardt was the first white explorer to pass through, in 1845, descending from the Arnhem Land escarpment near Twin Falls and heading north across the East Alligator River to the Victoria Settlement near Port Essington.

For me it is a week to celebrate the bounteousness of the Top End wilderness after 64 days on the road. At Yellow Waters, salt-water crocodiles sun themselves on the bank, magpie geese, rainbow bee-eaters and Burdekin ducks fossick among the reeds, and a long-legged Jabiru stork spears a barra-mundi with its beak. Jim Jim Falls, where the South Alligator River plunges off the Arnhem Land Plateau into a crystal clear pool the size of the Melbourne Cricket Ground, is enchanting, as is Ubirr Rock, where ancient Aboriginal rock paintings watch over Cahill's Crossing, the entrance to the Aboriginals' sacred Arnhem Land.

It is a time, too, to speak to fellow travellers. My next-door neighbour at the Yellow Waters campground, dressed in stubbies and a Darwin Crocodile Wrestling Club T-shirt, and cradling a can of VB under an awning, is on his way down the wild Nathan River Road to Borroloola on the Gulf of Carpentaria. 'The last time I was there, ten years ago, one bloke was shot, one was stabbed, and one reckoned he was lucky to be alive,' he says. 'I hope it hasn't changed.'

Among Kakadu's natural beauty, quite incongruously, is a uranium mine, Ranger, near the township of Jabiru at the eastern edge of the park. The building of Ranger, the third-biggest uranium mine in the world, began in 1979, the same year that Kakadu was declared a national park. The irony of this is not lost on the Australian conservation movement, which uses it to argue that Australian governments' collective commitment to conservation is, at best, highly conditional. Uranium mines and national parks are diametrically opposed, they say, and cannot, almost by definition, co-exist. Kakadu's rainfall, say the conservationists, creates difficulties that cannot be planned for. Last year, for instance, more than two-and-a-half metres of rain fell in the region, and the contaminated tailings dams were in danger of flooding. Already ore-body number one, mined out in 1994, houses 30 metres of contaminated water. Since it was built, conservationists argue, there have been 30 'incidents' at Ranger within Kakadu's boundary, including the contamination of Magela Creek with the release of radioactive waste. Equally ominous is that much of Ranger's production is sold to France, which has tested nuclear bombs in the South Pacific.

The mine, argues the mine's tour guide, is 'safe as houses' and management *does* recognise the historical significance of the region. All employees undertake cultural awareness training when they join the company, with refresher courses every six months. According to Aboriginal folklore the rainbow serpent lives in the nearby hills, so the mine has installed a vibration monitor to ensure the serpent is not disturbed unduly. Any employee caught on the serpent's side of the fence is instantly dismissed. Ranger would be wise to remain on the right side of the serpent; according to Aboriginal folklore the serpent, also known as Kurangali, can cause floods and earthquakes, and eats people.

On numbers alone, the mine is certainly an impressive venture. Construction costs were $388 million, 43 000 cubic metres of concrete were used, alongside 5000 tonnes of structural steel. Five-thousand tonnes of uranium oxide are produced each year, and 30 44-gallon drums of uranium, each selling for around $15,000, are produced each day. Since the mine started, $130 million has been given to local Aboriginal people, made up of 4.25 per cent of gross sales revenue plus an annual rental of $200,000 for the land.

In Jabiru busloads of students mill about, with Save-The-Whale T-shirts, three-week growths and keen eyes. They have been here for weeks, protesting against the development of another uranium mine, Jabiluka, 15km north of Ranger. Jabiluka has ore grades, in many places, nearly twice the richness of Ranger and, although it was discovered more than 20 years ago, mining the ore was prevented under the Labor Government's Three Mines Policy. John Howard's Coalition Government reversed the policy, and preparations for mining, which is expected to continue until 2027, are underway. Energy Resources of Australia believes Jabiluka has the potential to deliver $3.8 billion in earnings.

The students are taking a day off to swim in the Jabiru pool. For some it could be their first wash in some weeks, a fact not lost on the pool manager. 'They need a wash, but why does it have to be in my pool?' he says, concerned. The students are convinced their protest *has* made an impact, though are worried that none have yet been arrested. Their enthusiasm remains undaunted. 'We'll crush the bastards. Jabiluka will *not* happen,' one whispers to me conspiratorially.

I drive west along the Arnhem Highway to Darwin, via Wildman River, Annaburroo Billabong and Humpty Doo. From Darwin I will cycle south, back to Katherine, and then west along the Victoria Highway to Kununurra and Broome.

It is a strange feeling to be in Darwin, only 13 degrees south of the equator, seeing the sun set low over the Timor Sea towards Melville Island. I have not seen the ocean since Townsville, more than a month ago. The water looks inviting, were it not for the stingers and crocs. Life in Darwin, according to most of the people who live there, centres around the weather. In winter it is a beautiful place, with clear, warm days and mild nights. It shows its other side in summer when the rain thunders down, the humidity sends people troppo and cyclones thrash about. Although a quarter of a century has passed since Cyclone Tracy hit, destroying all but 400 of Darwin's 11 000 houses and killing 66 people, it remains firmly etched in the city's consciousness. In many ways, people say, the cyclone was the making of Darwin in both a physical and metaphorical sense. It gave the locals a chance to start again, demonstrating a true Top End resilience, to build a city smarter and sturdier than before, even if the new brick houses do not deal with the heat as well as the old, airy, stilted Queenslanders.

I spend five days there, another tourist wandering around alongside backpacking Belgians and didgeridoo-lugging Danes, and work for two of those at the Cancer Council office, writing to sponsors and liaising with drivers and cyclists for the weeks ahead. It is, in many ways, good to be in an office again, where I can use a computer and a normal phone instead of the expensive mobile phone. It is equally good to be spending time *not* on the bike. I have developed a burning case of jock-itch, a red rash on either side of the scrotum, on which I am spreading liberal doses of tea-tree oil which is recommended for this unfortunate affliction. Perhaps I have a particularly virulent strain; the panacea does not live up to its promise and I walk about with legs apart, like a wild-west gun-slinger.

One morning I meet some young cyclists from the Jingli Cycling Club and we cycle 15km from the city to the Casuarina shopping centre, where we collect money from shoppers, rattling tins. The smallest kid of all, no more than three feet high, is a fearless extractor of funds, raising $100 with a potent mixture of bravado, an angelic smile and Dickensian tricksterism. We feature on the TV news in the evening, alongside

▲ Day One. How long will the smile last? Sydney, NSW.
▼ Enjoying the waterfalls with sister Jenny at Comboyne, NSW.

'My physio doesn't know I'm here. Be gentle.' Steve, Flinders Highway, Qld.

Steve speeding towards Mount Isa. Flinders Highway, Qld.

▲ Queensland hospitality. A welcome to Mount Isa, Qld.

▲ Supporting the Spitfires. Local football match. Tennant Creek, NT.

▲ Edward Ah Toy, third generation Australian. Pine Creek, NT.

▲ The end of another 160km and feeling ok. Daly Waters Hotel, NT.

▲ Love those punctures. Gibb River Road, WA.

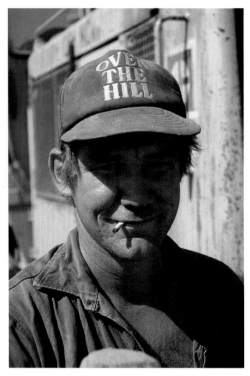

▲ A welcome sight for cyclists. Grader driver. Gibb River Road, WA.

▼ Robert and Valerie Newport cycling the Gibb River Road for the fifth time. Gibb River Road, WA.

▲ Drowning the dust in the world's longest cattle trough. Derby, WA.

▲ The perfect pet. Answers to the name of Cuddles. Broome, WA.

▲ Nick cools off. North West Coastal Highway, WA.

a story of ski-instructor Stuart Diver being extracted on a stretcher—blue-faced and shuddering in the freezing temperatures—after five days under landslide rubble at the Thredbo ski resort.

The next crew arrives from Melbourne: my cousin Caroline Walford and her three kids, Hugh, Eliza and Harriet, who range in age from seven to eleven. Caroline's mother, Patsy, and mine, were sisters. Patsy also died from cancer. 'Thought we'd come and give you a hand,' she said by phone last month. Her kids ooze enthusiasm. Tomorrow I tackle the Stuart Highway, this time heading south. I am aware that southerly winds have been blowing for weeks, and I cannot exorcise from my mind the image of Ken the Japanese cyclist straining into the wind, sweat running in rivulets down his forehead and splattering into the red Territory roadside dust. Tomorrow, more than likely, this will be me.

Day 78: Monday 4 August, Darwin to Batchelor
Distance: 117km
Distance so far: 5240km

On a journey it can be frustrating not making headway and I am glad to be back on the road, the kilometres slipping beneath the wheels. The past two weeks have been a tonic; my cold has recovered and Quasimodo's moving parts have been oiled. The only problem remains the nether regions, which feel like they are harbouring a hot poker.

The traffic is diabolical until I pass the northern entrance to Kakadu; then it is merely dreadful. My nerve seems to have deserted me in the fortnight, and I chicken out easily today, veering into the roadside dirt as road trains rumble past. It is now August and the weather has become noticeably hotter; twice I refill my water bottles and guzzle the contents. There is a head-wind, but not a strong one. At a café at Noonamah a local squints at a paper, a rollie hanging effortlessly from his lips. Judging by the number of butts in his ashtray he has been there some time. He doesn't look up. 'Where are you cyclin', mate?'

'Around Australia.'

'How many times?'

Pause. *What's this guy getting at?*

'Er, just the once.'

'I was working in Kununurra recently and met a Yank who was doin' it twice. You wouldn't want to let a Yank outdo ya, would ya?' He drags on his fag, gives me a challenging stare, turns a limp page and returns to his reading.

I feel strong despite an increasingly brisk head-wind. Batchelor, 5km off the highway at the entrance to Litchfield National Park and formerly the town servicing the Rum Jungle uranium and copper mine, won a tidy town award some years ago and deservedly so. It is a pristine Shangri-la, all manner of tropical plants flourishing in spotless gardens. Harriet, Eliza and Hugh spend hours in the campground pool and drag me in, where we toss a ball around.

Today's heat has made my jock-itch even worse and I realise I might need something more medicinal than tea-tree oil. As I sit in the darkness, legs open and fanning a copy of *TV Week* for all I'm worth, I wonder how it will recover. Rashes love hot, wet regions and there is no way that the bit of me that sits on the saddle is going to be anything other than that for the foreseeable future.

Day 79: Tuesday 5 August
Rest day: Batchelor

Last night the impossible happened, it rained. 'Well, I'll be buttered on both sides,' says the campground owner in the early morning, scratching his head and looking at the puddles on the road. Caroline, sleeping in her swag under the stars, got wet. For some reason I erected the tent; more good luck than any meteorological foresight.

We spend most of the day messing around in the pools made by the tributaries of the Reynolds River as it plunges off the Tabletop Range and winds its way towards the Joseph Bonaparte Gulf, west of Darwin. The kids, my first-cousins-once-removed, are wonderfully open and enthusiastic, and it is good to get to know them a little. I don't think they have quite wrapped their minds around the ride yet, or worked out why I am doing it. 'Do you think it could be just a *little* nutty?' asked Harriet last night.

Then disappointment. I speak to Diane Raymond from the Perth Lions Club, who is organising a fund-raising function for us in her city. She tells me she recently rang the Cancer Foundation of Western Australia who said they were not interested in supporting me. 'They told me that we should think twice about supporting you too,' she says, 'because people doing these sorts of things traditionally offer much and produce little.' I am devastated by the news, and confused; why would an organisation for which an event is raising money refuse to support that event, particularly when $170,000 is already in the bank? Why would a charity organisation turn its back on help? I ring my biggest supporter, Heather Le Roy at the Anti-Cancer Council in Victoria, for advice. She says she will make a few calls. 'Hang in there,' she says. 'You're doing a good job.'

Day 80: Wednesday 6 August, Batchelor to Pine Creek
Distance: 174km
Distance so far: 5414km

A day of 170km, but I feel strong. At Adelaide River I pass through 5300km, a third of the way. If it were not for yesterday's news I would feel on top of the world. Instead I feel steely, still irked and determined to prove the detractors wrong. 'Bugger them,' I say out loud.

It seems that even the most unlikely town in these parts is famous for *something*. Adelaide River, a sign announces proudly, is the home of Charlie the Buffalo from the hit film *Crocodile Dundee*. It is also the home of the ARSS Club—the Adelaide River Show Society. As I stop for a photo, an Aboriginal woman in a spotless dress, polished two-tone leather shoes, and carrying a new suitcase walks past me, heads out over the showgrounds and into the scrubby wilderness beyond.

I, too, head into the wilderness, opting to leave the Stuart Highway and take the back road to Hayes Creek. It becomes clear that the ride will not be straightforward: the road is hilly and there is no water. I have already drunk four litres this morning, and both water bottles are full. Farmers have been burning off and tendrils of smoke from wizened, charcoaled tree trunks curl upwards.

For two hours I have seen acrid smoke from a fresh fire billowing in the distance and as I get closer the smoke turns into flames, spitting and jumping among the eucalypt saplings, fireballs reaching into the sky, smoke obscuring the road ahead. I wait for ten minutes—the only alternative to backtracking—before throwing caution to the wind, taking a deep breath and riding into the blackout, hoping a car is not coming the other way. After five seconds I wonder whether I have made a big mistake, then emerge into the clear air, feeling silly. The scorched-earth policy seems to mock the common Top End sign, 'We Like Our Lizards Frilled Not Grilled'.

At Emerald Springs I fill my water bottles at the pub. Truckies tuck into huge plates of steak and chips and a handful of locals prop up the bar, a line of bottom cracks peeping over the top of Wrangler jeans. A sign asks people to tie up their dogs, not an unreasonable request, although a pig, presumably the pub owner's, roots around the tables at the patrons' feet. No-one takes much notice. This is, after all, the Territory.

Day 81: Thursday 7 August, Pine Creek to Katherine
Distance: 110km
Distance so far: 5524km

I have cycled this road before, from the opposite direction two weeks ago, and am keen to get today's ride over. Backtracking is no fun. There is no wind and I settle down on my aero bars, knocking over 60km in less than two hours. When cycling you don't notice the heat very much on account of evaporating sweat, and it is only when I stop to stretch that it hits me like a furnace. I put on more sunscreen and remind myself to do it more often. It is August and the heat will increase from now on. Skin cancer is one thing I *should* try to avoid.

I overtake a cyclist, another Japanese, Shiko, wobbling his way to Port Augusta. He looks like he has lost his marbles, a tea towel around his head and wearing two-sizes-too-big gardening gloves bought, he says, from K-Mart in Darwin. We cycle together and he tells me his story in halting English. His ride, I gather, is some sort of rite of passage—to prove his manhood—between leaving university and starting a job in Osaka. 'I love Australia,' he tells me with a grin. 'It is a tough place, but not too tough for me. I am strong.'

I'm not sure the feelings of love are reciprocated. I have been told that Japanese cyclists are loathed by the truckies on the Stuart Highway because of their flagrant disregard for the road rules, often cycling down the wrong side of the road, and occasionally down its middle. Shiko has half his home on his bike, as well as a substantial pack on his back. I persuade him to tie the pack to the top of his rear panniers to lower his centre of gravity and take the strain from his shoulders. Clearly he has no idea how to do this and seems amazed that I can. He sets off again, weaving about the road like a drunk. Every now and again he turns around to look at me and grin, which causes him to swerve more. I wish him luck and leave him behind.

We stay at the Springvale Homestead in Katherine which, like many other cattle stations, has had to move with the times to combat falling cattle prices and lure tourists. It has campsites, a pool, a bar, a restaurant, a visiting singer each night and a corroboree four times a week.

Day 82: Friday 8 August
Rest day: Katherine

My new companions the Walfords, in Katherine for the first time, visit Katherine Gorge while I write to supporters and friends. So many people have helped and I want to keep them posted on my progress. I also visit the bank and deposit $5,000 collected over the past four weeks. It is a nice feeling, but $1 million seems a long way off.

Best Western Hotels have agreed to sponsor the rest of the ride, providing hotel rooms where possible. It is not monetary sponsorship, but the accommodation will be a welcome alternative to camping.

I ring the public relations officer at the Cancer Foundation of Western Australia, Fiona Paice, and tell her of my progress and the achievements of the team. She assures me they *will* support me in Western Australia, organising media and alerting schools in the region. Can't understand why this wasn't the case originally. Got to sell yourself all the time. Buoyed by their change of heart we collect money in the Katherine supermarket. Harriet, Eliza and Hugh, supremely confident, are first-class collectors, encouraged by the lure of a prize for the most money raised. In two hours we collect $450. Many people saw us on TV the other night. The further I go, the greater the donations.

Day 83: Saturday 9 August, Katherine to Camp Oven Bore
Distance: 105km
Distance so far: 5629km

'Be careful out there,' says the campground manager as I set off heading west. I press him for information. 'Oh, there's just some weird shit between here and Kununurra. Odd folk, vagabonds, drifters, a few nutters. Just be careful.'

New day; new bitumen. The Victoria Highway, south-west from Katherine, is a refreshing change from the Stuart Highway and for the first time in three weeks I feel like I am making progress again. The road is white and hot and the sun beats down. I slap on the sunscreen. The small hills give way to stunted scrub and no views. The sky is a dazzling blue. 'Back on the road again,' I hum to myself. I stop at a roadside clearing where a fellow traveller tops up my water bottles. He is from Ararat in Victoria and knows a friend of mine. Small place.

Nothing but gum trees, termite mounds and long, wispy grass. Although there are cattle properties on both sides of the road—*Manbulloo* and *Carbeen Park*—I do not see a beast all day. Their carrying capacity, especially during the dry season, is low. With nothing to look at I search for other distractions. I sing songs, often at full blast, and quote poetry. Kipling's *If*, in particular, 'If you can force your heart and nerve and sinew to serve you long after they are gone ... ' Skerricks of Shakespeare, morsels of Monty Python: 'Amazing bird the Norwegian Blue, beautiful plumage ... What *is* the most popular cheese round here? ... Listen, strange women lying in ponds distributing swords is no basis for a system of government ... ' The countries of the world in alphabetical order: Afghanistan, Albania, Australia, Austria. Backwards—natsinahgfA, ainablA ... Their capital cities? Units of currency? Bordering countries? It is a long morning.

At a lay-by, Camp Oven Bore, we can see neither camp oven nor bore. It is good to be in the wilderness and away from campgrounds where we often find ourselves cheek by jowl with other campers. There are downsides though—the clearing has no toilets and smells come from people shitting in the surrounding bushes. There is a huge concrete water tank for washing and cooking.

In the middle of the night, a car pulls in and shines its headlights on us, idling for five minutes. Two men get out and have a piss, talk for an hour, laugh a bit, rev up their car and pull out, the wheels spitting out stones and gravel. Again, calm descends, though my heart is racing. 'Well *that* was interesting,' says Caroline, voice shaking, from her swag.

Day 84: Sunday 10 August, Camp Oven Bore to
Victoria River Downs station
Distance: 155km
Distance so far: 5784km

A tail-wind helps me cover 70km in two hours. At *Willeroo* station is an enormous obelisk, marking the turn-off to Top Springs at the north end of the Murranji Track. The thin bitumen road carves off to the left. Nearby a wedge-tail eagle picks at the remains of a recent road kill. Folklore says wedgies only eat animals they kill themselves but I have witnessed enough of them picking at dead 'roos to refute this. Cars have become the biggest predators, providing food for lazy carnivores.

I come to the top of a rise near Illari Hill and gasp. Waves of flat-topped hills—in reds, yellows and browns—march to the horizon, their flanks plunging into canopies of green. I am at the edge of the Gregory National Park which represents, in my mind at least, the beginnings of the Kimberley region. And the western edge of the Kimberley, I repeat to myself like a mantra, is halfway.

The escarpments play havoc with the wind, which swirls and eddies, preventing good cycling rhythm. I crank up and down the gears to find the right one. Now a tail-wind, now a side-wind, even, God forbid, traces of a head-wind. You have been good to me; don't give up on me now. Down a gentle slope and the first glimpse of the mighty Victoria River—100 metres across and bursting with energy—which forms one of the finest pastoral regions in Australia. Much of the land, geologically referred to as Cambrian Basalt, forms an extensive alluvial black-soil plain and can support a cattle population of between six and ten beasts per square kilometre: an agricultural gold mine.

The first European to see the mouth of the Victoria River was Phillip King, the son of the first Lieutenant-Governor of Norfolk Island, who sailed his boat the *Mermaid* as far as he dared up the river—which was not far—in September 1819. Twenty years later Captain John Clements Wickham took his boat, the *Beagle*, 220km upriver, his deputy John Stokes—not long after surviving an encounter with a crocodile which 'brought his unpleasant countenance much nearer than was agreeable'—declaring, 'as the Murray is to south-eastern Australia, so in value and importance is the great river Victoria, to the opposite side of the continent.' In the early 1850s gold fever gripped the continent and further exploration in the north-west was deemed irrelevant. Until, that is, brothers Augustus and Francis Gregory set sail up the Victoria River, becoming the first Europeans to lay eyes on the confluence of the Victoria and Wickham rivers. Today this is the centre of arguably Australia's most famous cattle station, *Victoria River Downs*, referred to in the Top End as *VRD*, or the *Big Run*.

Looking bedraggled at Victoria River Crossing Roadhouse is Greg Potter, a 41-year-old from the Victorian town of St Arnaud, near Bendigo. He has cycled up from Adelaide on a recumbent, a three-wheeled machine which he sits in, his pedals out the front, towing his luggage on a trailer. We swap cycling stories and it becomes clear he is not your average cyclist. He speaks with a slurred voice, the result, he says, of a brain tumour removed 16 years ago. He has two kids and lives on a pension. He has cycled 5000km, about the same as me, and is taking his time. 'No point hurrying,' he says. We bid farewell and I press on, sheepish that I have felt sorry for myself at times on this trip, given his challenges and achievements. He, too, is heading for Broome and I hope we meet again.

Fifty kilometres past Victoria River in an area of classic Australian outback—parched red earth with traces of green, giant termite mounds and boab trees (*Adansonia gregorii*)—is the turn-off to *VRD*. We have been invited to stay there by Cathy Holmes à Court whose father, entrepreneur Robert Holmes à Court, bought the station at the height of his acquisitive phase in the 1980s. When he died his wife, Janet, took over the company reins.

It has been a tough day, 155km, and I am glad to sit back in the car as we drive through two hours of bulldust to *VRD*. I take the precaution of taping up the caravan's vents but to no avail—by the time we arrive an inch of red talc covers everything. Dust is part of life in the Territory.

The *VRD* manager is Ken Hasted, a rough-talking, hipless Territorian who squints as if permanently looking into the sun, and talks without moving his lips. He refuses to let me take his photo when he greets us. 'Hate bloody cameras,' he growls. 'Take someone else's.'

Ken's is no easy job—*VRD* covers nearly 12 000 square kilometres (second in size only to *Brunette Downs*) and carries 80 000 head of cattle. There are 80 employees, a general store and a post office. In modern-day human resources parlance he is multi-skilled, filling the roles of manager, accountant, public relations coordinator, policeman, magistrate, psychologist and marriage counsellor. He looks very tired.

His wife, Vicky, has an effervescent ebullience and a wide Top End smile. She puts us in the guest house, usually reserved for the Holmes à Courts and other dignitaries. In the evening a fund-raising barbeque is held at the social club and people come from miles around: ringers, jackaroos and jillaroos, gardeners, wives, kids and chopper pilots (most of the mustering in the Territory is done by helicopter and a chopper company is based at *VRD*).

Ken conducts an auction of four 'mystery parcels'. The bidding is fast and furious and $1,100 is raised in 12 minutes, which he presents to me with a flourish and a wink. The winners look a little nonplussed when the parcels' contents are revealed: a leather belt and three water bottles that have quenched many a ringer's thirst. The place erupts with laughter. The party finishes at midnight and everyone pitches in to clean up. 'Best night I've had in years,' somebody says.

Day 85: Monday 11 August
Rest day: *Victoria River Downs* station

Over the decades, owners of *VRD* have won, and lost, fortunes and reputations have been built and smashed. The station used to cover 41 000 square kilometres, bigger than Denmark. At one stage, in 1934, it boasted the biggest herd in Australia, possibly the world, 170 000 head. Such was the distance between the homestead and outstations that the workers spoke of days travelling rather than kilometres. Today, musters still span weeks.

The job of stocking the station in the early 1880s was given to legendary stockman Nat 'Bluey' Buchanan, who drove 20 000 head of cattle from Queensland—encountering bogs, river crossings, crocs, bouts of Redwater Fever and murderous mosquitoes—opening up new stock routes in the process. The tough men working on the *Big Run* paid a high price for their pioneering spirit, enduring life-threatening diseases including malaria, one outbreak of which killed more than ten per cent of the station's population. Isolation, of course, was part of the job.

No man built up a greater reputation at *VRD* than the manager in the 1880s and 1890s, Jack Watson, known far and wide as the Gulf Hero. Watson's exploits as a Boy's Own–style fearless adventurer included the rescuing of a Chinese man who had fallen overboard from a lugger off the Carpentaria coast and was being mauled by a shark. Watson dived in and hacked at the shark with a knife, rescuing the victim and driving away the assailant. He thought nothing of jumping from a boat into a croc-infested river to rescue a hat. He refused to carry a gun, believing his reputation was enough to deter any assailants—human or animal—and the only time he used one, so the story goes, was to shoot cans from Aboriginal boys' heads! He died, on April Fool's Day, 1896, swimming stock over the flooded Katherine River, and was replaced as manager by his brother, Bob. Jack was a better horseman than diarist, and used to send the station's then-owners, English company Goldsbrough Mort, into a lather with the lack of detail in his monthly station reports. These reached a crescendo of brevity in June 1895 when he sent the following: 'Water, Pasturage and Stock same as last month.'

We spend the morning looking at the old *VRD* hospital, now in ruins, and wallowing in the Wickham River, 5km from the homestead, which we first check closely for crocs. On the way home, embarrassingly, we run out of petrol and are towed back to the homestead by a car-load of life-saving Aborigines.

A feeling of inequity at *VRD* surfaces among the white stockmen. 'The Aborigines get a bloody good deal here,' one told me candidly at last night's dinner. 'The Flying Doctor will come out to see one of them at the drop of a hat while we have to drive into Katherine if we get sick. We had our school closed down not long ago and yet they are getting a $600,000 school built for them. That's not fair, and that's what the people from the cities don't understand.'

In the evening, as the sun sets low over the downs, we are taken up in a chopper. Crocs bask in the river below while 60km to the south, beyond *Pigeon Hole* outstation, broods Mount Northcote. The green lawns of the *VRD* homestead are an oasis amid the bleak plains. 'It's swish but not as swish as *Newcastle Waters*,' says our pilot Paul. 'Kerry Packer owns that one, and Kerry likes his comforts.'

We are invited to dinner at the Hasteds' house. Vicky tells us she has had more than 100 visitors during the dry season. Over dinner their teenage son arrives, bleary-eyed after a 17-hour drive from the Mount Isa rodeo. He didn't do too well in the buckjumping but is enthusiastic about the Mount Isa strippers. Gets a clip over the ear from Ken, who retires, looking as bushed as his son. Later, I walk past his room and see him snoring on his bed, another child—a three year old—asleep beside him.

Day 86: Tuesday 12 August, *Victoria River Downs* station to Baines River
Distance: 142km
Distance so far: 5926km

Thirty kilometres west of the *VRD* turn-off is Timber Creek, nothing more than a BP service station in the scrub. I have 22 phone messages: schools wanting to meet with me in Western Australia; and sponsors and well-wishers. Greg Potter, bandanna around his head, sits in the shade, a busload of tourists showing interest in his recumbent cycle. For once it is nice not to have to field questions about long-distance cycling and I melt away.

Bikes seem to generate a lot of interest in the outback, mainly because there are so few of them. It has always been the case. In *Hell West and Crooked* Tom Cole writes of the days he was managing *Bullita* station, 50km south of here, in the 1930s.

At the end of a week, my bullock paddock was just about eaten out and I'd nearly talked Peg Leg into staying when Jack Noble arrived on a bicycle! It must have been the most sensational thing that had ever happened on Bullita; I reckoned it would have been a bigger sensation than the Crisp spearing. My stockboys had never seen a bicycle in their lives. I'm sure they wouldn't have been as impressed if Jack Noble had arrived walking up the river without wetting his ankles. I've mentioned that I thought there were only three motor cars between Katherine and Wyndham in Western Australia, possibly four—but there was only one bike, that was certain . . . and we had it here on Bullita!

Greg and I cycle together out of town and he gets up a good head of steam on his recumbent, especially on the down slopes, although he is less efficient going uphill. He has, after all, five tyres touching the ground while I have only two. We speak about his brain surgery and its ramifications. 'People don't take as much notice of what I say now,' he says. 'But one day they will realise that I still speak good sense. The hardest thing was having my kids taken from me when I got divorced.'

A campsite sits next to the Victoria River, which is a mesmerising and inviting blue. I am tempted to dive in. 'I wouldn't, mate,' says a camper. 'A croc took a person last year. Poor bastard wasn't even in the water but cleaning fish on the side. He disappeared in an instant, did the death roll, and that was that.' Greg decides to camp here and we say goodbye. I am aiming for Kununurra tomorrow which means I still have 100km to cover today. I feel like I am leaving a very special person and pay my respects in the time-honoured Aussie bush way, presenting him with half-a-dozen stubbies.

The Victoria River keeps me company for 10km before it peels off and meanders soporifically north, across the Whirlwind Plain to the Joseph Bonaparte Gulf 150km away. Boab trees, resembling giant sprouting beer bottles, have become more common. It is hot and humid. According to the locals August is the start of the build-up to the wet season and is often uncomfortable. There is a humidity and a frisson in the air and people, not that there are too many of them out here, get on-edge and jumpy.

The road is good, the wind negligible, and I make pleasing progress for 80km. Then 15km of gravel and sand on account of roadworks. Big earth-moving trucks and graders chug along, cumulus clouds of bulldust billowing in their wake. No-one takes much notice as I pick my way across the rocks, between the sand-drifts. Just a lonely fruitcake heading west.

We camp in the bed of the dry Baines River. There are waterholes nearby and Eliza is spooked by recent tales of crocodiles. As dusk descends an old Brahman bull wanders past, searching for water, and snorts. The kids scream.

Day 87: Wednesday 13 August, Baines River to Kununurra
Distance: 134km
Distance so far: 6060km

The campground is in a torpor this morning. None of us wakes until late and the kids walk around like zombies. Even Caroline and I feel lethargic. Perhaps a hangover from *VRD*, more likely due to the mosquitoes. The kids have been mauled. 'I've counted 32 bites,' says Eliza, peering into the mirror.

Mid-morning I clock up 6000km, which is worth a celebration as I steam towards the Western Australian border. How to celebrate by yourself? I smile, which is about it. Ten thousand to go. It seems only yesterday I left Sydney, and yet I have already passed through the best part of three states. Every day I have been moving, every day is new.

The Northern Territory–Western Australia border is nondescript, not surprising given this is pretty much the end of the earth. There is an enormous 'Welcome to Western Australia' sign, and the fruit-fly police. One emerges from a caravan with a box of vegetables to be destroyed. Somehow this is supposed to save Western Australia from the much-feared fruit fly, but I don't see how they stop the flies from *flying* over the border. 'Eight years ago the whole thing was pretty pointless,' he tells me. 'We weren't open 24 hours and people waited around the corner until we closed and then drove through. The sad thing is that most of the fruit we destroy is better than what you can buy in Kununurra, down the road.'

It is mesmerising to be in a new state. Western Australia, one-third of Australia's area, is one of the biggest states in the world. The land on the west side of the border seems to advertise the fact; the rocky outcrops seem bolder, the cliffs steeper and the grass somehow lusher. The state represents, for many people, everything that is quintessentially Australian: inhospitable deserts and gold mines, while the wild Kimberley region to the north represents the last frontier. Vibrant Perth, and the south-west region with its wineries and spectacular mountain ranges, are the modern face of this vast state.

Western Australians claim they are the most isolated people on earth and have no choice but to rely on nous and ingenuity to get ahead, celebrating their parochialism. No-one was particularly surprised that the Australian yachting syndicate to win the America's Cup in 1983 was based in Perth. Equally no-one was surprised when the syndicate's lynch-pin, Alan Bond, ended up doing time. Says a lot about life in the West: you have to sail close to the wind to make headway, and people who sail too close to the wind often stall. While it is energising to enter a new state, and a new part of the ride, I feel a sadness leaving the Territory. Territorians are salt-of-the-earth people in their own wacky, individualistic way and they seemed to *understand* why a person would want to cycle around the country.

It seems everyone has a bad story about Kununurra—violence, racism—and I cycle towards it with feelings of trepidation. I find, however, a friendliness, Aboriginal and white Australians mixing freely at the local pool, and broad smiles everywhere. The local paper, the *Kimberley Echo*, tracks me down for an interview and for the first time I feel there is something newsworthy about the ride. Six-thousand kilometres is no trifling matter. I spend the afternoon answering overdue messages and learn that Cynthia Glen, a friend of mine in her late-thirties, has died of cancer, leaving behind two children and a husband.

Caroline and the kids arrive after dark, raving about their tour on the giant Lake Argyle, which holds nine times as much water as Sydney Harbour. Kununurra residents, the kids say breathlessly as they prepare for bed, would have 23 minutes to vacate if the dam broke. It is hard to sleep without at least one ear listening for the sound of rushing water.

Day 88: **Thursday 14 August**
Rest day: **Kununurra**

We tour Kununurra's Ord River Project which is, depending on who you speak to, either one of the great agricultural feats of the modern age or a Jumbo-sized white elephant. That the project is large and audacious is undeniable: when Prime Minister Robert Menzies opened the dam in 1963 there were plans to develop 100 000 acres of irrigated land. Whether it has been economically successful is open to dispute. Certainly, the land of milk and honey that the government promised to the people lured there took a long time to materialise, if it ever did. Initial crops like cotton and rice encountered problems with tropical diseases, birds and the removal of government subsidies, and were abandoned. Higher-return products like cashews, peanuts, chick peas, bananas and rockmelons have been more successful.

There is no doubt that the bubbling canals and waterways today give year-round life to a land that would otherwise be bone dry half the year. Those not complaining are the hordes of students who stop here between May and September to pick fruit in the middle of their Australian wanderings, earning themselves ten bucks an hour, tax-free.

CHAPTER FIVE

The Gibb River Road, WA
A Hell of a Place

And the sun sank again on the grand Australian bush—the nurse and tutor of eccentric minds, the home of the weird, and of much that is different from things in other lands

Henry Lawson: *The Bush Undertaker*

Day 89: **Friday 15 August,**
Kununurra to *El Questro* **station**
Distance: 110km
Distance so far: 6170km

The Kununurra Primary School holds its assemblies early to beat the heat. The principal asks which route we are taking.

'Through Halls Creek and Fitzroy Crossing,' I answer.

'There's always the Gibb River Road,' he says with a smile I later discover to be that of executioner. 'It's one of the great roads of the world and most people only get the one chance. You'd be crazy to pass it up.'

I am haunted by the principal's words as I cycle out of Kununurra, across the raging Ord River lined by palm trees and pandanus, and along the Duncan Highway. Travellers have told me about the Gibb River Road, connecting the port town of Wyndham on Joseph Bonaparte Gulf and Derby on the west coast, and opinions are that it is nothing more than 650km of sheer misery. Undeniably, it cuts through some magnificent country, the renowned Kimberley, but it takes its toll on all who travel it.

Motorists speak of the road in hushed, reverent tones. There are tales of hardship and heartache, even murder. A 32-year-old German traveller, Joseph Schwab, lost his mind near the Pentecost River Crossing in June 1987 and killed three tourists. He was eventually tracked down by police and shot dead near Fitzroy Crossing.

The areas involved in the Kimberley region of Western Australia are prodigious. Although it occupies only the top bit of the state it is three times as big as England and twice the size of Victoria. It is home to only 15 000 people, most of whom live in Halls Creek, Fitzroy Crossing and Turkey Creek. It is, many say, Australia's last true frontier, a land of million-acre cattle stations, razor-back ridges, sprawling savannah grasslands and fertile river flats.

I have even met people who have survived the Gibb River Road, but they speak only of hardship and frustration. Many were towed out. Descriptions are repetitious: the road is 'awesome' and 'frightening', and people say they *change* on the Gibb River Road. Certainly, their cars are never the same. It is not the knee-high bulldust or the remoteness, nor the lack of water or fuel that most causes the alteration of mind and body. The corrugations, which appear mysteriously on the surface of many gravel roads, are the real problem.

Corrugations start as mere ripples and, over time, turn to large, unforgiving undulations which slowly consume cars and trucks. When you put a car, even a hardy four-wheel drive, under enough pressure, bouncing it about for days on end, it submits and returns, piece by piece, to the earth from whence it came. Screws unwind, wire snaps, rivets pop out. The car slowly disintegrates and, in many cases, the driver's mind follows shortly thereafter. Regulation cars are not forbidden, but are definitely not encouraged. I have heard of the tourist who took a welding kit when travelling the road to make running repairs and removed its casing after three days to find why it wouldn't work. The insides had been reduced to jelly. Or the couple who took an aluminium boat along the road only to have the four struts of their trailer hammer through the boat's hull. It was abandoned in a gully on the side of the road, a warning to those hoping to go fishing on the Mitchell Plateau.

Today we travel to *El Questro* station, 30km into the Gibb River Road, which will give me some idea of what to expect. As I think about my choice, the Deception Range staggers alongside me to the south, its name mocking any decision I am likely to make.

The roadsign at the start of the most feared road in Australia is all shiny metal and cheery letters, pointing the way to *El Questro* and *Mount Barnett*. It is not unlike a sign on the door to Hades saying 'Welcome', or Beelzebub wearing a T-shirt saying, 'What, Me Worry?' Even the name—the 'Gibb River Road'—is something Enid Blyton might have cooked up, leading perhaps to the Magic Faraway Tree. By reputation there should be blood stains on the sign, or at least a scrawny vulture hunched on the top, beadily eyeing the infirm, and probably those on bikes too.

The start of the road, as if a siren to lull the unsuspecting, is nothing unpleasant. It is smooth, hard gravel—not unlike poor bitumen—and I freewheel at 20km an hour, wondering what all the fuss is about. Two kilometres on is an even more promising sight: a grader. A workman takes measurements on the roadside and I stop, eager for information. He gives me a concerned look, the kind usually reserved for people swimming among icebergs or patting crocs. 'We're working on the eastern end of the road only,' he grunts. 'It deteriorates not long after the *El Questro* turn-off. It's bloody awful a hundred kilometres out and doesn't improve 'til you get to Derby. You'll have your work cut out on that thing.' He looks disparagingly at Quasimodo, and I bristle.

The *El Questro* driveway is 15km long and, if it is a portent of things to come, the next two weeks *will be* hard yakka. At times the gravel becomes deep, red sand and I have no choice but to walk. On the harder gravel the corrugations resemble a mini-rollercoaster. This, too, plays havoc with my speed, and my mind feels like a plate of spaghetti. Three four-wheel drives thunder past, en route to *El Questro* from the Kununurra airport. Each time the driver sticks his hand out the window and gives me the thumbs up.

Drained, I arrive at the station, wallowing first in a bubbling creek to wash the grit and sand from Quasimodo's pedals and chain, and from my ears and eyes. I stagger into the station, looking a sight. 'Jeez mate, we thought you'd never arrive,' says the manager as I stand in the doorway of his office, dripping. 'You're sweatin' like a pig.'

I have three days to make a decision, but now is not the best of times for objectivity; the bitumen to Halls Creek looks far too inviting. Caroline and the kids, who drove on ahead, have been here for some time and have bad news: the caravan's winding mechanism is broken and the roof will not lift. Eventually we jack it up, holding it with stacked cans of beetroot and soup.

Days 90–92: Saturday 16–Monday 18 August
Rest days: *El Questro* and Kununurra

For the Walfords it is the end of their trip and we make the most of *El Questro*'s waterholes, swimming in the hot springs and taking a boat tour in the stunning Chamberlain Gorge. No swimming in the latter, on account of the crocs.

Andy Mackinnon, a cousin on Dad's side, arrives from Melbourne as crew for the next leg, getting a lift to *El Questro* in one of the dust-making machines. I am mindful that he has volunteered for the most remote part of the ride and I appreciate his commitment. His mother, my aunt, is a diminutive septuagenarian and one of the most positive, enthusiastic people around; I hope Andy has brought along plenty of both qualities. We discuss the options for the next fortnight and decide the Gibb River Road is an opportunity not to be ignored. I guess I was swaying that way anyway, but it's nice to agree.

It is not a decision we take lightly. We must be in Broome in two weeks to meet the next crew and Andy has a plane to catch. I have no real idea, despite yesterday's taste of the road, whether I will be able to make the 650km in that time. Don't know whether the car will make it either, to say nothing of the caravan, even if it *does* have 'Off Road' written boldly on the side. We have heard too many horror stories to imagine the driving will be hassle-free. Still, we are prepared, with spare fuel, two spare wheels, two extra 25-litre water tanks and expansive tool and first-aid kits. Already, for the sake of simplicity, we have decided to sleep outside and use the caravan's outside cooker. The downside is that the fridge will be out of action, which means canned food and warm long-life milk.

I drive Caroline and the kids to the Kununurra airport. Another team is disbanding and I feel saddened by it. They have been wonderful, happy support and I will miss their smiles and laughter. I shed a tear as they wave goodbye from the plane's steps. 'See you in Melbourne,' yell the girls.

I spend the night in Kununurra and the following day buy food for the next fortnight, aware that the fruit and vegetables are unlikely to last more than a week at best in the heat. In the Kununurra library I log into my e-mails and receive 47. Responding to them is overwhelming. Two of the e-mails are from the cancer councils in Western Australia and South Australia, which report that there has been a good response from the schools in their states.

On Monday afternoon I return to *El Questro* where Andy has been waiting patiently. The Gibb River Road waits too.

Day 93: Tuesday 19 August, *El Questro* to *Home Valley*
Distance: 35km
Distance so far: 6205km

The accepted wisdom of getting along the Gibb River Road unscathed, we have been told, is to travel slowly and enjoy it, as much as you can. The corrugations are the key—many tourists go fast, hoping to skim over the top of them. The locals say this approach eventually wears out the driver, passengers and car. No-one seems to know of anyone who has cycled it before so advice is a little thin on the ground for me.

There is no guidebook, and therefore no rules. This is difficult for me to fathom; I've lived in cities with rules and regulations all my life. Here people can do what they like, so long as they realise that if things go wrong they're on their own. 'The best thing to do,' says the *El Questro* manager, 'is not to hurry. It's a great spot and the road will still be there tomorrow. Take your time.' On the whole, I don't feel I have much choice.

Andy and I look along the red-earthed ribbon of road to the west, shimmering in the rising heat and making strange, primeval shapes of the bloodwood trees and the already odd-looking boab trees. Scanning a horizon which shows only trees, rocks and grass, and knowing it continues that way for the best part of 700km is intimidating at best.

146

I know that, at a pinch, I can cycle 200km a day on bitumen, but have no idea what this converts to on gravel and sand. Fifty? Twenty-five? Ten? Our goal, 620km in a fortnight, amounts to about 50km a day. I know that if the cycling becomes impossible I can walk, although walking in sand is like walking in treacle.

I think of all sorts of things, still gazing west. *Carpe diem* and the rest. In my mind I quote Robert Frost:

Two roads diverged in a wood, and I—
I took the one less travelled by,
And that has made all the difference.

With a deep breath and a small sigh of resignation I mount the bike and bounce off down the road, heading towards a group of distant, precipitous cliffs, bathed in blue. The impressive ramparts hang downwards like a giant sheet, resembling something Christo may have wrapped.

Not even giving me time to settle into a stride the corrugations begin. Like a batsman getting a bean ball first up. Even at the edge of the road, where the razor grass cuts into my legs and slashes at Quasimodo's tyres, they are relentless. My speed is down to below 10km an hour and I cycle with teeth gritted. Before long I am yelling in frustration.

A few four-wheel drives pass going the other way and people wave. One stops and takes a photo of me. I feel like an exhibit. Perhaps they will be showing the photo to the Kununurra cops in a few weeks and grainy posters will be plastered on billboards and lonely telegraph poles: 'Last Seen On Gibb River Road, Heading West.' *Silly bastard.*

A few stop for a chat, evidently pleased to be nearing Wyndham. They have, they all say, enjoyed their time, though they confirm my worst fears. 'The road is corrugated to hell, and there are cars broken down the length of it,' says one, a

Pom with long white socks, sandals and a Foreign Legion hat. 'Getting help's not easy either. The only mechanic works at the Mount Barnett Roadhouse, 300km west of here.' I leave them behind with their untimely tales of woe, wishing we had never met.

The temperature is well into the 30s. I have already drunk four litres of water and need every drop. My speed is down to 7km an hour and the road seems interminable. The view is unquestionably magnificent—impressive ramparts of the Cockburn Range rise to the north—though it is hard to appreciate as I pick my way through the potholes and fissures.

I had a conversation with a man in Kununurra who was convinced that the best way to tackle the corrugation problem was for people to drive on the left side of the road for six months, then the right for six, the theory being that cars travelling both ways would cancel out the corrugations. Perhaps the idea has merit, but would drivers keep their nerve when a car approached? How would they know whether the other driver knew the rules?

After 24km I reach the stony waterbed of the Pentecost River. I feel I am crossing the River Styx, Quasimodo my Charon. The river has its origins at the north end of the Durack Ranges near Speewah Mine and 15km from here it flows into the West Arm of the Cambridge Gulf. Today it is as dry as a James Bond martini. In five months it will be a raging torrent, and impassable. The Kimberley deals only in extremes.

An hour beyond is the entrance to *Home Valley*, my destination. Although I have cycled only 35km I am shattered. Andy is there and has clearly had troubles of his own. 'How was it?' he asks.

'A bitch.' I slump in the shade.

'Same with the car. The caravan swayed across the road the whole way, and dragged the car with it. The car also sometimes speared across the road, ignoring the wheel direction. It was as if it had a mind of its own.' He looks drained but, as ever, has a ready smile. We come from the same stock and I suppose this means we will tackle this with like minds. At present my mind is a jangled mess. I look like the unwilling participant in a pagan ritual, red all over from the dust sticking to my sunscreen and sweat. Quasimodo, my faithful friend, also looks weather-beaten, cogs and gears glued up with dust. The gears have been slipping and another spoke is broken. When the manufacturers, Avanti, told me this was a touring bike, I wonder whether they had the Gibb River Road in mind.

A couple has set up in the ramshackle spot designated as the campsite at *Home Valley*, and we join them. As I go through my laborious stretching exercises we talk. 'Are you sure that's a good idea, mate?' says the bloke when I tell him I'm aiming for Derby. 'The road's a Barry Crocker.' Another car arrives and the driver, a Japanese man, eats his dinner quickly before climbing into his car to sleep. He must be suffering a severe case of culture shock.

A wizened lady in an outsize floral dress runs *Home Valley* and its tourist tea room complete with dog-eared maps of the area, old books and posters. 'There's not much water between here and Derby, love, so make sure you've got enough,' she says. We can carry 150 litres and I have modified the bike so that it carries four. Still, I wonder whether this will be sufficient. Andy and I agree that he should drive within a kilometre of me at all times, and that we should meet up often during the day to replenish water supplies. I am mindful of a writer who said that the real heroes on round-the-world walker Ffyona Campbell's journey were the succession of drivers who followed her, day after day, at 4km an hour. While my drivers have often driven on ahead, we decide it is important to keep in close contact here.

Home Valley is owned by the Sinnamon family of Darwin, who also own *Karunjie* station further west. Made from corrugated iron and timber, the homestead is a converted aircraft hanger—without walls—a perfect design for stifling summer heat. 'If there's a big wind the rain comes into the house, but that's a small price to pay for sanity,' says our host. As with all houses out here there is no electricity, and a generator throbs in a shed out the back.

The campers' shower block is a Heath Robinson contraption of hissing pipes, corrugated iron and 44-gallon drums. As night falls the showers and toilets are inundated by green frogs feasting on the insects attracted to the lights. As we sit around the fire, Andy expounds a Darwinian theory, suggesting that, just as the frogs have collected to feast on the insects, so snakes should gather during the night to feast on the frogs. We have set up camp next to the shower block, but agree we are too tired to move.

An enormous full moon rises over the Cockburn Range to the east and there is a panoply of stars in a sky the colour of lapis lazuli. At nearby Bindoola Creek our torchlight cuts through the clear air, revealing seven pairs of red eyes gazing languidly from under the pandanus palms. The lady has told us of the crocs, salties. 'Don't go in for a dip,' she chuckled. 'You won't be cycling much further if you do, unless you're good at cycling with one leg. The crocs sometimes visit the camp site at night, so if you hear one wandering around, don't breathe. Sleep well.'

Day one on the Gibb River Road and there is no turning back. I now know two things, and they are not a pleasant combination: cycling on the corrugations *is* possible; and it will be frustrating and painful. With this in mind, and the possibility of visits tonight from both vipers and crocs, sleep does not come easily. At ten o'clock the generator stops and the camp plunges into silence, interrupted occasionally by the satisfied croaking of the frogs in the shower block. The shadows flicking overhead become giant bats. Only 585km to Derby.

Day 94: Wednesday 20 August, *Home Valley* to *Jack's Waterhole*
Distance: 62km
Distance so far: 6267km

Up at six and the sun has been up for ages. The Japanese man has already left and I think of him lazing in a Wyndham pool tonight. The couple wish us luck, before they too head off. I drink two litres of water before mounting Quasimodo and hit the corrugations as soon as I reach the main road. The pain starts shortly thereafter. It is very hot.

By mid-morning I can categorise the three surfaces that make up the Gibb River Road and each means profoundly different things to the cyclist. The white gravel, hard and smooth with small stones, carries no corrugations. The grey gravel, rocky and semi-corrugated, is tolerable. The red gravel is the worst—loose, all-consuming sand, and corrugated to buggery. I could draw up a chart, create a sort of Beaufort scale of gravel; it would not bring me untold riches, but there is little else I can think of this morning.

The road crosses the Pentecost Range, providing views of the Cockburn and Milligan ranges and the Steere Hills to the north. I then cross Palmer Creek—dry—before tracking Bindoola Creek due west. On both sides of Palmer Creek the road converts to 2km of bitumen, to prevent wash away during floods and to give drivers something to grip, but it provides only temporary respite. Beyond, the red dust is like talcum powder and the loose gravel grips like quicksand.

Occasionally, when there are no corrugations, I can appreciate the terrain *off* the road. The horizon stretches away like an ocean. In addition to the boab and bloodwood trees, the Kimberley is renowned for its superior grazing grasses, including Mitchell, Flinders, kangaroo and spear grasses, as well as species of spinifex.

Andy, up ahead, is clearly having trouble. I come across two of the caravan's bed struts on the road and lash them to my bike. Already, on day two of the road, I sense the corrugations are having a deleterious effect on the car and caravan and I wonder how much of it they will take. I catch him at the top of the range, where he has stopped to look at the view. He had not realised the door was loose, and we fix it.

Descending the Pentecost Range into the depths of the Kimberley seems to sever our connection with civilisation. It is hard not to think of the early explorers and pioneers in these parts, and the hardship they endured. For the European settlers, the Kimberley region was the last Australian frontier, although it was discovered well before that. A map by Coronelli of Venice, dated 1618, gives the first indication of European awareness of the Kimberley area. Although he called the region *Terra de Concordia*—'land of peace and harmony'—when sailing past, he was not enamoured enough to actually land here.

Dutchman Abel Tasman and British buccaneer William Dampier also sailed around the Kimberley coast in the mid-to-late 1600s. In 1699 Dampier anchored at the southernmost part of the Kimberley coast (near today's Broome) and named it Roebuck Bay, but left with unfavourable impressions.

The first European to show any interest in *inland* Kimberley was 25-year-old George Grey, who anchored his schooner *Lynher* near Prince Regent River in January 1838. Although it was the wet season Grey set off with horses and men to explore inland. He enthused about the 'wild beauty of the scenery which was as lovely and picturesque as impetuous torrents, foaming cascades, lofty rocks and a rich tropical vegetation could render.' Grey reported on the richness of the land and made several important discoveries including the Glenelg River. This despite hostilities with the Aborigines, including being speared in one episode.

The first attempts at settlement were undertaken in the mid-1860s by pioneers hoping to establish sheep stations near Roebuck Bay. They were defeated by the unsuitability of the grasses, the oppressive heat and unwelcoming locals. Following exploration of the region by Alexander Forrest in 1879 (who recommended it be named after the British Colonial Secretary, the Earl of Kimberley), there were more attempts to settle. In the 1880s several families—the Duracks, Emanuels, Buchanans and MacDonalds—set out from Queensland and New South Wales on epic overland cattle drives, some approaching 6000km in length, and settled near the Ord River. At the same time sheep farmers from Western Australia settled further west. By the start of the twentieth century the townships of Broome, Derby, Wyndham and Halls Creek had sprung up, followed closely by Fitzroy Crossing.

The discovery of gold provided a huge boost. Prospectors Charlie Hall and Jack Slattery travelled along the Fitzroy River in 1885 until they came across Forrest's tracks, which they followed to Mount Barrett, north of Halls Creek. They returned to Derby with ten ounces of gold and in the ensuing two years 10 000 men landed in the Kimberley, hoping to find their fortunes. Many died in the waterless plains, or in the jaws of crocodiles.

Mateship was important and the story of Russian Jack still does the rounds in the Kimberley. He arrived at Halls Creek to prospect for gold and teamed up with another prospector, who fell ill. The nearest medical attention was in Wyndham so Jack loaded his mate, with provisions for the two of them, into his wheelbarrow and pushed him the 300km to the port.

The early afternoon drifts along, punctuated by long stretches of corrugated redness, until I arrive at *Jack's Waterhole*. The station sits on a lazy shimmer of water on the Durack River, lined by reeds, hibiscus, acacia and pandanus. I collapse next to the caravan in the cool shadow of a paperbark, shaking the dust from my shoes. It has been a long day, 62km, taking the best part of seven uncomfortable hours. Through my fatigue I recognise the beauty of the waterhole, though I marvel at the contrast; how such a glorious place could exist next to such a dreadful road.

Smatterings of people camp in glades and openings along the river bank. Members of a group of German and English travellers lie about in states of shock. The bonnet of their massive vehicle, a cross between a bus and a Sherman tank, is up and the driver looks under it disconsolately. Some of his clients offer help and encouragement while others moan and mutter among themselves. They have come cross-country from Fitzroy Crossing and look like they have gone over Niagara Falls in a barrel.

One of them, an Englishman, comes over to talk, though I am not the best company. My legs have seized up and I can hardly move. 'I'm travelling with my sons and they're learning a lot, about Australia and themselves,' he says. 'If nothing else they will leave here with a bit of independence, which is difficult to get in Gloucestershire.' He fishes into his pocket and peels off a $100 donation. I am amazed at his generosity, having only met him ten minutes ago. 'My mother died of it. It's the least I can do,' he says.

Andy has been talking of catching dinner for some time, and about his prowess with rod and reel. 'Tonight we shall eat barramundi cooked in olive oil and herbs on the open fire,' he says, hiring a canoe and unfurling a handline. He lolls about in the canoe for an hour or so, without even a nibble. Tinned tuna isn't so bad.

Day 95: Thursday 21 August, *Jack's Waterhole* to *Ellenbrae Homestead*
Distance: 56km
Distance so far: 6323km

Two punctures within an hour of setting out. One is bearable but the second smells of a conspiracy. The corrugations re-appear like a nightmare and stretches of deep gravel make the going slow. The secret of cycling long distances is rhythm, which is impossible when I have to dismount every 3km to walk beside Quasimodo. Although I have been on the road for nearly a hundred days I feel like a novice here. No amount of training can prepare a cyclist for this. It's like asking a rowing eight to paddle around Cape Horn.

A handful of vehicles pass and each stops to see if I need help. I am touched by the camaraderie and get the feeling that everyone realises we are all in this together. Although I enjoy the chats I am annoyed by the people who stop to look, some-times even take photos, without saying a word.

In a 15km stretch I count seven abandoned cars, insides stripped and blackened with fire. Elsewhere, bits of car—lights, handles, pieces of grille, even the odd roo-bar—lie abandoned on the side of the road. I stop for a breather under a tree and two giant trucks pull up, laden with drills, pipes and pumps of various description. Three men, bearded and mad-eyed, climb down and view me suspiciously. They are dressed by the same clothing company: blue singlets, torn stubbies and workboots turned red from the dust.

They are heading north for six weeks, up Drysdale River way, towards Kalumburu on Napier Broome Bay. Their quest: diamonds. They are not new to the wilderness, having just finished two years in the Tanami Desert north-west of Tennant Creek—to most people the end of the earth. 'Mate, that was civilisation compared to here,' says one. They disappear in a cloud of dust which hangs in the air.

The corrugations continue and I curse and scream at them. I curse the road, the trees, the birds and anything else that moves, and quite a few things that don't. My resolve is being battered to bits. I tell myself, as I have done many times in the past three months, to keep my head down and pedal. I battle lethargy and ambivalence.

I perk up 15km from *Ellenbrae Homestead* when Andy appears on a bike from the opposite direction to escort me in. We say little to each other and I can hear him puffing. When we arrive I collapse in a heap. Andy has made a pot of tea and I drink five cups leaning against the caravan's tyre before I feel remotely like moving.

Ellenbrae Homestead is a million-acre cattle station on the west side of the Mosquito Hills. It sits above a tributary of Ellenbrae Creek which in turn runs into the Durack River. The station is run by Byrne and Ann Terry, a forty-something, no-nonsense, angular couple from Hughenden in Western Queensland, who hold the lease until 2015. They bought the land for $1 an acre and have spent the past ten years building a house from local stone and wood. Like the Kimberley personality the house is open and solid, to withstand searing heat, tropical downpours and cyclones. It seems *Ellenbrae* is a modern-day Noah's Ark. 'We have frogs in the wind-chimer, lizards behind the oven, and a variety of bush marsupials come for a bite most tea-times,' Byrne says with a smile. 'Even snakes drop in from time to time.' Ann, cooking, shudders.

The Terrys make the best of what they have—a common approach in the Top End. These days the cattle business is poor. 'We didn't even bother mustering this year because prices are so low,' Byrne says. 'Mind you someone is making money out of it. A steak still sells for $15 in a restaurant. *That* doesn't come down when cattle prices fall out of the sky.'

Tourism is helping them make ends meet, and the Terrys have built a business attracting ornithologists. An English couple is here, enthusiastic about the bird life, including the black grasswren, the white-quilled rock pigeon and the effervescent rainbow bee-eater. The Terrys are also keen artists, an old railway carriage in the garden displaying a collection of homemade paraphernalia.

They have a happy, relaxed outlook that comes from knowing you are living the right life for you. This despite, perhaps because of, being cut off from the rest of the world three months each year during the Wet. Last year it rained 35 centimetres in 24 hours and a dead donkey was found four metres up a tree. It was worse in 1986, when they had to camp on the roof for the night in the drumming rain, floodwaters lapping at the gutters. 'We were sharing the roof with every critter for miles,' Byrne chuckles. 'We had snakes, mice and lizards on the roof with us but there was no nastiness between them. It was as if they had all made a pact to get along because of the desperate straits we were all in. We were OK, because we had a slab of beer with us.' The story requires great imagination from us—the ground outside looks like it hasn't seen rain in decades.

Ann's parents, Norm and Shirley, in their 70s, live at *Ellenbrae* during the dry season, spending the other six months in Blaxland on the outskirts of Sydney. They resemble Ma and Pa Kettle, both whippet-thin with weathered faces, their clothes hanging from them. At *Ellenbrae* they tend the garden and clean the shelter that has been erected for campers, which includes a boiler, showers, armchairs and a serviceable book collection. While we set up camp, Norm has a shower, and Shirley dries his undies on the boiler. Norm is recovering from cancer and is on a strict diet of nuts and cereal, which he has for breakfast, lunch and dinner.

We are invited to the homestead for dinner: soup, roast beef and fresh fruit. Having a home-cooked meal is a thrill. We have become used to canned food and the lack of a fridge is wearing thin. The topic of conversation, naturally enough, turns to the road and its future. Byrne and Ann tell us horror stories about people coming unstuck. Despite their affection for the local indigenous population they say Aboriginal people are the worst offenders. 'You see them driving through here with no jack, no water and no spare tyres,' Ann says. 'Sometimes they blow their tyres and keep driving on the rims of the wheels. They always seem to get rescued.'

The road's future is problematical as it comes under pressure from increasingly adventurous tourists. 'It would be a tragedy if they bituminised it because it would turn it into a highway and would seriously change the area,' Byrne says. 'Of course, only a politician would do that; but that's what scares me.'

I wouldn't knock back a few hundred kilometres of bitumen at the moment, but keep my mouth shut.

Day 96: Friday 22 August, *Ellenbrae Homestead* to Gibb River
Distance: 75km
Distance so far: 6398km

During last night's conversation Ann mentioned they had run out of antiseptic cream, so I give them a tube from our first-aid kit. It is good to give something to someone else for a change. They then insist on donating 30 litres of fuel.

I know it is going to be a long day as soon as I leave *Ellenbrae*. The road is sandier than ever, which presents the usual problems. Five cars stop and offer help, including a lift. Tempting. The dust causes mechanical problems too. I am using clip-on pedals—my shoes are attached to the bike pedals, which need to be swivelled sideways to unclip—and the dust has clogged them something chronic. Twice I fall off Quasi-modo when he stops abruptly in thick sand and I am unable to unclip in time. Quite apart from the problem of being covered in dust, the embarrassment is acute—it happens once when a car is approaching. The occupants applaud as I wallow around in the sand like a beached whale.

Early afternoon, after 50km, two people appear like a mirage on the road ahead, pushing cycles. The effect of the heat makes them look like they are walking in mid-air, and as they get closer to me they descend gently to the ground. They are salt-stained and red-faced through exertion, with thin-lipped, crooked-tooth smiles. I am not sure who is more surprised to see whom.

Robert and Valerie Newport, from Katherine, are in their fifties and have cycled more than 100 000km, the equivalent of seven times around Australia, since they sold their car in 1981. Occasionally, they say, they cycle from Katherine to Mildura in north-west Victoria, to pick fruit. 'This is our fifth time on the Gibb,' Robert says matter-of-factly. I am astounded, and wonder whether he is having a lend of me. How, *why*, would anyone do it more than once?

They have just cycled from Katherine to Derby, 1300km, to look at a house. 'It was too expensive, so now we're heading home again,' Valerie says. Their bikes are laden with clothes, pots and pans and 45 litres of water. They no longer carry a tent. 'People ask us where we sleep and we always reply, 'Where do you think? Under a gum tree of course,' Robert says.

Their last tent was washed away ten months ago. 'We were camping on a dry creek bed 100km west of Katherine and we spent the evening watching two electrical storms over *Willeroo* station,' Valerie says. 'We went to bed and woke six hours later to the sound of roaring water. I poked my head out of the tent to see our bikes and everything we owned being washed down the river. We jumped up to the bank before we went as well. There we were standing on the side of the river in nothing but our nightclothes, three pieces of chewing gum our only possessions. We went back three weeks later, when the river had gone down, and found a plastic bag. We haven't camped in a creek bed since.' They laugh crazily.

Hearing them explain their simple approach to life is both confusing and a joy. I admire people who turn their backs on society and do entirely what they want. Their life is, I muse, the antithesis of my own, no meetings, no deadlines, no traffic jams—certainly not here—and no smog.

Their determination reminds me of the Englishman who ran the New York Marathon dressed in a rhinoceros suit, raising awareness for the Save the Rhino Fund. At the 20km mark he was flagging, sweltering in the high temperatures and humidity, inside 20 kilograms of grey papier mache. A television journalist ran alongside, microphone in hand, and asked whether he would finish. The Rhino stopped in indignation, replied, 'Of course I will. I'm British aren't I!' and tottered off.

Robert and Valerie bid me goodbye and I watch them walk their bikes into the distance. After a hundred metres they stop and spend a minute looking at something off the side of the road. They hold hands for a moment, kiss, and wander on.

An hour later another couple stop for a chat, driving a well-appointed Land Cruiser. I immediately pick them as Victorians on account of his well-worn Aussie Rules football socks. Robert and Linda Brown are teachers from the Victorian town of Seymour, spending four months driving around the country. He is as tall and quiet as she is bubbly. They heard on the bush telegraph that we were around, and we agree to camp together tonight at the turn-off to the Mitchell Plateau, on the banks of the Gibb River.

After another two hours cycling and walking, the sun belting through my helmet and threatening to fry my brain, I reach the campsite, shaded by giant paperbarks rustling in the steady breeze. Robert has strung up a mobile shower. After stretching for 20 minutes I go for a slow walk along the dry river bed to regain the shattered senses. Four days on this road seems like four weeks, and we are only one-third of the way.

I feel like I *have* lost my marbles when I hear the echoing sound of an Aussie Rules football being kicked about. The diamond drillers are having a kick in their steel-tipped work boots before heading north. 'We always have a kick in the evening,' one says. 'I reckon this is the most travelled footy around—been booted from Rabbit Flat to Wilcannia. Kicked it off Ayers Rock last year. Almost hit a ranger who wasn't too happy. I told him I dropped it accidentally and he gave it back.'

The Browns invite us to share dinner and we while away the evening discussing their travels, the road, the bike ride and Robert's football career. 'He played in 12 premierships with Seymour before winning his first one, didn't you Darl'?' says Linda. Rob grunts. I wonder whether he would be the same laid-back fellow if he hadn't registered that one victory. They provide the spaghetti and Andy makes serviceable pancakes and bananas. We spot seven comets beetling through the clear sky overhead. The pressures of the day are momentarily forgotten.

Day 97: Saturday 23 August, Gibb River to
Mount Barnett Roadhouse
Distance: 115km
Distance so far: 6513km

Two nights ago Byrne described the road west of the Gibb River as 'good'. I can find no way of describing it as anything other than diabolical. I guess a person's perception of some-thing depends on what they are used to. Just as Scottish golfers describe gales as zephyrs and Eskimos think mid-winter in Finland is warm, so the residents of the Kimberley have unique perceptions of road conditions. I realise in a moment of mild panic that I am unlikely to ever get used to this road. I know I would never, *could never*, describe it as 'good'.

I cycle at 6km an hour much of the morning, and clearly am not the only one experiencing difficulties. Over the course of the morning I find: two swags; a small bag containing a thermos, cups and a tin of sugar; two pairs of pliers; a screw-driver; and a tin of sardines (unopened). The tools must have been left accidentally following roadside repairs and I figure the finders–keepers rule applies. The swags and bag must have bounced off the back of a truck and I leave them on the side of the road, presuming the owners will discover their loss before Wyndham. The sardines I pocket: never know when they'll come in handy.

The sun is piercingly hot and there is no shade. The coun-tryside is low-lying scrub with the odd, stunted eucalypt. One lonely cloud floats to the north like a dirigible. Gaining some relief from the corrugations by sticking to the extreme edges of the road, which many cars have not yet discovered, I ride like an automaton. Three cars on the side of the road are undergoing repairs. I offer my new tools—aware that they may be *their* tools—but they seem well kitted-out. One man, a tourist from the UK with a sweat-soaked shirt and a sweat-soaked wife, voices his frustration: 'I've tried going fast over these corrugations, I've tried going slow and I'm slowly going mad,' he says. 'I feel like I'm being beaten about with a sledge-hammer.' His wife slumps beside their car, clutching a water bottle to her chest, her head wrapped in a towel, looking like the aftermath of Desert Storm.

Early in the afternoon I am stopped by a driver and told that Andy has had some troubles of his own. Ten minutes later I see him hunched under the caravan, bum in the air, hammering away at something. 'The leaf springs on the axle fell out and the caravan slewed off the side of the road,' he says. He has managed, with the help of some passers-by and some old wire, to put the springs back in place. Even a mechanic who has stopped to help says he has done a 'bloody good job'.

I am amazed at both his ingenuity and his dexterity. Longer-term problems remain. The U-bolts that connect the axle to the caravan have been twisted beyond repair and we will need heavy-duty help. We are only 30km from Mount Barnett Roadhouse where our guidebook says 'minor repairs are available'. If we push, we could make it tonight. Andy drives off like a snail, showing the patience of Job, picking his way along the road as if through land mines. Despite his pace, he soon leaves me behind.

The Mount Barnett Roadhouse is owned by the Kupungarri Aboriginal Community and is an oasis in the middle of the Kimberley. When I limp in late in the evening, having covered 115km, Andy is speaking to the manager, despite the sign on the roadhouse: 'Absolutely no trading outside store hours. 9 am—5.30 pm'. Clearly, begging is not categorised as trading.

The manager is New Zealander Angus Graham and he agrees to look at the caravan tomorrow, Sunday, his day off. Andy and I realise our good fortune: we could easily have broken down 150km either side of here and I dread to think how much a tow truck would charge to come out here.

We have dinner at the roadhouse and drive 7km to the picturesque Manning Gorge, listening to the dying minutes of the final Australia–England Test on the radio—an odd feeling hundreds of kilometres from a city in the far north-west of

Australia. The Aussies capitulate to the Poms and lose an unlosable Test. Seems to sum up the day.

Day 98: Sunday 24 August
Rest day: Mount Barnett Roadhouse

The croc-free Manning Gorge, at the south end of the Manning River, which runs off the Gardner Plateau, is one of the great attractions of the Kimberley. Today, despite its obvious appeal and the recuperative power of its waters for lethargic limbs, we have our minds on other things. If Angus is unable to fix the caravan we will have to get it transported, somehow, to Derby, and that will throw the itinerary asunder.

Despite the early hour, Angus is working on the axle when we arrive, up to his arms in grease and wielding a monkey wrench. He has, he tells us with his head buried under the van, a varied job description. He not only runs the roadhouse for the Aboriginal owners, but is also postmaster, gravedigger and distributor of the social security. Each Tuesday he drives to Derby to collect stocks for the roadhouse, including 20 tyres for ill-equipped tourists like us. Tyres are a good business and he has a monopoly. 'The road,' he says, 'has a habit not so much of puncturing them as mangling them completely.' I wonder whether he makes more money from tyres or fuel. He sells fuel for $1.10 a litre and, as he squeezes his generous frame once more under the rim of the caravan's wheel, I don't begrudge him a cent.

Five hours later he looks like he has won the World Bog-Snorkelling Championships, covered in grease and dirt. Most importantly he has fixed the caravan. It sports a brand new set of U-bolts which we have to tighten at the end of each day until we reach bitumen. He lends us a heavy-duty spanner for the job. 'Leave it at the Mobil service station in Derby when you get there, and don't bloody forget,' he says. I shudder to think of the cost of Angus's labour on his day of rest and reach for my wallet. 'You blokes are doing a good job,' he says. 'But Christ knows why you chose to come along here.' He charges us nothing. I come very close to kissing him.

Day 99: Monday 25 August, Mount Barnett Roadhouse to
Imintji Roadhouse
Distance: 80km
Distance so far: 6593km

Yesterday, as I walked back from the roadhouse after buying some bread, a female voice barked, 'Come and stay with me tomorrow night if you like.' The owner of the voice sat with an open book in a clearing on the other side of the courtyard, a statuesque lady with a skinhead, the torso of a sprinter and smoker's teeth. Gwenda Freudenstein, 37, drives the school bus each day 80km from the Imintji Aboriginal Community, where she lives in a tent, to the Wananami School at Mount Barnett. Once she drops the kids she either reads or does odd–jobs around the school until it is time to drive them home again. I accepted her offer, of course.

Today's ride is hillier than recent days. I scale the Phillips Range, leaving the 500-metre-high Divide Hill on my right. There are spectacular views of Mount Felix and the King Leopold Range to the west, and Mount Clifton overlooking Old Man Lagoon and Barnumbah Yards to the south. Again, it is hot as an oven.

Things are on the up: for once I am not covered in dust, although my gears are still cranky and slip constantly. Most importantly, rumours are circulating that the grader is in the vicinity and coming our way. At midday I see it in the distance and the driver dismounts. 'Heard you were coming,' he says, taking the words from my mouth. 'The road ahead should be a little smoother for you.' He is right, and after three hours I come to bubbling Saddlers Spring, pausing to wash down Quasimodo's gears, cluster and pedals.

The Imintji Roadhouse, 100km north of Fitzroy Crossing over the King Leopold Range, is run by members of the local Aboriginal community, whose houses appear from the scrub off the road. I am surprised to find a white man behind the store's counter. Shaen, pig-tailed and stocky, is keen for a chat, while I drink two cans of Coke in under a minute. He wears a sleeveless shirt, the name 'Cassie' tattooed prominently on a muscular shoulder.

'Your wife?' I ask, pointing.

'No, mate, my daughter,' he laughs. 'Never tattoo your wife's name because she might not always be your wife. But your daughter will *always* be your daughter.' Looks like he made the right choice: his ex-wife, he tells me, lives in Green Head, between Perth and Geraldton, 2000km away.

Shaen and Cassie live together in a ramshackle donga behind the shop and invite me in for a beer. Inside are all manner of electrical appliances, including a new computer connected to the Internet. 'Cassie is the computer whizz and just about lives on the Net,' says Shaen. 'I'm learning about it slowly. It's a long haul.'

I tell them I didn't expect white people to be running the store. 'The Aborigines did before us, but the store was humbugged to death,' Cassie says.

'Humbugged?'

'They find it very hard to say no to each other,' Shaen says, without a hint of prejudice. 'Essentially the place was being run on credit and eventually the shelves were empty. They asked us in to try to fix things up and we're getting there. The first thing we did was get rid of credit.'

The driveway to Gwenda's camp is marked by a battered oil drum and the camp itself is 200 metres down a windy track. She has not yet returned from her school run and her two massive dogs eye us suspiciously. I always think a friendly attitude with dogs is best and I approach them with a smile. They growl. I retreat.

The three of them live in a collection of tents and awnings held together with ropes, halyards and bits of twine. Her bed is out the back under an industrial-strength mozzie net, which hangs from an old man gum. The house looks airy and fun, although seems a disaster waiting to happen. I picture a wind picking it up and blowing the whole thing into the Never-Never, like some giant out-of-control zeppelin.

Although Gwenda seems to live a spartan life, closer inspection reveals home comforts: a generator, bookshelves and a few chairs. A fridge makes gurgling noises in the corner. Candlesticks are everywhere, dripping wax. Clearly we will be cooking out tonight—there is no stove to be seen and a fire smoulders in front of the main tent.

It feels odd being in the house of someone I have met only once, and then only fleetingly. Bush hospitality is legendary in these parts—helping others as much a part of Australia as outback dunnies and damper. As Henry Lawson wrote:

If a man's in a hole you must pass round the hat,
were he a jailbird or gentleman once.

Gwenda arrives with a scowl on her face, and grabs a beer. 'I hope you've made yourselves at home,' she says. 'Sorry I'm late but the bloody kids were playing up something shocking in the bus, and I had to stop until they quietened down. The worst thing is that some parents were on the bus and did nothing. It drives me crazy.'

Gwenda introduces her dogs: Wasim, named after a Pakistani cricketer and Tess. I ask her why they don't run away while she is away each day. 'They usually run after the bus for a bit when I leave in the morning, but they always come home,' she says. 'There's plenty to interest them around here.'

And there is. Waist-high grass conceals all manner of interesting creatures, including king browns, Gwenda says. A small mountain range rises a kilometre behind us and Saddlers Spring is a short walk away. The spring serves as Gwenda's water supply and bath, though it's a breeding ground for the mozzies. She tells us she will live here until the rains come, then move to Derby for four months. 'During the wet season the school, obviously, is isolated and the students have a few months off,' she says. 'It's a good time for me to get a dose of civilisation.'

We are covered in dust and Gwenda offers us a shower. Again there is no pretension: the shower is a bucket with holes hanging above a tub in the middle of the main tent. We take turns stripping off and washing away the day's grime. Gwenda is not perturbed to have two strange men in her house and we make easy conversation. I suspect we are not the first she has invited to stay on a whim, and she seems happy with the company. She has a ready smile and I like her immediately.

We stoke the fire and prepare dinner. Light from the fire flickers off the nearby eucalypts and the dogs lie at our feet, occasionally growling at night noises. I had assumed Gwenda would be a vegetarian and am surprised when she produces three enormous steaks from her fridge. We can only provide canned food—including a tin of sardines—but a bottle of wine makes up for our paltry offerings.

Before coming to the Kimberley, Gwenda drove safari vehicles in the outback for six years, which explains her camping skills. She then worked in a bar in Derby before landing the bus-driving caper. 'I've lived with Aboriginal people for years, and I love them,' she says. 'This is the best job I've ever had.'

She has two teenage daughters living down south and one of them came to stay recently. 'She found it hard to come to terms with,' Gwenda says ruefully. 'I'm not sure she was entirely comfortable with the concept of her mother living like a hobo. It was a challenge getting to know each other again.'

Gwenda speaks plainly about her Aboriginal friends and their way of life. 'There's no doubt grog remains a huge problem for them but as much of a concern is the growing incidence of racism, on both sides of the fence. In the past two years things seems to have got worse between the Blacks and the Whites around here. There's now racism coming from the Blacks and a lot of resentment, especially from the blackfellas in their twenties and thirties. The young, male Aborigines are angry and frustrated.'

The Imintji Community is struggling without a car, and Gwenda says a heavy dose of candidness is required, difficult in these days of political correctness. 'The fact is that they once had three cars and wrecked them all,' she says. 'Despite that they can't seem to realise that they don't deserve another one. They often come down here and ask me if I will drive them to Derby in the school bus, but I refuse. The bus is for the kids, not the adults.

'As much as I would like to say I feel positive about their future I don't. We seem to have pushed them into a welfare society, and I don't know how we can stop that now it's started. Although it's good to have sympathy, the poor old blackfella has to get off his arse and do some work. The Imintji Community actually is a good one, because some of the people have taken the plunge and left to find work. I just wish more of them did it.'

'Is there an answer?' Andy asks.

'I wish I knew,' she says, staring into the coals. 'They live in communities where physical conflict occurs on a daily basis. They refuse to live inside their houses, which are falling down. Many of their dogs, which are precious to them, spread disease. People say that education is the key, but education today sends the blackfellas conflicting messages. They get educated in a whitefella way, and then they return home and live the black-fella way. For 30 years they have been told they have to learn to live like whitefellas, and now they are being told they should celebrate their Aboriginality. They're just bloody confused.'

Gwenda asks whether we would like to spend a day at the school tomorrow and speak to the kids about the ride. I accept, Andy opting to stay behind and relax. Gwenda crawls under her mozzie net while Andy and I curl up in our swags under the stars. Wasim and Tess pad around the camp, growling occasionally, until they too, evidently satisfied, turn in.

Day 100: Tuesday 26 August, Imintji Roadhouse to
Lennard River Gorge
Distance: 20km
Distance so far: 6613km

I wake to find one of my shoes missing. Wasim looks guilty.

Gwenda picks the kids up from their community, ten minutes away, then collects me from the side of the road. I take my bike on the bus and the kids, ranging in ages from six to 12, eye it suspiciously. 'All right, we have a visitor with us today, so you better be on best behaviour,' Gwenda yells from the front of the bus. The kids take little notice of me, and spend the entire hour jumping over seats, wrestling and pinching each other's rulers. Music from the Spice Girls blares from the sound system. Occasionally giant smiles light their faces, revealing rows of white teeth.

The bus trip goes quickly, largely because Gwenda drives

fast. With her bald head and heavily-toned arms poking from a sleeveless denim jacket she looks like something from a Mad Max movie. The corrugations hold no fears and she takes the corners like a Formula One champ, fishtailing and correcting as if she has done it for years. The kids are unperturbed while I am scared witless, trying my best to hide my white knuckles. We do the distance that took me six hours yesterday in under an hour.

The school is a comfortable wooden and tin structure in spotless grounds. The kids pile out of the bus yelling and swinging bags, joining a game of cricket underway on the pathway with a tennis ball and a couple of plastic bats. There is not much subtlety involved: the bowlers bowl as fast as they can and the batsmen try to smash the ball into the stratosphere. The girls seem more adept than the boys and there is no quarter given. A little girl comes up and holds my hand at square leg while her contemporary cops a bean ball on the head, and laughs.

The bell goes and 40-odd kids troop into the classroom. Gwenda tells me the attendance varies a lot, depending on whose parents are around at the time. Gwenda has organised for me to speak to three classes and the principal, a white man, tells me not to expect too many questions about either cancer or the ride. The line of questioning is more about relationships: Am I married? Do I have children? Brothers and sisters?

The Wananami School at the Kupungarri Community was opened in 1990 and has had its fair share of challenges, and changes. At lunch the principal explains the principle of code switching, where kids are expected to 'change to white man's thinking when they come to school each day.' The kids, he says, are long on enthusiasm and short on attention span. His teachers' efforts are frustrated because many of the kids, just when they seem to be making headway with the three Rs, are taken away from school for periods up to a month by parents who go walkabout. 'When they return it's back to square one,' he says.

'What can you do about it?' I ask.

'Not a lot. It's very frustrating.'

Clearly he cares for his pupils, but says the lack of application is endemic. Not long ago, he says, a Kimberley cattle station, *Tirralantji*, was bought, fully-stocked, by the government for the Aboriginal people. 'They were supposed to breed cattle but that never happened. They killed the stock one by one until there were none left, and then they all went back into Derby.' He shrugs, then introduces me to two health inspectors, here to check the kids' ears.

After lunch I retire to the roadhouse to read a book. There is a commotion: a kombi van arrives on the back of a truck. Not one of its windows is intact and its front is caved in. The owners, two hippies, stand next to the wreck, looking sheepish. 'Panel beater job,' mutters someone, a major understatement. The car is a write-off and they are lucky to be alive.

A siesta has clearly not dampened Gwenda's enthusiasm for speed. I hang on grimly during the manic ride home, while the kids jump about in a frenzy. One attempts homework in the back of the bus, brow furrowed in concentration, but unless homework is an abstract drawing I don't hold much hope. The Spice Girls play on. 'Who wants a swim in the water tank?' Gwenda yells. The screamed response is deafening. 'We are not supposed to do this but the kids have been good and the farmer probably isn't about,' she says to me. A minute later we pull up and I glance over my shoulder. Twenty naked Aboriginal kids stand in the bus's aisle, looking expectant, their clothes scattered over the seats.

They swim like dolphins and dive from the edge of the giant tank, trying to outdo each other with somersaults and backflips, their laughter infectious and unselfconscious. It is a moment of simple joy and Gwenda smiles at me, watching the shenanigans. 'I really love these kids. They are so unaffected and affectionate. I just hope they have good lives,' she says.

One kid climbs down from the tank and shies a stone at a cow. He picks up another and Gwenda shouts: 'It's a long walk home, Billy.' He thinks for a bit then drops the stone.

The mood changes perceptibly when Gwenda pulls up at the community. Adults sit outside their houses on broken beds and chairs, dogs skulk about in the shadows and there is rubbish everywhere, in bags on the side of the road, and scattered around their gardens. The sight both horrifies and saddens me. I am also confused. I knew there were desperate conditions among many Aboriginal communities in the Top End, but I did not expect this. There *are* two Australias: the cities and the wealthy country towns occupying one half, and places like this the other.

'It's not always like this,' she says. 'They haven't collected it for two weeks because they don't have a car. They asked me to take it away in the school bus, but again I refused. If they want to have cars, they have to look after them. It sounds tough, but it's the only way I can see around the problem. The school bus is for taking the kids to school only. Period.' We return to Gwenda's in silence. I can understand the bind that she is in, and respect her reasoning.

It is four o'clock and I want to cycle some distance this afternoon in order to make it to Windjana Gorge tomorrow. We say a sad goodbye to Gwenda, who has opened our eyes. 'I might see you in Derby on the weekend,' she shouts as I leave. I cycle hard into the setting sun, which turns the cirrus clouds above a bright orange.

We camp in a clearing on the side of the road. Nearby a dead bull is beginning to putrefy and the flies are fearsome.

Fires flicker on the side of a nearby hill. We have not seen or heard a car for hours. The Kimberley is silent as a graveyard. Today is my 100th day on the road and Andy and I celebrate with a bottle of warm riesling, secreted in the caravan for just this occasion. I am heartily sick of not having a fridge and we speak longingly of cool drinks and ice.

We are woken by the sound of an animal rooting around in a rubbish bin. Andy, doing a passable impersonation of Richard Attenborough, stalks towards the bin, torch in hand, to investigate. 'I know what's going to happen,' he says. 'It will be one of those spotted quolls, and it will jump out of the bin and scare the shit out of me.' He is right on all three counts.

Day 101: Wednesday 27 August, Lennard River Gorge to
Windjana Gorge
Distance: 80km
Distance so far: 6693km

The road changes dramatically during the 80km between Lennard River Gorge and the turn-off to the famous Windjana Gorge. I cycle over the King Leopold and Napier ranges, where vertical rock formations stand like sentinels, and there are striking views over the gorges leading to *Mount Hart* station. Escarpments plunge and the sky is impossibly blue. We take a detour to Lennard River Gorge to swim in the crystal water.

Afterwards, the cycling is difficult, into a searing head-wind. I lather on the sunscreen and am passed by an adventure safari truck and two motor cyclists. The chasm of the Napier Range does strange things to the wind: a willy-willy rushes past, lifting leaves and sticks into the air which then fall back to earth. Queen Victoria's Head, a rock formation outlining the monarch's fierce countenance, scowls from the middle of the range. Frustrated by the head-wind I scowl back at her.

I reach the turn-off to Windjana Gorge National Park feeling like I have been hit by Gwenda's bus. We strap the bikes to the top of the caravan and drive 20km towards Fitzroy Crossing to the gorge campsite.

Windjana Gorge is managed by the Department of Conservation and Land Management (CALM) and covers more than 2000 hectares. A gorge more than 3km long formed by the Lennard River snakes its way through the Napier Range, an ancient limestone reef of black and red cliffs which used to be under water and is, the guidebook tells us, 350 million years old. When white settlers came here in the 1880s they found the bones of an extinct wombat-like animal, *Diprotodon australia*, which wandered these plains 20 000 years ago.

A week ago Derby seemed a lifetime away but now, despite my delicate disposition after today's head-wind, it feels eminently reachable. As much as it is physically possible I have a spring in my step as we set up camp. A shower block at the campsite is the first we have seen for days. The water is cold, but I couldn't give a stuff.

At the gorge silver archer fish (*Toxotes oligolepis*) lurk under the overhanging branches of the river gums, and freshwater crocs, supposedly harmless ('so long as you don't tread on one,' says a ranger), wallow in the greenish shallows, their snouts protruding from the surface. There are a lot of croc jokes among those swimming but I notice that most people stick close to shore and swim together.

We are only 150km east of the coast, which means we are now back among the day-trippers, travelling out from Derby, Broome and Fitzroy Crossing. The campsite at Windjana has more of a holiday atmosphere about it, campervans and cars alongside the four-wheel drives. Rob and Linda Brown, who we haven't seen for six days, are here, and we join them for dinner. Again we can offer little in the way of food: tuna and a tin of (still uneaten) sardines. Linda somehow conjures a jam rolly-polly from the open fire. 'Necessity,' she says, 'is the mother of invention.'

Day 102: **Thursday 28 August**
Rest day: Windjana Gorge

We join Rob and Linda for a trip to Tunnel Creek, 30km to the south-east. As the name suggests Tunnel Creek runs, for the best part of a kilometre, through a tunnel underneath the Napier Range—and it takes some courage to walk from one end to the other, bats flitting overhead, torch-light flickering off the walls like in a horror movie. Half-way along the roof has collapsed and huge roots and vines creep upwards to the trees overhead, twisting around themselves like Rapunzel's giant locks.

Nearby, at the base of the Napier Range, are the ruins of Lillimilura Police Station. The station has a grisly past, the site of the murder of Police Constable Richardson in October 1894. The murderer, a Bunaba Aboriginal called Pigeon or Jandamarra, began his war against the white invaders in the late 1880s, stealing stock and raiding settlers' properties. He led a large party of Aborigines which killed two white settlers about to drive their cattle through Windjana Gorge. A fierce battle ensued and many were killed—but Pigeon escaped and, legend has it, spent many months holed up in a cave near the western entrance to the gorge, now called Pigeon's Cave. For years he played the outlaw and was eventually killed by police on April Fool's Day 1897.

I read in the afternoon under a gnarled gum tree over-looking our camp, a pleasant activity after the past few days. In 1968, aged 28, English writer Bruce Chatwin began his study of nomads, travelling in places like Afghanistan and

Mauritania. He spent several months with Aboriginal people in central Australia and, in 1987, wrote *The Songlines*, about ancient Aboriginal tracks and culture. Two years later he died, too young, aged 49. In the book is the line, a quote from a rickety old stockman, 'being lost in Australia gives you a lovely feeling of security.' A flock of cockatoos rise with madmen screeches and the turrets of the Napier Range glow crimson and ochre in the dipping sun.

Day 103: Friday 29 August, Windjana Gorge to Derby
Distance: 130km
Distance so far: 6823km

A hard-of-hearing English couple yell at each other all night in the tent next to us. By the time I get up they are gone. They can't have had more than four hours' sleep. I have had less.

On the road by seven for the final push to Derby, 130km away. The sun is like a furnace, and, despite drinking two litres of water early in the morning and carrying another three litres with me, I am out of water by the time I reach the bitumen— still 65km from our destination. Making matters worse the shoe cleat (holding my foot to the pedal) breaks, and the cage snaps that holds a water bottle. Quasimodo has performed heroically so far, but it feels like even *he* has had enough of this road. I am thankful these things didn't happen a week ago. I scrounge some wire from the side of the road and fix the water bottle cage and, with some practice, learn to cycle while resting my foot, unattached, on the pedal.

Forty kilometres to go and I curse my dumbness—thought I had worked out this water caper. I now understand how people die of thirst in these parts. My throat is parched and my mouth sticky. A hot westerly wind has sprung up and every breath further dries my throat. No saliva, breath rasping. I pass by the turn-off to *Kimberley Downs*, *Meda* and *Birdwood Downs* and think of calling in for water but I have no idea how far the homesteads are from the road. Eventually Andy cycles out from the car and tells me I have 15km to go.

There is no water in the car when I arrive and I unscrew the tap to the water tank under the caravan and guzzle insatiably. I lie there under the caravan, admiring its spanking new U-bolts, and laugh deliriously. Andy arrives.

'What's so funny?' he asks.

'We did it! We did the bloody Gibb River Road!'

As I lie for several minutes in the dirt under the caravan, smelling of sweat and grime, I dissect the past fortnight. I have no doubt we escaped the Gibb River Road lightly. Aside from the caravan's springs and U-bolts we had few mechanical problems. Quasimodo performed like a good cattle dog, doing the job without fuss or bother, and Andy drove with care, the car, too, coping admirably with the conditions. A sign where the Gibb River Road meets the Derby Highway suggests caravans should *not* be taken on the road. We take a photo of it, a testament to foolhardiness and idiocy, before I cycle the final 7km north to Derby.

Derby, on King Sound, we have been told many times, is a Jekyll and Hyde town. 'Ugly place, nice folk,' is a common description. Others say it leaves Broome for dead. Bombed by the Japanese in 1942, it is renowned for its tides, which rise and fall more than ten metres each day. Although it is on the ocean there are no beaches to speak of, just miles and miles of meandering mudflats. The town serves as the centre of the beef cattle industry in the Fitzroy Valley and King Leopold Range but others say it has another major purpose. 'Everyone likes to talk Derby up, but the real reason the town exists is Aboriginal welfare,' we are told within an hour of arriving.

As Gwenda warned, alcohol is clearly a problem. Bottles are

everywhere and silvery innards of empty wine casks lie flat against wire fences. Aboriginal people loll about in the sun, many yelling and swearing; kids are clipped over the ear. As in Tennant Creek there are no takeaways on Thursdays, welfare day, and pubs keep strict hours on weekends.

'It's all the whiteman's fault,' says a white man in the pub. 'The Derby Aborigines used to be jackaroos on the Kimberley cattle stations, working for their keep. It was a perfect arrangement. Then the bloody do-gooders came and buggered things up. They demanded equal pay for equal work and the station owners had no choice but to sack many of the Aborigines. Many were transported from their traditional homelands to the Mowanjum Aboriginal Community south of here.' Today, people talk of Mowanjum as being among Australia's most depressing and shameful places.

I am surprised to find the pubs segregated by colour; Whites have the front bars, Blacks the back bars. 'The areas aren't enforced, and not even planned, but the colours simply don't mix,' says the bloke. 'They are happy keeping their own company if they have the choice, though they get along if they are forced together.' While the Australian Government is doing its best to work out ways to reconcile Aboriginal claims on pastoral leases—via the Wik case—and to improve black–white relationships in the lead-up to the Olympic Games, when the spotlight will be on Australia, it is clear that there are no easy solutions.

We meet Liz Kelly, one of 11 Aboriginal women searching for their own solutions at the Ngunga Women's Group which provides child-care, family support services and counselling. Liz is adamant that progress is happening among Derby Aborigines that is not immediately apparent to visitors. 'Problems remain—alcoholism, housing and health—but there have been big steps taken in recent years,' she says. Health is on the improve, though the life expectancy of Aboriginal people is still well below that of white Australians. Aboriginal houses are simply the wrong design because the Perth-based building authorities are far removed from the realities of Aboriginal life in the Kimberley. 'We tend to have big families in the Kimberley, and most of the houses have no more than three bedrooms,' she says. 'People have no choice but to live outside.'

She says she is 'angry, sad and frustrated' at the level of alcoholism in Derby, though she is convinced that things are improving. 'Not selling grog on Thursdays was a good idea, because it means more money is now spent on food. Derby is a strong community and we are all—Black and White—trying to tackle the problem. But it's not something that can be solved with a click of the fingers. You have to chip away at it slowly, with educational programs, and getting more people back to their homelands, where there is no grog available.'

She thinks the same approach must be taken with reconciliation—which must be tackled in small steps at a local level. 'I think the commitment is there from the Aboriginal people, though it will take a long time for us to come to terms with the Stolen Generation (Aboriginal children taken from their families and fostered by white families) and losing our land. There has been no equity with the Aboriginal people historically.'

Liz, 38, is a born-and-bred Derby girl, a mother of three and grandmother of one. Her eldest son works for BHP in Port Hedland, 1200km to the south. She says more and more young Aboriginal people are finding work in Derby as shop managers, office staff or artists, especially in sewing and screen printing. 'We are definitely going up the ladder and we are in a better position to be able to help our people. More and more Aborigines are becoming educated.' She quotes a recent study which found that Aboriginal communities brought more money into the Kimberley region than any other group except the Argyle Diamond Mine. It is an uplifting statistic.

It is delightful to arrive at the campground, shower, then go in search of fresh food. Rob and Linda join us for fund-raising, buckets in hand, in the pubs. At each one I make a quick speech and we walk about to gather donations. We encounter nothing but kindness and enthusiasm—most of the locals have spent time on the Gibb River Road and know the challenges. Many, too, have cancer stories of their own. We raise close to $1,000 in less than two hours. 'I haven't got any dough but I've got four mud crabs I want you to have,' says a man, all skin and bone with a Caterpillar Tractor cap perched jauntily on his head. 'They're in a bag out the back.'

I lie in my swag under the sparkling Derby night sky and reflect on the past ten days. Although we were in the wilderness, I never felt friends were far away. All welcomed us without condition. I will never forget Angus Graham, who spent half a day sweltering under our caravan and waved away our thanks. Gwenda had us to stay, unconditionally, and fed us. It was as if, by the very fact that we had bothered to make the trip to their uninhabited region, eager to see how they lived in *their* land, we were OK by them. The people of the Kimberley have an honesty and an openness that is intoxicating. They are a fine lot, the people of the Gibb River Road. Having said that, I'm glad to have left them behind.

Day 104: Saturday 30 August, Derby to Willare Bridge Roadhouse
Distance: 60km
Distance so far: 6883km

Gwenda, Wasim and Tess are parked in the main street, chewing the fat with the locals and examining the *Kimberley Echo*, which sports a large colour picture of me on the back page. 'Surprised the camera survived the shot,' says Gwenda. I have had a dream run with the media and this coverage should give me credibility down the west coast.

Gwenda agrees to help us eat the mud crabs for lunch. 'Can I bring the dogs?' she asks. 'I'll hide them under a tarp when I drive past the office.' Eating the mud crabs is a messy business, and we put to good use the collection of pliers and hammers gathered from the Gibb River Road.

Our camp overlooks Derby's mudflats shimmering at low tide. Nearby is a giant, brown four-wheel drive with 'Bush University' painted on the side. Several people sit around in walking boots and khakis, reading books on Aboriginal art and customs. One of them, Graham, explains that this after-noon they leave for a camp on *Gibb River* station to learn about Aboriginal food, medicine, art and spirituality as well as tribal lore and law. Thirteen Whites and 20-odd Aborig-inal people will do the week-long course. 'The course covers everything from birth to death,' he says. 'It gives Whites the chance to be positive about Aboriginal culture and the young Aborigines the chance to learn about their culture and customs from the elders.'

Mid-morning an Aboriginal elder David Mowaljarlai drives up in a ute. He will be leading the course, and his pupils flock to him in adoration. I can see the attraction. He has eyes like pools of water, a smile that lights up the camp, and a tattered Akubra hat perched on his silvery head. Mowaljarlai is the heart and soul of the Bush University. A Ngarinyin elder, he was born at the Kunmunya Mission in 1928. He was a United States Marine during World War II and an early member of both the Aboriginal Arts Board of the Australia Council and the Australian Institute of Aboriginal and Torres Strait Islander Studies. He was Aboriginal of the Year in 1991 and received an Order of Australia in 1993. In recent years he has actively spoken against alcohol abuse among his community. Recently, his travels took him to a UNESCO meeting in Paris where he said: 'Once we old fellas die, with our history and our stories, and we are buried with it, well, it will be burning, burning for the rest of time and no-one will ever know of it.' *(Later: less than one month after I met this elder, on 24 September 1997, he died of a heart attack shortly after one of his sons died in custody.)*

By three o'clock it is time to go and we say our sad farewells to Gwenda. Rob and Linda will spend some more time in the region before driving on to Broome.

A stiff, honest northerly blows all afternoon and, heading south for the first time on the ride, I make good time down the Derby Highway, saluting the entrance to the Gibb River Road as I pass. It is beautiful cycling, the sun low on the horizon and Quasimodo hammering along like a train. I am aware that I have entered a new phase of the ride—I am not only heading in a new direction but have knocked off the most notorious road in the land.

Cycling on a main road again requires adjustment. It is wonderful to have a smooth surface—the bitumen is like granite after the Gibb River Road—but no more can I hog the middle of the road or wobble down the right-hand side. I must remember to use my mirror more. Road trains thunder past ominously, 60 wheels spinning together. We stop at the Willare Bridge Roadhouse on the north side of the mighty Fitzroy River. 'Jeez mate, it's easier with an engine,' says one of the truckies.

Day 105: Sunday 31 August, Willare Bridge Roadhouse to Broome
Distance: 163km
Distance so far: 7046km

The pristine beaches of Broome beckon like a siren but they will not be won easily. The wind comes from the south-west and I am cycling into it. Even in the best of conditions 160km is a long way; it's harder still into a head-wind.

Within minutes of leaving the roadhouse I cross the Fitzroy River, one of the country's great watercourses. Its catchment covers the lower half of the Kimberley and the northern part of the Great Sandy Desert, drawing water from the slopes of the Barbwire, Millyit, Jones and Hicks ranges. At the height of the wet season the Fitzroy can be 30km wide; today it is barely 100 metres across, flowing lazily into King Sound 10km away. Refuse sits in the upper branches of trees high on each bank, testament to its wet season fury.

There are plans to develop an Ord-style dam on the Fitzroy River, which would irrigate a quarter of a million hectares to the south of Broome. The plans have been drawn up by a local, John Logan, owner of *Nita Downs*. He quotes impressive numbers: a $2 billion development returning $1 billion a year in export revenue and creating 400 jobs, in addition to indirect employment. It will, naturally, be environmentally sustainable and economically viable. The plan has attracted lots of opposition, principally from conservationists, pastoralists and Aboriginal groups and it looks like a decision will not be made on it for 15 years.

Bitumen or no bitumen, today's cycling is tough work, with nothing to break the monotony of spinifex, dwarf mulga and low, rocky hills. The head-wind is even more monotonous, a cruel joke after the horrors of the Gibb River Road. Which is tougher? Bitumen and a head-wind, or corrugations and no head-wind. A toss up. The wind is hot as hell, and my energy is drained. Nothing to do but keep the legs turning. The road stretches to infinity, but towards civilisation. Bloated cattle and kangaroo carcasses line the road, alongside giant shavings of blown tyres and remnants of shattered windscreens.

After six hours in the saddle I arrive at Roebuck Plains

Roadhouse. It has few redeeming features: caravans dot the unkempt reserve behind the main building, where old oil cans and plastic bottles sit in piles and dogs lie panting under low-slung, wiry bushes. Andy appears out of the roadhouse looking downcast. Princess Diana is dead, killed in a car accident in a Paris tunnel. I feel sick, and sit at the concrete table outside the roadhouse for the best part of an hour. The roadhouse TV is on and the reactions from people to the news differ widely. Some stare at the TV screen in disbelief while others cast their eyes up for a moment before walking off. I met Princess Diana briefly when I was at university and she was in Melbourne following her wedding. She transfixed me then and I am trans-fixed, macabrely, now, as report after report is beamed from all parts of Europe.

I drag myself onto Quasimodo and set off for the final 30km to Broome. The wind has eased but the road passes beneath me in a blur, whether owing to fatigue or the latest news I cannot say. Broome appears, whitewashed houses sparkling against the impossibly blue water. I have passed 7000km and in another thousand the ride will be half over. I have been through the most challenging parts of the continent and have arrived in Paradise. Yet all I feel is a numbness.

Chapter Six

The Pilbara, WA *Head-winds and Heartache*

My mother owned a sheep station in North West Australia and had 80 000 sheep. I inherited a quarter of these and never saw one of them. Now I've got about 30 and see them all the time.

General Sir John Hackett

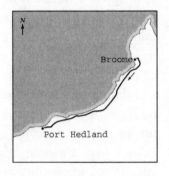

Days 106–112: Monday 1–
Sunday 7 September
Rest days: Broome

To wake up in a bed, in a hotel room, is strange indeed. Broome, azure water and friendly faces, nestled on the edge of Roebuck Bay, is like a fresh breeze after the trials of the Gibb River Road. I am five days ahead of schedule and can put my callused feet up. Andy returns to Melbourne in four days and a new team arrives this week. I write overdue letters and e-mails, largely to schools that have shown interest in participating. Most importantly, I am able to wash away the dust and frustration of the Kimberley.

I can also take stock after more than 100 days on the road. I feel surprisingly well and invigorated, fit, delighted—and a little surprised—to have crossed the breadth of this country. I still have trouble reconciling the size of Australia; after 100 days I still have 9000km to cycle. How can you cycle around a country for a third of a year and still not be halfway? The best course of action, I decide, is not to think about it.

There will be a group of five travelling down the Great Northern Highway south from Broome. Brothers Robert and John Joyce arrive for two weeks from Perth and Melbourne respectively and will drive the car. Nick Jones and Emma Eade also fly in from Melbourne and will cycle, both assure me, to Perth. I have known the four for many years: Nick is a computer programmer, Robert is an industrial officer for the *West Australian* newspaper, John is an accountant and Emma a vet nurse. It speaks volumes that all four have been prepared to travel such distances to join the ride. I consider all sufficiently unstable to cope admirably with the task ahead.

Their reasons for coming are varied: John and Robert wish to spend some fraternal time together, Nick is an avid cyclist and wants to put in some hard miles, and Emma is motivated by the money-raising angle, her father, John, having died of cancer early this year. She has already raised $6,000 in the weeks leading up to her arrival, pushing the total to $190,000.

I am, I concede, concerned about Emma. She is not a cyclist, though she assures me she has trained hard in the past two months, up to 80km a day. We have a punishing schedule ahead and I hope her training, circling Albert Park Lake in Melbourne, will be adequate. On her side is the fact that she has ridden horses for many years and therefore knows about hanging onto unpredictable beasts. Horses, of course, only need a kick to get them going, while bikes need a lot more.

Andy and I clean the caravan, which looks like it has mud-wrestled the Sahara. When a mechanic arrives to fix the winding mechanism he views with distaste the red stains leading to the gutter; it looks as if a particularly nasty garrotting has been carried out. When we get the car serviced, only the

Shoo-Roo, an obscure electrical device which emits a high-frequency squeal to scare kangaroos, has shaken loose and needs to be re-attached with electrical tape. We have not hit a 'roo yet, so it must be working.

The new team shoehorns into the hotel room which looks like a bomb site, covered in cycling gear, provisions, dirty washing, clean washing and, somehow, five bicycles. All concede they are nervous, not so much at the thought of covering up to 150km a day for the foreseeable future, but more at the fact that we will be travelling largely through uninhabited regions.

Broome, population 10 000, is an oasis on Australia's arid north-west coast. Founded in 1883, it built its wealth on the pearling industry. While pearling in the traditional sense is finished, luggers remain, the owners diving for young pearl oysters to supply stock for the cultured pearl farms at Kuri Bay and Cygnet. The industry peaked in 1925 when 300 luggers employed 3000 men—Japanese, Malays, Chinese, Indonesians —to supply 80 per cent of the world's mother-of-pearl. The 900 divers' headstones in the local cemeteries indicate the perils of the profession: cyclones, the bends, drowning and sharks.

Artificial pearls and plastic buttons killed the industry in the late 1950s, but tourism saved the town in the 1980s, largely inspired by the English entrepreneur Lord Alistair McAlpine and the sealing of the road from Port Hedland. Today Broome is a captivating mixture of old buildings with wide eaves and stilts, and more modern structures that have retained the corrugated iron theme. The town, spiced with bougainvillea and hibiscus, now boasts up-market shops, up-market people and the camel rides on the world-famous Cable Beach. I bump into the barmaid from Mataranka. 'I decided I needed to see the ocean,' she says, a smile white with zinc cream. 'Three days ago I put my hitching thumb out and here I am.'

At the Crocodile Park all manner of salt-water crocodiles do their bit for the tourists, including jumping for dead chickens dangling from overhead ropes. Their reptilian dumbness (they have pre-historic brains the size of peas) contrasts with their ferocity, and I make a mental note not to wander across any streams in the weeks ahead; after three months on a bike my legs bear too close a resemblance to a chicken's for comfort.

The media is showing interest in the ride. My cycle along the Gibb River Road raises eyebrows and the publicity we get aids the fund-raising profile. Linda and Robert Brown help us collect $3,000 at pubs, caravan parks, at the local crab races, the rodeo and the circus, which is in town for the week.

The fund-raising is a case of swings and roundabouts. While members of the public continue to show startling generosity, corporate Australia has closed the shutters. I receive a call from Tattersall's saying they will not take up naming-rights sponsorship, which is disappointing. The battle for the sponsorship dollar is clearly a fierce one, and there are some slick marketeers out there.

The issue of sponsorship is raised again in Broome when I meet John Harcourt, marketing consultant for Uncle Toby's, who says the company, maker of high-energy foods, could be interested in sponsoring the rest of the ride. He suggests I write a proposal. After the Tattersall's experience I am sceptical. I have spent, literally, weeks writing to companies about naming rights sponsorship but the response is always the same: 'Nice idea but our sponsorship money is already committed. Good luck though.' I like to think that because the media has shown so much interest so far companies will realise the ride is worth backing. It's hard to convince companies of this without completing the event, and by that stage it is too late. Getting sponsorship for charity events is all about overcoming Catch-22s.

The Broome Lions Club sends a representative, Chris Mitchell, with a $200 donation. Chris works for the WA Fisheries Department prosecuting illegal fishermen and has his hands full at the moment with proceedings against 67 Indonesians from the island of Roti caught last week inside Australian waters. Their methods of obtaining valuable shark fins are, he says, 'barbaric'. 'They catch sharks, club them over the head with a baseball bat, then cut off their four pectoral and anal fins with a machete. They then heave the sharks back into the water where they either sink to the bottom and drown or get eaten by the other sharks,' he tells us. The 20 prahaus impounded were carrying 50 kilograms of dry shark fin—from 100 sharks—and loads of kepang, or seaslugs.

Last year, Chris's department prosecuted 300 Indonesians caught between Darwin and Broome and burnt 40 prahaus. 'On one of the boats we found an 18-year-old kid who had the bends so bad he had lost control of his bladder,' he says. 'The Perth medicos could do nothing to help him and sent him home. No doubt he will continue to dive, and he will die. A lot of the Indonesian divers don't service their equipment and dive with faulty regulators. Others simply shove a hose in their mouth and go down a hundred feet or more. It's a pretty basic set-up.'

Chris is fighting the Australian justice system as much as he is the Indonesian fishermen. Captured fishermen are put in jail for a month, either in Darwin or Broome, then released. In prison they get free medical and dental attention, watch videos and play sport. Amazingly, they get an allowance, which they can spend in town. 'One fisherman was here so often he saved enough to buy a TV,' Chris sighs. 'Took it back to Indonesia with him.'

We have a team meeting, discussing issues like food, hydration, stretching and team dynamics. With a team of five, possibly tolerance will be the most important—two people can work well together but five is more difficult. We will have different cycling speeds, different ways of cooking, cleaning and sleeping, and different privacy requirements.

There is no Coles supermarket in Broome and the Darwin supermarket has agreed to send six boxes of food to our hotel. Five of them have arrived and I ring about the missing one containing, ominously, meat, cheese, salami and butter. Coles promises to 'look into it.' Three hours later they ring back. They have located the missing box, in Kununurra.

Day 113: Monday 8 September, Broome to
Roebuck Plains Roadhouse
Distance: 35km
Distance so far: 7081km

Coles rings at sunrise. The missing box is on its way.

I drop Andy at the airport and mourn his departure. Never has one who had so much reason to complain complained so little. He had a tough job—the road from hell, a collapsing caravan, searing heat and dust, and a grumpy cyclist to look after—and he never showed anything other than ardent enthusiasm for his task.

Today is a short day, 35km, but there is the bane of administration before departure: post letters, bank donations, buy fruit and vegetables, last-minute repairs to the bikes. Despite my pleadings for frugality everyone seems to have brought enough clothes for a year.

It's exhilarating to be back on the saddle after a week on shanks's pony and we whoop like madmen cycling towards *Roebuck Plains*. Nick sets off like a greyhound lure, looking aggressively fit and conditioned, while Emma is sedate and controlled. I am, simply, thankful to have some company after six weeks alone on the bike.

The Roebuck Plains Roadhouse has not improved in the past week: grimy walls, and dirty and cracked plastic seats. Desultory travellers sit about with long faces. Above the pool table, its cloth torn, is a sign: 'Anyone found playing pool when pissed . . . is lucky—the Manager'. The Roebuck Plains Roadhouse is a place you stay at only through necessity. A truckie props up the bar, fag defying gravity, belly hanging from too-tight shorts, and watches me guardedly, trying to place the scrawny bloke in lycra. 'Nev's the name,' he coughs, proffering a sandpapery hand.

'Have you come up from Perth, Nev?' I ask him.

'Yep.'

'How's the wind?'

'Put it this way, I used a bee's dick of petrol between Perth and here,' he says. 'The southerly's as tough as a whore's heart out there this time of year. Hope you're cycling north.'

I know of the debilitating effects of head-winds and wonder how Emma and Nick will handle it. Equally, how *I* will handle it? Today, we cycled on adrenaline. Tomorrow, with 140km to cover, will be a different matter altogether. My guidebook says that the 600km between here and Port Hedland is 'a contender for the most boring length of road in Australia.' Unless you're a kite.

Day 114: Tuesday 9 September, Roebuck Plains Roadhouse to Bidyadanga Aboriginal Community
Distance: 140km
Distance so far: 7221km

Highway Number One—the Great Northern Highway— south of Broome tracks Eighty Mile Beach while out east the inhospitable expanses of the Great Sandy Desert shimmer like jelly, an arid and featureless wasteland. A roadsign confirms another of Nev's assertions: that there is 'absolutely sweet bloody Fanny Adams' between *Roebuck Plains* and Port

Hedland. Sandfire and Pardoo roadhouses are it. Between here and the coast farmers eke out an existence, a beast to God knows how many acres.

Nev's wind is not as strong as predicted. Emma and Nick give themselves sideways glances as we stop for photos next to the distance sign—Port Hedland 570, Geraldton 2000—realising now what they have signed up for. We set off and I hang back to let them make the pace. We cover 60km in two hours with no problems.

Emma, also on a touring bike, has a classic cycling technique: lots of leg movement, good cadence (pedal spin) and balance born, I guess, from her equine experiences. On first impression Nick's technique has flaws: his cadence is low and his body sways from side to side. Must remind him to lower his seat this evening. Why did he opt not to buy aero bars? Since I bought my aero bars I have been hunched over them 90 per cent of the time and I feel he will rue his decision. He is, however, on a racing bike, which is faster than mine. Perhaps the two will cancel each other out.

Past *Roebuck Plains* station the Great Northern Highway turns to the south-west, through scrub burned by the sun. Wiry cattle stand around half-empty turkey-nest dams, looking for inspiration. To the south-east the low dunes of the Great Sandy Desert track 700km to the Canning Stock Route down near Lake Disappointment on the Tropic of Capricorn. It is one of the most inhospitable regions on earth, explored for the first time in 1873 by Peter Warburton who, battling dehydration, trekked from Alice Springs to Port Hedland in one of the great, but little known, feats of Australian exploration.

Mid-afternoon, 140km later, we arrive at the Bidyadanga Aboriginal Community on Lagrange Bay and set up camp on the playground next to the school principal's house. Nick and Emma are ecstatic with their efforts and I am delighted for them. It has been no pushover and they have done admirably.

The temperature is the best part of 35 degrees and we drive to nearby Lagrange Bay to swim in the sea. The tide is out— 2km over undulating tidal mudflats pockmarked with crab tracks. We massage our aching muscles in the shallows, planning for tomorrow, and watch an angry sun sink into a grey, restless ocean.

Most teachers at the Bidyadanga school, both White and Aboriginal, hail from Darwin or Perth. They teach by day, chill out by night, and escape to either Port Hedland or Broome on weekends. This time of year the weather is temperate but summers are thunderous and hostile—roads are cut off by flooded rivers and the community can be marooned for weeks. Largely, they say, they enjoy their work in this challenging environment, though few plan to be here long. 'The tyranny of distance plays havoc with your life,' one says.

The community is undergoing a time of potentially damaging transition. Bidyadanga has been alcohol-free for years, and the community is polarised as to whether it should remain that way. 'The women and elders have voted for it to stay dry while many of the men want grog to be allowed,' says a teacher. A recent vote yielded no clear result and the status quo will remain, for now. 'The kids will have the most to lose if grog is allowed,' says another.

Despite the week's rest today was not easy for me. I feel crushed and slip away from dinner with the teachers, erecting my mosquito net under an old eucalypt. Emma and Nick seem full of beans; perhaps I have underestimated their stamina.

Day 115: Wednesday 10 September, Bidyadanga Aboriginal
Community to Sandfire Roadhouse
Distance: 150km
Distance so far: 7371km

It is a moot point whether we are woken first by the Aboriginal
kids or the mozzies. Both swarm in at first light and make lots
of noise, the kids kicking a footy about dressed in nothing but
bare feet and Chicago Bulls T-shirts.

Later I speak about the ride and cancer prevention to the
school assembly. Like the Imintji students on the Gibb River
Road the Bidyadanga kids are not big on asking questions and
most questions come from the teachers. One kid looks like he
has his hand up, but is only scratching his head. They show
lots of interest in Quasimodo, one girl weaving a precarious
path around the trees and building posts until she is reminded
that she should be sitting a maths test. There is a feeling of
good-will and generosity between teachers and pupils; many
hold hands, and students lean on teachers' knees during the
talk. One girl has her arms around the principal's neck until he
chides her for also playing truant. 'The majority of the kids
here won't use their education once they finish school,' he tells
us later. 'They don't want to go to places like Broome and get
jobs, even though they can get paid twice as much as white
people. In fact, many of them will stay in the community for
the rest of their lives. Why leave here, the beach and all? It's
got everything.'

The township, where we buy bread, is a depressing sight.
Mangy dogs skulk about, with their heads low and growling
at everyone and everything. A car drives up without a wind-
screen, sounding like a B-52 bomber, disgorging eight people.
A woman, in town to teach the bank staff how to operate
computers, donates $20. 'Don't be fooled by this town's

appearance,' she tells us. 'This is a great community.'

It is ten-thirty before we are on the road, a distance similar to yesterday's to cover. Today there *is* a strong head-wind and we will not make Sandfire Roadhouse until late in the day.

On the road Emma scoots ahead and Nick and I pass the time by asking each other capital cities. Nick astounds me by knowing Iceland's. I amaze him by knowing Burkina Faso's. Neither of us knows New Zealand's.

The wind batters us and the afternoon kilometres pass slowly. The horizon is as flat as the Republican debate, broken only by termite mounds looking like ancient monuments, spindly salt-bush and spinifex circles spread out like disjointed Olympic rings. We pass the lonely entrance to *Frazier Downs*, on our left is the scorched expanse of the Cudalgarra Claypan. The Joyces meet us after 65km and we shelter from the wind and scorching sun in the shade of the caravan, eating like hyenas.

The afternoon brings no relief from the heat, nor the wind, and I concede that today's ride on top of yesterday's is a big ask. Again Emma and Nick seem to handle it better than me. We see no car for several hours until the circus, all 20 trucks of it, passes on its way to Port Hedland, a motorised Noah's Ark wobbling down a highway in north-west Australia. The last truck contains two lions, the Kings of the jungle, bored stiff.

Conversation dries up. Emma and Nick cycle on ahead and my mind wanders. I think of a teaching colleague who went on expeditions in the Arctic. Often, he told me, his team would go for hours, sometimes days, without speaking. Occasionally a question would be asked and a response would not come for several hours. 'At the time,' he said, 'there didn't seem anything odd about this. Time meant nothing.' Marcel Proust wrote in *Remembrance of Things Past*: 'Distances are only the relation of space to time.' Today the distances are long, the space vast, and the time interminable.

Mid-afternoon we agree to make for Sandfire Roadhouse, still 70km away, powered by the thought of a shower. Past *Nita Downs* to the east looms Mount Phire which, although only 90 metres high, looks gargantuan on the flat horizon. The Sandfire Flats consist of sand, saltbush and a few stringy beasts wandering the fence-lines. Its name, I read somewhere, was taken from the diaries of an early explorer, who wrote that it was so hot during the height of summer, 'the sand looked like it was on fire'. Today the flats are dead, neglected by nature and offering nothing to interest humans.

Dusk envelops us with 10km to go. John drives out and follows us in, lighting the road ahead. At the roadhouse, little more than a box-like corrugated iron shed, we collapse, having battled a head-wind for more than seven hours. Nev *was* right; we'd be better heading north.

Nick says he is buggered and disappears into the roadhouse for a sugar fix. He returns ten minutes later having consumed, he says, three milkshakes, two Mars Bars and a packet of Jaffas. Emma looks fresh as a daisy and I have no doubt, if pressed, she could do it all again. Her technique and rhythm, on top of her training, is obviously having a huge bearing on her ability to handle the distances and the wind. I dread to think what I look like. I *feel* terrible.

The remnants of a fiery sunset glow over the spirit-level flats making them look, more than ever, like the end of the earth. We are 300km from the nearest town. I suppose there are other places in the world as isolated as this but I have never been there. I cook the old faithful, Tuna Surprise, which gets the thumbs up from the team. They are not hard to please; 'I'm so hungry I could eat a road-kill,' says Robert.

(Nine months later, in one of the great stories of survival in modern Australia, Aboriginal Cyril Jackson walked 200km in thongs to get help for four friends after their four-wheel drive broke down near Cotten

Creek, Jiggalong, in the Little Sandy Desert, as they headed for Bidyadanga. He ate bush tucker and collected water in his vinyl jacket, enduring freezing wet nights with no protection. On the fifth day he stumbled across two telephone technicians, who took him to Sandfire.)

Day 116: Thursday 11 September, Sandfire Roadhouse to
Eighty Mile Beach
Distance: 60km
Distance so far: 7431km

We are late getting away, at least according to Robert, who is a committed yoga disciple in Perth and rises each morning at four-thirty. I convince him that long-distance cyclists need more than five hours' sleep.

Yesterday's head-wind put paid to Nick's plan of cycling without aero bars and he purloins the set from the spare bike. Five kilometres south of Sandfire, Quasimodo's chain breaks and we spend 30 minutes on hands and knees looking for the missing link. An odd sight greets the single passing motorist: five people criss-crossing the road like myopic crabs.

The wind is strong again, screaming in from the south-west, directly into our faces. Despite it we average a healthy 22km an hour. The countryside remains tediously flat, though today we see the first semblance of wildflowers, a dusting of purple and red. Despite his new aero bars and a seat ratcheted a notch or two lower, Nick has fallen behind and arrives at our lunch stop ten minutes after Emma and me, slumping into a chair, distressed. I tell him I think he is not drinking enough water, compounded by the fact that he can only carry one-and-a-half litres on his bike. By contrast I can carry three and Emma three-and-a-half. I am surprised at his cavalier attitude: he is an experienced mountaineer and bushwalker, activities where hydration is crucial.

After lunch we toss in the towel early, taking a detour to a campground at Eighty Mile Beach. We are running short of bread and find, to our amazement, not only an oasis of palm trees and hedges, but a small and productive bakery. The owner refuses us more than nine loaves.

Eighty Mile Beach must be longer than 80 miles—white sand tracks in both directions as far as the eye can see. We troop down to the water for a swim and see, to our horror, hundreds of sea-snakes swimming just off the shore, their heads poking out of the ripples. Sea-snakes are poisonous. 'I wouldn't worry much,' says a nearby fisherman. 'Their mouths are so small they can only bite humans on the finger webbing or the ear-lobes. If you swim with your hands and ears out of the water you'll be fine.' I can't tell whether or not he is joking.

We rattle our collecting tins for half an hour in the evening, with some success. If nothing else it proves we are clearly getting good coverage. Some of our fellow campers already donated in Broome, and one couple tells me they have donated *four* times: Tennant Creek, Katherine, Timber Creek and Derby. 'I haven't got any money for you, but I will donate *this*,' says a fisherman, pulling a fearsome-looking snapper from a cool box. We decide this donation would be better eaten here than slapped on the Cancer Foundation's front desk in two weeks.

Shane, an American attempting his own cycling circum-navigation, joins us for dinner. He did the Gibb River Road two months ago and we swap horror stories. Unlike us, Shane has no itinerary to stick to, and plans to spend summer in Perth before tackling the Nullarbor. 'The prevailing wind on the Nullarbor this time of year,' he says, sounding assured, 'is an easterly.' After the past two days this is not what I want to hear, and quickly change the subject.

'At least we're all doing it the easy way,' says Shane later.
'Eh?'

'Anti-clockwise . . . on the left-hand side of the road. We're on the inside lane right around Australia! It's 40km shorter!'

Day 117: Friday 12 September, Eighty Mile Beach to
Pardoo Roadhouse
Distance: 120km
Distance so far: 7551km

Cirrus clouds hover above and we have a tail-wind, a godsend. Before we leave, Nick, who concedes that insufficient water could have caused yesterday's problems, drinks enough water to drown an elephant. We have entered the Pilbara, renowned as one of the hottest places on earth. There is no place hotter in Australia than Marble Bar, 200km south of here. In the 1920s it had 160 consecutive days over 37 degrees and in 1905 the mercury hit 49. The hottest months start in October and we will, thankfully, be in Perth by then. The region is famous for its iron ore. Red earth stretches away into the scabby, scar-ified horizon, host to famous mining towns like Newman, Tom Price and Paraburdoo. To our right, occasionally, we see the coast but more often it is low-lying dunes, punctuated by wells and bores. It is disappointing that the road does not follow closer to the ocean on such a spectacular coastline.

After 80km we arrive at the Pardoo Roadhouse, where 18 dismembered and decaying 150-tonne Shay dump trucks stand like a row of battery hens. A Brobdingnagian car lot. Each has done a generation's service tearing into the Pilbara's dusty red ranges, providing vital foreign exchange for Australia and no-one could deny they have earned their retirement.

I speak to ABC radio in Sydney and the journalist seems as interested as he did before I left, although his line of questioning suggests he thought I would have chucked it in by now. We make a date to speak again on the Nullarbor in two months. Again I wonder whether such interviews, even when hundreds of thousands of people are listening, result in donations.

Although it is tempting to call it a day here, we decide to ride a further 40km then return to the roadhouse in the car. Billowing smoke in the distance becomes flames chewing at the roadside undergrowth. The ground is scorched, but no-one seems concerned. There is no-one to *be* concerned and spinifex is not in short supply hereabouts.

Mining aside the Pilbara is not famous for much, except, that is, the northern end of the Number One Rabbit-Proof Fence at Cape Keraudren near Pardoo. The fence was started in 1934 and took six years to complete, costing £205,000 and requiring 560 camels for its construction. Until it was abandoned in 1948 this section of the fence was maintained by the Rabbit Department staff based in Jiggalong in the Little Sandy Desert. The other end of the fence is at Starvation Bay, near Esperance, 1200km away.

European wild rabbits were introduced to Australia in 1859 by Thomas Austin, who let 24 of them go at *Barwon Park*, near Geelong in Victoria. It was a monumental mistake and a century later trial runs for the introduction of *Myxomatosis* were introduced in the Murray Valley. In the interim their population ballooned, farmers calling their march across the land the 'grey tide'. Within 30 years of their introduction they had spread along the river systems into central New South Wales and southern Queensland and across the Nullarbor into Western Australia. Rabbiting became a big business: in the first six months of 1887, for instance, more than 600 000 were killed in the Wilcannia district of New South Wales, and in the same year more than ten million were destroyed in that state. In 1906 more than 22 million frozen rabbits were exported, earning more foreign exchange than the export of frozen beef. Others set out to control the vermin, erecting rabbit-proof fences like this one.

At Cape Keraudren little of the Number One Rabbit-Proof Fence remains, except a few concrete blocks disappearing into the ocean. Hundreds of kangaroos and wallabies share the area with some intrepid, wind-blown campers. But there is *no* sign, the 1940s Rabbit Department staff at Jiggalong would be pleased to know, of rabbits.

Day 118: Saturday 13 September, Pardoo Roadhouse to
Port Hedland
Distance: 110km
Distance so far: 7661km

An early start, eager to reach Port Hedland. The discovery of a scorpion in the crotch of my cycling shorts leads to wholesale ribbing (which of us would have suffered more—me or the scorpion—had I been bitten?) but I notice everyone gives *their* shorts the once-over before putting them on.

The head-wind batters us again, but the frustration is diluted by drivers stopping to make donations. The radio interviews in Broome clearly reached a broad audience. The wind picks up during the morning, no hills to impede its progress. We join a train line, the first for weeks, used to transport iron ore from Shay Gap to Port Hedland. As if on cue, a train, 100-carriages long, rumbles past, closely followed by another.

Still 30km to go and Nick is struggling. I urge him to draft behind me, remembering my tough first week when I attempted nothing like these distances, and without a head-wind. There is no doubting Nick's tenacity—he has climbed mountains in Nepal and only last week completed a 42km cross-country ski race in Victoria. Today he is distressed, victim of both heat and head-wind. We struggle to maintain a speed of 10km an hour approaching Port Hedland's two enormous salt piles, and occasionally dip to 8km an hour. I maintain he is still not drinking enough water but he is adamant he is, so I don't labour the point. Twice he has covered distances of 150km this week and whichever way you look at it, that is a grand achievement. We reach the others on the outskirts of the town and a police car escorts us for the final 5km. 'Can you get a move on,' one of the cops urges. 'We want to catch the final quarter of the footy on the TV.' Not even a hurricane could move Nick faster.

Port Hedland seems dull and featureless, with grey weatherboard houses and brown, motley nature strips. The exception is BHP's iron ore plant, the town's lifeblood, which sits in a sea of green lawn and native trees. The company has vast petroleum, steel and mineral assets and its iron ore operations centre around this region of Western Australia. It is currently spending billions of dollars building a hot bri-quetted iron plant in the town, to treat ore from Newman's Mount Whaleback, transported here on the world's longest privately owned railway.

We have another profitable night at the gates to the circus, raising $700, and add another $300 later in the evening on a tour of the pubs. Most of the donors work for BHP; 'I don't care what you hear, the letters stand for Broken Hearted People,' says one. At the Pier Pub late in the evening a group of locals buys us beers. 'Port Hedland is a great town,' one says. 'You can dress like a dickhead and no-one cares. People don't pre-judge you.' Troy, a very drunk BHP employee, slurs that he will ring us tomorrow to organise collecting in the BHP plant on Monday. On his way out he trips up and lands in the gutter. His drinking chum, displaying the best in Australian mateship, picks him up and he is led home, singing Sinatra.

Day 119: Sunday 14 September
Rest day: Port Hedland

The phone rings at first light and it is, unbelievably, Troy. Equally unbelievably, he seems not to have had his stomach pumped. When I later ring the BHP public relations manager, who doubles as the Mayor of Port Hedland, he says Troy's suggestion of a visit to the plant tomorrow, though worthy, would be 'too difficult', a disappointing result given the obvious trouble, and pain, that Troy has gone through.

At the final of the Rugby League competition donations are slow at the gate, until we are approached by a man from the Cook Islands—Grasshopper—who announces, with scant modesty, that *he* is our salvation. 'I've been watching you guys and you're doing a good job, but you need some professional help. You are in luck, because *I* am that professional help.'

Grasshopper turns out to be a fund-raiser par excellence, convincing passers-by to donate with a subtle blend of heart-rending stories, extortion, threats, promises and bare-faced lies. American multi-billionaire Ted Turner recently vowed to donate $1 billion to the United Nations and I have no doubt Grasshopper was involved in the deal somehow. 'Who's going to pick you up when you get sick, guys, who's going to pick you up?' he demands from spectators.

Within an hour we raise $1,000 and Grasshopper announces his departure with the words: 'Keep up the good work. I think you are doing a wonderful job, and until my dying day I'll support the Royal Flying Doctor Service.' We look at each other in bewilderment as he skips off to watch the final minutes of the game.

CHAPTER SEVEN

The Mid-West, WA *The Long and Lonely Road*

Speewah folk consider that a drought has ended only when they're able to have water in their tea.

Bill Wannan:
Crooked Mick of the Speewah and Other Tall Tales

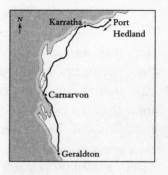

Day 120: **Monday 15 September,**
Port Hedland to Whim Creek
Distance: 128km
Distance so far: 7789km

Last night Nick was ceremonially presented with a two-litre plastic bottle which he promised to fill with water every morning and drink before cycling. This morning as we pack up he wanders about dragging the near-empty bottle, looking pregnant and groaning.

On the way out of town, after another radio interview and a trip to the supermarket to buy provisions for the next three weeks, we get stuck behind a ten-storey building, part of the hot briquetted iron plant inching its way on the back of a gargantuan semi-trailer. By the time we are out of town, heading south-west on the North West Coastal Highway, it is hot and windy, and I am grimfaced with annoyance. We have another head-wind which has vengeance written all over it, whipping up from the south-west and throwing at us a collection of dust, leaves and frustration. I reason with Emma and Nick that I have had my fair share of tail-winds so far and a head-wind or two is to be expected. 'But we haven't had any tail-winds, so *we* don't deserve the head-winds,' they wail. We take turns to lead and draft, but the morning is nothing less than a battle of attrition.

Cycling into a head-wind is not complicated, nor technically difficult. It's a bloody grind, a lot slower than normal, and bags more painful. Letting my imagination drift, the haven of the long-distance cyclist, is not an option today: every pedal shoots pain up my legs and every breath seems to constrict my chest. My speedo, comfortably sitting on 30km an hour in the Territory, hovers frustratingly between ten and 15. We fight disillusionment, speaking in grunts and sighs, as the kilometres pass in slow motion. Beyond Poverty Creek, an apt name under the circumstances, small hills bring relief to the monotony of the spinifex. The sun goes down, replaced by an enormous moon which casts our elongated shadows across the faces of the hills, creating giant, willowy spectres.

We cycle the last 20km in the half-light like robots, arriving at the Whim Creek Hotel eight hours after leaving Port Hedland. Our campsite is an ordinary one, a motley gravel car park behind the hotel. The Joyces have been there for some hours and greet us with large mugs of tea, careful not to aggravate our delicate states. I am annihilated and spend the best part of an hour stretching my legs, which have contracted several sizes. My knees hurt like hell.

The Whim Creek Hotel arrived in Australia as a pre-fab structure from England and is big and airy. The town—though the word implies people and, as far as I can make out, Whim Creek has only one—was established as a copper mine late last century when there were two hotels. The other, Dunns, was knocked down by a cyclone and never rebuilt. Up the hill from the hotel is a graveyard, one of the graves that of union worker Thomas Darlington. Darlington had his throat slit on Christmas Eve 1911 when a brawl developed between scabs, who had been called in to operate the mine, and the union. Twenty-two witnesses had to attend a court hearing in Roebourne but most of them were killed en route when a cyclone overturned their boat. The hearing was abandoned.

The copper mine lies dormant today but Australian company Straits Resources has suggested it may breathe new life into it. 'At the moment an Aboriginal land rights claim has delayed the re-opening,' says the hotel owner. 'A big green turtle seems to have wandered up there.' Her cynicism reflects a deeper malaise. She has had Whim Creek 'up to the bloody eyeballs,' and is looking to sell up. 'Any of you guys interested?' she asks. Behind her even the potato chips are in the fridge. It was 35 degrees today, and it gets much hotter than this.

Distance-wise I am halfway around Australia, and I lie in my swag taking stock of my feelings, which resemble the curate's egg, good in parts. I am pleased to have got this far, and the team is pulling together well despite the hardships. I am staggered at the reception people continue to give us and the money that we have raised. However, I am worried about the wind, and haunted by Nev's warning at the Roebuck Plains Roadhouse. Emma, Nick and I agree categorically that we would prefer to cycle 150km with no wind than 75 into a head-wind. Perth is still 1700km away; a head-wind all the way would make things very difficult.

Day 121: Tuesday 16 September, Whim Creek to Karratha
Distance: 120km
Distance so far: 7909km

Like a manic stalker the wind is already up when we start. Again it is from the south-west and again the morning is a misery. A road train stops and the driver, who heard the Port Hedland interview, donates $20. 'Wind's a prick,' he says, more statement than question. We grunt in agreement.

The town of Roebourne, 80km on, is a depressing sight, graffiti covering the walls and windows barred. The windows without bars are broken. The only building of any presence is the police station, surrounded with Colditz-like barbed wire, its only inhabitant a gleaming police car which sits facing the front gate like a watchdog on alert. The town's service station displays a sign:

'Long-range weather forecast: Hot, hot and damned hot

Last rain: 5 September

Last snow: The Ice Age'

Eager for some respite in the middle of the day we drive to the nearby ghost town of Cossack. This once-thriving pearling town, run predominantly by Europeans, Japanese and Chinese, drips with history, its restored bluestone buildings indicating a way of life very different to that which exists today in the nearby iron ore town of Wickham. The grave-yard tells many stories: 'Henry Truslove, Nov. 12 1893, Aged 34 years. Sarah Ramsay, 3rd September 1903, Aged 34 years. In loving memory of ZB Erikson, his wife Minnie and their child Pearl. Drowned in the Foam Passage, Jan. 10 1894. Dora E. Snook, born 16 September 1899, died aged 14 years'. If Dora were still alive, she would be 98 today.

A photographer from the *West Australian* newspaper, responding to a press release, arrives from Dampier and we pose in the middle of the road, trying to manufacture smiles, squinting in the swirling dust. Despite plans to lead and draft for the afternoon we drift apart, seemingly in keeping with this disjointed, frustrating day. I can see Emma in the distance, a small dot of yellow battling the elements, head down and focused. Nick struggles gamely. I have time to think of my vow to break the ride into achievable bits. In past weeks a day seemed both achievable and realistic, but today requires further segregation. I break the afternoon into 5km lengths.

Complete one, look to the next. Ditto.

Then 5km seems too much. Two kilometres. One kilometre. The next tree. The next white line on the road. Eventually, I reach Karratha. My legs are shot. All I can think of is sleep.

The town has got behind the ride. We are put up for the night in a flat owned by Dampier Salts, and two members of the Lions Club, Colin and Adrian, unfurl a four-page itinerary outlining tomorrow's fund-raising plans. It looks frightening.

English buccaneer William Dampier described the area around the present-day towns of Karratha and Dampier as 'desolate' when he sailed past in 1699, and a succession of explorers passed it over as worthless land. Decades later this region is one of the most important as Australia tries to make it in the global marketplace. Iron ore railed from Tom Price and Paraburdoo is shipped off at Dampier, bound for overseas furnaces. Gas from the North-West Shelf is piped ashore at the nearby Burrup Peninsula and transported to Perth or the Pilbara, or exported in liquefied form to Japan or South Korea.

Robert, who has not cycled for years, vowed last night to complete today's ride and set off at first light with a steely eye. He achieved his aim. He also wanted to prove he could cycle 120km into a head-wind fortified only by a can of SPC pear halves. We don't see him all day and discover he did one better: he forgot a can opener.

Day 122: Wednesday 17 September, Karratha to
Fortescue Roadhouse
Distance: 70km
Distance so far: 7979km

The phone rings at six-thirty. It is Adrian; I am due on radio
in 15 minutes.

Shit.

This media work is beginning to get to me, particularly
when it involves six-thirty wake-up calls. Was desperately
looking forward to a lie-in. I drag myself from bed.

The Year Two students at the Tambrey Primary School are
enthusiastic and ask probing questions. 'I was with my parents on
the Gibb River Road a month ago, and did you see the cyclist
who was lost?' After some clarification I realise he is talking about
me. The kids are impressed with the distance we are covering,
although one seems unimpressed by our mode of travel—he says
he saw a person recently *crawling* to Perth. Troy?

We do not leave Karratha until two, the late departure and
another head-wind rendering impossible our plans to cycle
100km. Again, the head-wind is tortuous and my speed gets as
low as 14km an hour. In a fit of prima donna-ish pique I think
of tossing the bike into the roadside spinifex and calling this
whole ridiculous thing off.

A pale figure appears on the horizon. In my frazzled state
of mind I am sure it is a ghost, the Pilbara poltergeist, or the
Grim Reaper to take me away. Closer inspection reveals a
woman, wearing a grubby yellow tank-top and little else,
carrying a small bag over her shoulder on a stick. 'Humping
her bluey' is the Aussie expression and I wonder where she is
humping it to, given we are two days' walk from habitation.
She walks as if late for an appointment, hips waddling, a stern
expression on her face. Emma pulls up alongside.

'Are you OK?'

'Yep,' she replies, without breaking step or taking her gaze from the middle distance. 'I sure am honey. Thanks for asking.'

Pause.

'Where are you going?'

'To see a friend,' is the curt reply.

Something in her demeanour points to a woman scorned and something about her answers points to a score about to be settled. If her 'friend' is the bloke behind it all, I hope he's running.

The head-wind increases as the afternoon drifts along aimlessly like a bad cricket match. I spend a lot of time cursing under my breath and can hear Emma and Nick doing the same. At one stage Emma screams, 'Bloody wind! Stop, you bastard!' Her words are buffeted and whipped away.

To the east is nothing, pure and simple. I feel for the explorers who set out looking for an inland sea or arable land in the early days, battling dehydration and disillusionment. David Carnegie, an English explorer in Western Australia, writes about the constant battle for water in his autobiography *Spinifex and Sand*:

A little water was visible, which I quickly baled into the canvas bags we had brought for the purpose. The bottom of the hole was filled in with dead sticks, leaves, the rotting bodies of birds and lizards, bones of rats and dingoes. Into the ghastly mass of filth I sunk up to my middle, and never shall I forget the awful odour that arose as my feet stirred up the mess.

The Joyces stop to give encouragement but by mid-afternoon even their well-chosen words have no impact. I am duelling the open road alone, and no-one else can get involved, or help.

We stop after 70km, 30km short of our target, as dusk descends. Everyone is testy, reserves of endurance depleted, showing their soft, vulnerable underbellies. Crumbling further

our morale the wind drops as we set up camp, a full moon
rising over the Fortescue Valley and bathing it in brilliant
luminescence. Today has been a day I would rather forget.

Day 123: Thursday 18 September, Fortescue Roadhouse to
Peedamulla outstation
Distance: 120km
Distance so far: 8099km

On the road by seven and it is still as a morgue. We celebrate
by hammering out 35km in less than an hour, crossing the
Fortescue and Robe rivers, which both gurgle happily as if
pleased for us. There is an urgency about our cycling, like ants
raiding a lunchbox—all in a line, heads down and bums up,
completing the task—fearing wind could spring up at any
moment and blow us backwards.

The morning is the antithesis of yesterday. The North West
Coastal Highway, which yesterday seemed nothing short of the
road to hell—and not a good intention to be seen—is benign
as a baby. The only people we encounter are two employees
of the Roads Board, stopping every kilometre or so to heave
dead kangaroos off the road. They doff their blood-stained caps
as they pass.

At midday we call a halt and drive up an orange Pilbara
side-track to pitch camp near *Peedamulla* outstation. Where
yesterday afternoon was full of frustration and frowns, today's
is relaxed. Importantly, we have not let yesterday's hardships
affect our approach to the trip, or to each other. It is as if the
elements were testing us, and relented because we were able
to meet the challenge. The evening is full of laughter and we
sleep outside on the tarpaulin, lined up like a picket fence,
marvelling at the clarity of the outback sky as Nick tries to
explain to us Einstein's theory of relativity.

In 1977 Queensland-born writer Robyn Davidson took four camels across the western half of Australia, starting at Glen Helen, west of Alice Springs, and ending at Hamelin Pool on the west coast, 2700km away. In her book *Tracks* she writes of her changing relationship with the arid landscape:

The self in the desert becomes more and more like the desert. It has to, to survive. It becomes limitless, with its roots more in the subconscious than the conscious—it gets stripped of non-meaningful habits and becomes more concerned with realities related to survival. But as is its nature, it desperately wants to assimilate and make sense of the information it receives, which in a desert is almost always going to be translated into the language of mysticism.

There is a mysticism about this place too, scaly spinifex under a night sky brimming with stars. We see Orion and the Southern Cross, Mars, satellites and shooting stars. In cities, stars are dulled by smog but here they are alive, glittering like diamonds on a black cape. I feel alive, vital and euphoric in the space of our surroundings.

Day 124: Friday 19 September, *Peedamulla* outstation to Nanutarra Roadhouse
Distance: 110km
Distance so far: 8209km

Another early start to beat the wind, but it has our measure, springing up the moment our backsides hit the saddles, mocking our clumsy attempt to outwit it. I am buoyed by yesterday's headway and we cover 70km in three hours, despite the mongrel wind. Enthusiasm will only carry me so far and, by mid-morning, I am washed up. An earache thrums inside my head, aggravated by the wind gusts, and my knees are hurting again. Nick and Emma press on like machines and I watch them in the distance, hoping they don't get too far ahead. The shimmering heat does strange things to their distant shapes, lifting them into the air like an illusionist's volunteers, then dropping them to earth. At times they wobble and stretch outwards, like a pool of oil expanding on a slab of concrete.

The deeper we press into the Pilbara the more hills we see. Mount Minnie appears on the right and, although only 200 metres high, looks more like Kosciuszko. To the east, Mount Amy, as high again, cuts a daring solitary figure in a sea of red earth. The Hamersley Range, 50km beyond, sits low in greys and dark greens.

At Nanutarra Roadhouse we wolf down tea and fruitcake and decide, on account of the early hour and the wind that has dropped, to do another 30km. It is easy going and we cover the distance in under an hour, leaving our bikes among the spinifex clumps and returning to the roadhouse. As ever, when backtracking by car, it seems an insignificant distance. While cycling we are kept company by an emu, which runs alongside us with seven-league-boots strides, dodging clumps of scrub, eventually peeling off and heading out to the ranges.

I pluck up courage to ring John Harcourt, the Uncle Toby's sponsorship consultant. He says the company prefers to concentrate on swimming sponsorship in the lead-up to the Olympics, and thanks me for the application. My faith in companies and the whole sponsorship game has been dealt a severe blow and I spend half an hour wallowing in the shallows of the Ashburton River, which bubbles next to the roadhouse. Nothing to do but complete the ride and prove to potential sponsors what they have missed out on. A pyrrhic victory.

At dinner Emma stuns me by asking whether she can stay on the ride until Melbourne, two months longer than planned. 'I couldn't fly home from Perth, knowing that you would be doing the Nullarbor,' she says. I am ashamed I questioned her stamina when she arrived—she has handled the conditions better than any of us and now she's volunteering to do *more*. I dips me lid.

Day 125: Saturday 20 September, Nanutarra Roadhouse to Exmouth
Distance: 90km
Distance so far: 8299km

Another early start is rewarded with a tail-wind and we cover 70km in two hours with the momentum of road trains. Mid-morning Quasimodo begins to show more signs of wear and tear. A screw integral to the pedal mechanism breaks and the pedal falls apart. A problem with all things technical: they're wonderful when they work, but when they fail you wish you had opted for something simpler in the first place. The corrugations of the Gibb River Road continue to haunt, and I cycle the remaining 10km using only one foot. We hide the bikes in the scrub and drive to Exmouth for a break. Not a moment too soon.

The people of Exmouth are a charmed lot. Their town sits at the north end of the North West Cape and is surrounded by natural wonders expansively beautiful even by Western Australian standards: the Cape Range National Park and the Ningaloo Reef Marine Park. The latter, the locals will tell you, betters even the Great Barrier Reef for aquatic life. At dusk on the top of the Cape Range there are views of the sun setting over the Indian Ocean unmatched the world over, including the twinkling lights of prawn trawlers and oil platforms.

The secretary of the Exmouth Lions Club, ex-Pom Pat Andrews, could have had no idea what she was letting herself in for when she volunteered to have us to stay. Two new recruits—Eric Graham, the Scotsman I met in Pine Creek, and Sydney nurse Margie Mort—have arrived, which makes our party seven. Somehow we squash into Pat's house. Eric has already raised $1,000 down the coast of Western Australia and assures us he has brought his bagpipes. Margie, whose parents both died of cancer recently, has arrived for two weeks and seems remarkably composed on now finding herself at the far reaches of Western Australia, about as far away from Sydney's plush North Shore as you can get.

Days 126 and 127: Sunday 21 and Monday 22 September
Rest days: Exmouth

Pat used to work for Darwin politician Steve Hatton and knows about pressing the flesh. She organises us like a military campaign and we raise more than $2,000 at pubs, caravan parks, the RSL, and the golf, bowls and yacht clubs. Eric plays the pipes at each and the locals get in the swing. At the golf club a woman dances a jig, and the members of the bowls club farewell us with a song from *The Sound of Music*.

On Sunday night we drive to Pap Hill, 30km north of Exmouth, for a barbeque. The wind howls from the south, sending the sparks of our fire scuttling like fireworks. It does not augur well for tomorrow. Nearby are 13 giant towers of the US navy's low-frequency communication station, 12 of which are higher than the Eiffel Tower. The station was once a major communication site for US submarines, one of six such stations in the world. 'Exmouth had 600 Yanks stationed here in the past, and was a nuclear target during the Cold War,' says Pat's husband, Rod.

Day 128: Tuesday 23 September, Exmouth to Minilya Roadhouse
Distance: 115km
Distance so far: 8414km

Again the team changes. Robert and John, who have filled the support roles with care and consideration during the past fortnight, return to their respective cities from the Exmouth airport—a runway of flat sand, the departure lounge a corrugated iron lean-to—and a new team is born: Eric, Margie, Emma, Nick and me. Hard saying goodbye to Pat, who has opened her house to us. 'I just believe in what you are doing,' she says as we hug her goodbye.

Back on the bikes by nine-thirty but a southerly wind has already been gusting for an hour. A lime-green kombi van, 'Love Turtle' painted lovingly in adventurous, dope-inspired swirls, chugs past, a reposeful thumbs-up appearing from the driver's window. Half an hour later we pass through the Tropic of Capricorn, marked only by a simple sign above a yellow 44-gallon drum rubbish bin. I last saw this latitude—23 degrees from the equator and the southern boundary of the Torrid Zone—at Rockhampton on the other side of the continent.

The wind gains strength during the morning and when we call a break near *Winning* station—wonderfully optimistic for such a desolate area—it has a kick on it like a mule. Margie, who opted to drive in the car for her first morning—'just to see what you idiots are really on about'—sees us crawling towards the lay-by, all sweat and cursing.

Patches of wildflowers appear in the parched, red earth: parakelias with small, pink flowers; mulla mulla the purple shrub; Sturt's desert pea; orchids; and the purple vetch creeper. Up ahead a bloke in overalls tosses a large shaving of tyre into the back of his ute. He peels $5 from a roll of notes as we approach. 'Heard on the radio you were in the area. Keep it goin' ... ya' mad bastards,' he cackles.

Margie is five feet in her stockings so I adjust the spare bike's seat to its lowest setting. Although we give her an hour's head-start we catch her up within two. She is struggling stoutly and I wonder whether today was a good day to start. On the other hand, if she waited for favourable conditions she might *never* start. We cycle together and talk about her folks, and how her brothers and sisters are coping. Her nursing training comes to the fore when we arrive at Minilya Roadhouse; a lady trips over near the petrol pumps and gashes her head.

Takes all types. The owner of the roadhouse is adamant that we should pay full price for camping, saying discounts for charity event like ours are 'against the rules'. 'Why don't you camp down by the river, it's F-R-E-E, spells free,' he says challengingly. We do just that and a roadhouse employee comes down to see us later, looking over her shoulder. She tells us the 'rules' are the boss's rules. 'He sits out the back and watches customers on a closed-circuit TV,' she says. 'Doesn't trust a soul.' She donates $50, the proceeds of a whip-round by the staff, and sneaks us the key to the showers.

Day 129: Wednesday 24 September, Minilya Roadhouse to
Boologooro station
Distance: 68km
Distance so far: 8482km

Groundhog Day meets the Gascoyne. Another morning, another head-wind, threatening to snap the trees like matchsticks, and break our resolve. Emma says she's beginning to regret her decision to stay. Try as I do, I can't wrap my mind around anything other than I am travelling at less than 15km an hour and that 100 divided by 15 is seven hours of torture. Time

▲ On the road again. Nick, Robert, John, Emma and me heading south from beautiful Broome, WA.

▲ More outback generosity. North West Coastal Highway, WA.

◀ Leaving the Tropics. North West Coastal Highway, WA.

▲ The first hill for 1000km. North West Coastal Highway, WA.

▲ Pit stop. Repairing another puncture! Margie and me on the
North West Coastal Highway, WA.

◀ 'Until my dying day I will
support The Royal Flying
Doctor Service.' Grasshopper.
Port Hedland, WA.

▲ Eric, entertaining the masses. Geraldton, WA.

▲ Spreading the anti-cancer message in Ravensthorpe, WA.

▲ 'I'm as blind as a bat ... cycling for me is very exciting.' Enthusiast David Sharpe heading west at Caiguna, WA.

▲ Ian Cunningham, after three by-pass operations, en route to Rabbit Flat. Streaky Bay, SA.

▲ Environmentally sensitive and weatherproof. Chandada, SA.

▲ Reflecting on the journey, 13 000km down and still 3000km to go. The Head of the Great Australian Bight, SA.

▲ Emma, Kate and Tooey on the last day. No bikes allowed!
▼ Made it! Tooey, Kate, Emma and me break out the bubbly and celebrate. Sydney, NSW.

stands still, the only thing keeping my spirit up is that we have two days to cycle 150km to Carnarvon. Piece of cake, if only this wind would let up.

Off the road we see the roof of *Boologooro* station nestled among trees, and reason that 70km under the belt is as good a reason to stop as any. We have heard that the family here often allows people to camp on the station. Our knock is answered by Jo Symonds, 40-something-years-old, who looks us up and down and says we can camp on her front lawn and she'll cook us dinner so long as Eric serenades her at dusk with the pipes. The offer is hastily taken up.

Helping anxious cyclists is one of Jo's specialities. 'Every now and again Japanese cyclists call in, heading north in mid-summer,' she says. 'Always out of water and on their last legs. No idea about the distances around here, or the heat. They do their cycling in the summer because they think it snows here in winter I s'pose. One afternoon I heard a splash in the pool and it was one of them. Didn't even bother to knock—just saw the pool and collapsed into it. When I came out he was groaning, "water, water".'

Jo has been running *Boologooro* for 15 years. She has hard work written all over her face and her hands look like walnuts, her fingernails harbouring enough dirt to start a small nursery. Clearly, she is no friend of the owner of the Minilya Road-house. 'He's a miserable bastard,' she says when we tell her of last night's encounter, 'and next time I see him, I'll tell him that. The road flooded once and he was charging people three bucks for a piece of toast. I almost punched his lights out.'

Jo's family, the Maslens, are a big force in the district and own most of the land between the Minilya River, 70km to the north, and Carnarvon, the same distance to the south. Clearly they are good breeders. 'Shake a tree around here and a Maslen will fall out,' I am told later. *Boologooro* is 200 000 acres and carries 15 000 sheep. Although the land seems sparse, only red earth and spindly trees so far as I can see, Jo assures us the sheep have plenty to eat.

It seems we have arrived at a difficult time: Jo's husband, Simmo, has just been thrown from the top of a two-storey cattle truck by an angry bull. He has a broken leg and will be laid up for several weeks. We offer Jo our condolences. 'Oh, he's a big bloody sook,' she growls. 'It'll be good to have him in hospital for a bit. Give me a chance to get some bloody work done around here.'

'Dad's a big man,' says Jo's daughter Billie, wincing. 'He would have hit the ground very hard.'

Billie and her sister Farrar take Margie and Emma horse-riding. Milo, a testy stock horse that was rescued from the glue factory at the eleventh hour, bites Margie before they set off, firmly establishing the chain of command. Emma's horse, Rebel, was originally a buckjumper at the Carnarvon rodeo but was sacked because he wouldn't buck.

Jo collars Nick and me to collect snakewood: vicious, twisted hardwood which covers *Boologooro*. Each of us is skewered half a dozen times. 'You're getting off lightly,' says Jo. She warns us to watch for snakes, a little slow at the moment because they are coming out of hibernation, but 'bloody crabby' nevertheless. She reels off an impressive list: copperheads, king browns, death adders, gwardars. This morning she killed one noseying around her back door.

An emu flits around in the next paddock. 'If it was on this side of the fence I'd run down the bastard,' she says. 'Emus are a bloody nuisance around here and they're dumb too. They wreck fences and bash themselves against gates until the locks break.' We pass two men erecting a meat shed near the homestead, replacing the last one, wrecked in a cyclone.

There are 14 for dinner, including the girls' governess, a

jackaroo, the meat shed builders, Jo's cousin and her boy-friend—Bo and Neil—and other odds and sods who happened to be in the district at dinner time. City folk would despair at such a challenge but, as far as I can make out, Jo counted up the numbers at five o'clock, got a side of beef from the freezer, and whacked it in the oven. 'I had 27 for dinner last month,' she says without a hint of bragging. 'Whoever's around in the evening ends up here for dinner. That's the country way: if someone needs a feed, you feed 'em.'

The frustrations of the day are forgotten as Jo entertains us with local tales, including the way she deals with Perth politicians. 'If I have a problem I go straight to the top,' she says, punching the table hard enough to make us jump. 'I ring the Premier whenever I get the urge and if some dizzy blonde tries to palm me off I tell her I'll wait till he's free, thankyou very much. Politicians love forgetting about out-of-the-way places like *Boologooro* and Carnarvon. It's my job to remind them we exist.'

Before dinner Eric kilts up and belts out 'Scotland the Brave' and 'Bonnie Galloway' against a desert backdrop, the haunting echo of the pipes bouncing off the sheds and outhouses. Jo calls him the Maestro, a nickname which sticks, and issues a standing invitation for him to return. 'Any day,' she says. 'You and me, the tourists. You play, I'll cook, we'd make a bloody killing.'

Day 130: Thursday 25 September, *Boologooro* station to Carnarvon
Distance: 80km
Distance so far: 8562km

'Get up ya' slack bastards. Thought you'd be on the road by now.' Jo's voice cuts through the pre-dawn chill like a bugle. Over breakfast she tells us she has persuaded the owner of the Carnarvon supermarket to donate a box of food, while Neil and Bo promise to organise a function when we come through their town, Apollo Bay in Victoria, in two months. Their support is staggering. No questions asked, just honest, open-handed hospitality.

The 80km to Carnarvon pass quickly in a light head-wind. I am excited at the prospect of a large town nearly two weeks from Port Hedland and I crave fresh food. On the outskirts of town next to the Gascoyne River—no more than a sea of sand—piles of fruit are stacked next to bulging vines: tomatoes, bananas and red peppers. It is the first fruit I have seen growing since Kununurra six weeks ago. Carnarvon's main road is lined with eucalypts, all of which tilt precariously, and ominously, to the north.

There are not many kind words said about Carnarvon. The guidebook says it is non-descript, its main street a dragstrip for hoons in cars. Jo told us it is an 'OK spot, so long as you stick up for yourself.' More commonly I hear it is a town without a soul, sometimes showing a nasty side, occasionally descending into violence. 'Ahh, it's not a bad joint,' says the Maestro, who passed through some weeks ago.

After last night's piping performance Eric was appointed head of fund-raising, and early indications are he will take his role seriously. In the evening we visit four campgrounds, Eric playing his pipes and the rest of us rattling buckets. One camp-ground owner is undergoing chemotherapy. 'Keep at it,' she tells us. A Japanese girl, on exchange for a year, insists on collecting with us, though I am convinced she hasn't the slightest idea what we are doing. She certainly gives every indi-cation that she has never heard the pipes before. 'God's own sound,' the Maestro tells her. We raise nearly $500.

Day 131: Friday 26 September
Rest day: Carnarvon

A southerly wind blows mightily all day and for once I couldn't
care. A day for more collecting and speaking on Carnarvon's
School of the Air. Our host is John McCloy, originally from
Rylstone, near Mudgee in New South Wales, and a teacher
here for the past four years. 'It's the best place to teach in
Australia,' he says. 'Seventy kids from 45 families tune in each
day and meet periodically during the year for camps. Many of
the students have governesses, although falling meat prices have
forced a lot to be laid off. Then it's hard on Mum, who has
to swap between being the bitchy school teacher during the
day and the loving Mum when they switch off their radio sets.'

The evening money-collecting in the pubs challenges our
momentum. Despite the Maestro's best efforts people seem dis-
interested and donate sparingly. We are told by one man to
'fuck off'. We raise $350, a paltry sum for such a big town.
'Can't win 'em all,' says the Maestro.

Day 132: Saturday 27 September, Carnarvon to
Wooramel Roadhouse
Distance: 130km
Distance so far: 8692km

On the road before seven to beat the wind, but no chance. It
attacks us like a pack of dogs, snapping at our clothes and
clawing our resolve. The only good thing about cycling into
the wind is that it is taking us away from Carnarvon.

We battle gamely for six hours, with one ten-minute break.
It is another tall order, the relentlessness broken only by wildflowers, emus strutting about, and a flock of wild goats picking
at some low branches. The meat shed makers from *Boologooro*

pass us on their way home to Geraldton, a Bachelors & Spinsters Ball to attend tonight. 'Get a move on, it's just a breeze,' they yell.

'Bugger off!' we respond in unison.

After 130 unrelenting kilometres we limp into the Wooramel Roadhouse. Like other roadhouses it looks like some giant hand has just plonked it here in the outback. We arrive in time to watch the showcase of Australian sport, the Australian Football League's Grand Final between St Kilda and the Adelaide Crows. Adelaide wins the match at a canter. Nick drinks three chocolate milkshakes in seven minutes.

A light plane lands on the highway and taxies to the petrol bowsers. Two mechanics have flown in to fix a road train, the driver of which welcomes them like prodigal sons. He has been waiting the best part of the afternoon, 20 palettes of fresh chickens to deliver to Port Hedland. 'They've been stewing in the sun all afternoon, and they'll be ready cooked by the time I get there the way things are going,' he tells me. The mechanics have to return to Perth for a 'special part', taxiing down the highway before taking off, and the driver sits down in the dust, head in hands. The wind blasts all night and the caravan feels like it could become airborne any moment. This must be the windiest bloody place on earth.

Day 133: Sunday 28 September, Wooramel Roadhouse to
Overlander Roadhouse
Distance: 80km
Distance so far: 8772km

The driver and his road train, front cabin still tilted forward revealing an engine still missing the 'special part', are still there. 'I've no idea what's going on,' he says with exasperation. 'I know one thing—the plane never returned.' Although early, mirages are already wobbling in the distance. It's going to be a stinker of a day and I wonder how his chickens are faring. We wish him luck. I glance back to see him kicking rocks across the road, gazing occasionally to the heavens.

The wind has let up and we average 24km an hour, almost supersonic after yesterday. The days of the Barkly Highway, when I was routinely averaging more than 35, seem a distant memory. I have not given up hope that they will return.

The saltbush disappears, replaced by a moonscape of red and brown dust. Occasionally we get a glimpse of the sea, Hamelin Pool, to our right, but mostly the road tracks the coast a frustrating distance inland. There is minor excitement when we come to a small rise, the first for some days, but the crest reveals more of the same: a long straight road disappearing dispiritingly to the horizon. When we stop after 60km to replenish drink bottles and stretch, Nick hangs a wet towel over his head, looking like a morose Bedouin.

At the Overlander Roadhouse, another hotch-potch of corrugated iron buildings with peeling paintwork, the owner says she has been expecting us for several days—Chinese whispers on the bush telegraph—and donates $25. A posse of Mercedes with tinted windows cruises in, diplomatic plates glowing, and ten Japanese disgorge. The Maestro, sensing the mother lode, grabs the pipes and strikes up. People donate from all quarters but the Japanese studiously ignore us. They load up on burgers, squeeze themselves back into their machines, and hum off.

Bikes tethered to a cobwebbed ute at the Overlander we drive west across the Taillefer Isthmus to Denham, the westernmost town in Australia. It is located on the Peron Peninsula which, for such arid country, has a colourful history. The first recorded landing by a European on Australian soil took place here in 1616, when Dutch explorer Dirk Hartog beached on the nearby island that now bears his name. He nailed an inscribed plate to a stump on the beach, but a Dutch tourist pinched it centuries later and it now sits in the Rijksmuseum in Amsterdam. At the time there could have been little to interest Hartog, so he left the continent to the Poms. Names in the region—Useless Loop, Disappointment Reach and Hopeless Reach—suggest that later explorers had similar reactions. Today, tourists flock to the Peron Peninsula, mainly to see the tame dolphins at Monkey Mia.

The owner of the Denham campground views us with suspicion, having recently been ripped off by people collecting for cancer research. We show him our receipt book and he gives us a campsite at the ocean's edge. The low sand dunes of Dirk Hartog Island glow over the water and jet vapour trails swirl through the heavens like gold thread.

Denham, smelling of fish and diesel, is a busy little town with enough wooden fishermen's cottages remaining to retain an attractive seaside character. In the window of the Sandalwood Craft Shop is a sign: 'Old Bastards Meeting. 5.30 pm— 7 pm. Thursdays. Shark Bay Hotel'. Also visiting soon is Paul Andrews PhD, Professor Emeritus of Zoology at the University of Calgary, who will speak on 'Shark Bay Dugongs—Past, Present and Future'. Looks like we will miss it.

Days 134 and 135: Monday 29 and Tuesday 30 September
Rest days: Denham

At Monkey Mia not even a dorsal fin is to be seen. Cormorants do their best to provide an alternative underwater show, shuffling around the sandy ocean floor beneath the jetty like ice hockey pucks.

Driving home disappointed, a turquoise lake appears on the right and I take a detour to investigate. In a moment of idiocy that will haunt me forever I veer off the track to ford a narrow creek and the car becomes bogged in a foot of water. Panic reversing digs us deeper into the muddy bottom. Salt water leaks in through the doors as the tide rises. King Canute was right. We are pulled from the stream by two four-wheel drives, water pouring from the car like a colander, but the damage has been done—the car's computer, which sits under the driver's seat and drives all sorts of crucial things, is making nasty fizzing noises. With the electrics buggered the car refuses to start.

At the service station the mechanic shakes his head. 'If I had a hundred bucks every time I'd seen this I wouldn't have to work here any more,' he says dispiritingly, vowing to look at it 'first thing tomorrow'. Breaking the news to Eric, who stayed in Denham for the day, is difficult: he would no sooner bog the car than burn his bagpipes. I feel like a young, impetuous, idiotic fool.

Next morning I get the bad news. A new computer will have to be flown from Perth. The car's seats sit on the greasy floor of the workshop, next to the carpet, and everything stinks of salt and seaweed. It is a sad and decrepit scene and I can see the bike ride slowly collapsing around me, all because of a silly rush of blood. 'Next time make sure you drive through fresh water,' says the mechanic. 'Car engines and salt water don't agree with each other.'

We do our best to take our minds off the car by visiting a pearl farm pontoon off Shark Bay coast. The Maestro plays a stirring rendition of 'Scotland the Brave' to our fellow tourists, who seem confused. He looks like he is doing an advert for whisky. The pontoon's radio crackles into life and the message is for me, requesting I call the mechanic. Why is it that calls to mechanics never result in good news? Like: *Hey Mack, you know how we thought you'd be up for $2,000. Well, we made a mistake. It's only a faulty spark plug. The bill's $12.60.*

I leave the pontoon to make the call with a heavy heart.

Ten minutes later the heart is heavier still: there are no computers in Perth and one has to be flown in from Melbourne—cost $1,500. Again I curse myself for bogging the car in such a remote place, and pray that our sponsors, Custom Fleet, will help out. How do you explain getting bogged in a stream without sounding like a fool? My contact at the company is quiet on the phone, then says he will 'look into it'. I go for a long walk on the beach and get mauled by sandflies. If today was a sick dog, I'd shoot it.

Day 136: Wednesday 1 October, Overlander Roadhouse to Billabong Roadhouse
Distance: 47km
Distance so far: 8819km

John the mechanic, who I know like flesh and blood by this stage, says he cannot be sure whether the car will be ready by the weekend, which causes a conundrum. How long do we wait and what will this do to the itinerary? The decision: hire a car and continue cycling, Eric returning to collect the car when—if—it is repaired.

The Shark Bay pearling family, the Morgans, have asked us to dive for shells with them before leaving today and Nick, Emma and I chug through the shallows towards Guichenault Point, seeing sharks, rays, cormorants and a giant turtle flopping about. A few drops of rain fall, the first I have seen for months.

Jamie Morgan, a 25-year-old with wild hair and a buccaneer smile, explains the derivation of the family business. His father, Peter, and his uncle used to dive for pearl shells at Broome until plastic buttons belted the pearl market in the 1950s. The brothers went their separate ways, Peter ending up at Shark Bay, his brother at the Monte Bello Islands north-west of

Dampier. The staple activity is diving for albina shells, into which plastic shapes are inserted. If all goes well, pearls appear within a year or two. The Japanese are the biggest buyers and, at the right price, may order four years of production in advance. Necklaces bought for $12,000 on the Western Australian coast sell for $60,000 in Osaka.

Jamie's uncle has done well at his island hideaway, and now owns a private jet, a sea plane and a flotilla of boats. His employees have three weeks on, then a week off. 'I spent six months on the islands once and went troppo,' he says, as he checks the boat's depth-finder for possible shell sites. 'There's nothing to do on Monte Bello but dive and watch videos. There's only so many times you want to see *Beavis and Butthead Do America*.'

The British conducted nuclear tests off the islands in the 1950s and the effects are still apparent: two underwater craters the size of football fields surrounded by glazed rocks where the heat melted the sand. Geiger counters still register radiation there. 'You get two-headed oysters at Monte Bello, and the pearls glow in the dark,' he says. 'Bloody Poms.'

Peter Morgan, with a pugilist's nose and a ready smile, still runs the diving business, but is handing more responsibility to his sons. At 55 he has spent 20 000 hours underwater, more than two years of 24-hour days in a world of silence. 'Dad got cancer of the throat three years ago and had surgery and chemotherapy,' Jamie says.

Jamie and his offsider, Rob, squeeze into wetsuits, grab a large string bag each, flop overboard, and descend to the bottom, trusting Emma, Nick and me to steer the boat and drag them along the bottom. The divers breathe via rubber pipes, air pumped by a generator, and hang onto ropes that trail behind the boat. Jamie surfaces after an hour, though regularly spends eight under water in a day. Both men get $4.50 for each full-sized shell recovered, earning $1,000 on a good day.

The boat has the latest infra-red technology to locate rich stores of shells, and above the wheel is a list of morse-like codes so divers can communicate with the boat driver. The codes mean, among other things, Left, Right, Emergency, Shark, Snagged, Scary Monsters Down Here, and Stupid Bloody Job, I Quit, Want to Become a Sex Instructor.

We squeeze into wetsuits and flop overboard. Diving for shells can be a dangerous occupation, sharing a world with sharks, octopus, rays and sea-snakes. The sea-snakes are the most dangerous. 'A local pearl diver died recently from a sea-snake,' Jamie says. 'It came up in his shell bag and it bit him. He died two weeks later.' We find no sea-snakes, but two blue-ringed octopuses emerge from our bags.

We do not leave Denham until three and do not start cycling from the Overlander Roadhouse until after five. Another head-wind and we average under 20 down a gun-barrel-straight road. At dusk Eric, trailing us, turns on the headlights and illuminates the road. He is a trooper.

The Billabong Roadhouse is a tacky pile of lego bricks with dribbling showers. Like other roadhouses it seems long on functionality and short on charm. Travellers are encouraged not to sit inside unless buying something and, once they have finished, to move on smartly. It is not on the electricity grid and its generator throbs all night like a bad rock concert.

Day 137: Thursday 2 October, Billabong Roadhouse to Binnu
Distance: 147km
Distance so far: 8966km

We pay for yesterday's leisure. One hundred and fifty kilo-metres into a head-wind, through country becoming hillier, is no trifling matter, and I struggle from the moment my bum hits Quasimodo's intractable saddle. Everything is against us today. In addition to our traditional antagonist, the wind, the flies are in plague proportions, stickier than in past days. I wave them constantly from my helmet and they return with an audible thud. Two fly up Emma's nose.

Three snakes slither across the road in front of us and we discover we have reached bindy-eye country. These spiky seed pods are the bane of cyclists Australia-wide and I have been warned of them often. Nick and Margie get punctures within 1km of leaving the roadhouse.

It is a seven-hour day of head-down, bum-up road-slogging. There is nothing delicate about it—a day of sweat and swearing, protesting quadriceps and burning lungs, exasperation, self-doubt and blasphemy. I think of that chap Sisyphus, the King of Corinth from Greek mythology, who wronged the gods and spent eternity pushing a rock up a hill. The North West Coastal Highway has become my rock, the ride my private Sisyphean struggle.

We talk little, sinking into our own internal worlds, searching for panaceas and calling on tricks for how best to cope with situations like this. Nick has a stern look on his face, as if trying to remember chemical compounds from distant days. Emma yells and screams and Margie looks, simply, like she is about to expire.

For me it is a morning of lists:

African countries and their capital cities, Australian prime ministers, Olympic winners. Colours of the rainbow, elements of the periodic table, planets of the solar system. Wives of Henry VIII. Some lost their heads and I know how they feel. Bugger this wind.

The wind is as uncompromising as an incoming tide and the afternoon becomes a simple test of endurance and bloody-mindedness. The temptation is to toss it in and drive to Binnu.

I could almost live with my conscience, but Eric would never let me forget . . .

Were it not for the intemperate wind it could be a pleasant day. The eucalypts are taller now and she-oaks and wattles keep me company. The wildflowers bloom in brilliant reds, purples and yellows, especially bright in the Kalbarri National Park south of *Nerren Nerren*. Among them are prickly Moses (*Acacia pulchella*), Sturt's desert pea (*Swainsona formosa*), pixie mops (*Petrophile linearis*), cockies tongues (*Templetonia retusa*) and summer star flowers (*Calytrix fraseri*).

Mid-afternoon my odometer clicks over 9000km and I am, momentarily, alarmed at how quickly the trip is going. Three-fifths of the way. Despite this brief moment of semi-happiness, it is without doubt the most unpleasant day's cycling I've ever had, anywhere.

After 100km Emma and I have forged ahead of Nick, while Margie has retreated to the support car. We come over a rise and see fields of wheat to the south, tossing in the wind. It is a defining moment, signalling our passing from the arid north-west to the arable south-west. From the Never-Never to civilisation. Twenty kilometres into the wheat belt, on the south side of *Mary Springs* and Galina Mines, we cross the Murchison River, which has its beginnings on the Robinson Range north of Meekatharra 600km away. The wind is unrelenting and it is a feeling of release and relief to reach Binnu, nothing more than a service station, a school and two enormous wheat silos. I am not bothered by the bleakness; at least I have stopped. As we collapse outside the service station, too tired to stretch, the owner tells us we are lucky not to be cycling through here in two weeks' time. 'It'll be harvesting season and the road trains will be thicker on the ground than the flies,' he says.

There is no campground and he directs us to the back of the

tennis courts, which outnumber the town's inhabitants. The showers in the clubhouse are cold.

A TV news crew arrives en route from Kalbarri, desperate for a story after one on whale migration fell flat because the whales had already left. Who better to provide an alternative than the Maestro? There are, after all, not too many septuage-narian pipers in these parts. It is a sight for sore eyes, and legs: Eric doing his wandering minstrel routine at a haulage siding, dressed to the nines, wheat silos looming above him.

Day 138: Friday 3 October, Binnu to Geraldton
Distance: 100km
Distance so far: 9066km

Sleeping outside in a swag, I am woken at four o'clock by raindrops. Confusion reigns, not least because the sky is as clear as perspex. The lawn sprinklers at the Binnu tennis courts are the culprits and, within seconds, I am soaked. When calm is restored the Maestro announces he is driving back to Denham—300km—to collect our car, leaving *now*. We grab our cycling clothes before he takes off in a cloud of sprinkler spray. It is not until he has gone that I realise my cycling shoes are in the hire-car with him. I have no choice but to cycle in work boots, a nice look with lycra.

Miraculously we have a tail-wind, a reward perhaps for yes-terday's persistence. That good things seem to follow bad, and vice versa, reminds me of the words of a wise businessman who, when asked what he has learned from his decades of business, replied: 'Things are never as bad as they seem, and things are never as good as they seem.' Could be a good thing to remember.

At Northampton 'Bluey' Burden—a grandfatherly figure missing his right index finger, and president of the Lions

Club—tracks us down with a cheque for $250. We reward ourselves with a visit to the local café, where Emma eats a portion of black forest cake the size of the nearby church. Her capacity for food stupefies me, not that I am any slouch on the food front. Yesterday I ate nine Vita Brits, seven pieces of toast, four sandwiches, two apples and three bananas, two packets of chips, three muesli bars, two Mars Bars (giant size), two sizeable plates of spaghetti, and a significant slab of apple pie.

Things are never as good as they seem. Just when the day seems to be progressing nicely my rear tyre, which has survived since Mount Isa, explodes with a loud report. The spare tyres are, of course, in the car which is, of course, in Denham. I improvise with a tube of electrical tape provided by a friendly service station owner. I wrap it around the tyre 20 or 30 times—trying hard to give the impression that I do this most days of the week—aware that the man is watching me intently. 'How far have you come mate?' he asks.

'From Sydney.'

'And you're going to ... ?'

'Er, ditto.'

I can sense his eyes boring into me as I stand there, biting the electrical tape with my teeth, hard to achieve with any sense of elan.

'Hmmm,' he says, before walking away. 'Bloke out there in work boots reckons he's cycling around Australia. He's taping up his bloody tyre. Silly as a wheel,' I hear him say to someone inside. Laughter follows.

The electrical tape gives protection for an hour or so, although I have to put up with the 'ker-thump, ker-thump' every time it hits the ground. We cycle through plunging valleys and over luscious, green hills, with occasional glimpses of the ocean to the west. The paddocks of wheat, lupins and oats contrast with purple fields of the despised Patterson's Curse.

Geraldton, population 34 000, is a delight to behold as we crest a hill, not least because we are booked into a hotel tonight.

I have no idea how the Maestro is getting on in Denham, and wait with increasing nervousness for a call. Eventually Eric rings: our car will be ready ... tomorrow.

Days 139–141: Saturday 4—Monday 6 October
Rest days: Geraldton

Another call from Eric reveals that the car is indeed ready, and he is leaving for Geraldton. I feel a surge of relief, hoping this will be the end of our troubles. John the mechanic gives no guarantees. 'The funny bloody thing about cars that get salt water in their electrical systems is that they tend to have ongoing troubles,' he says ominously. 'We had a bloke last year who did the same thing in a new Pajero and the insurance company wrote it off. Others are OK. You just can't tell.'

Things are never as bad as they seem ... they're worse. Three hours later Eric rings from the Overlander Roadhouse. 'Stopped to stretch my legs and now the car won't start. A mechanic says the alternator's buggered and we need an electrical engineer and his testing equipment.' Needless to say, electrical engineers, and accompanying gadgetry, are as thick on the ground at the Overlander Roadhouse as nuclear submarines.

As I sit morosely in Geraldton, wondering for the thousandth time why I tried to cross that stream, I curse car manufacturers and their never-ending quest for things technical. Why do manufacturers' advertisements show four-wheel drives ploughing through mud, fording streams and generally being the hairy he-men of machines, when ours has not been able to handle two inches of water under the driver's seat? Why the hell does Nissan put computers under drivers' seats in the first place? If something hates water, wouldn't you put it as high as possible in the car, under the dashboard for instance? Swear I'll write a letter to them, if we ever get out of here. I ring transport companies to see if any trucks are passing through to bring the car down to Geraldton. Nothing until Tuesday. I can see my carefully planned itinerary unravelling like a dunny roll in the Binnu wind—we have commitments in Perth this coming weekend, 500km away, and *must* be there.

Some luck. Eric stops an elderly couple driving south in an empty truck and they agree to bring the car to Geraldton. They will be here this evening. I book the car into an auto-electrician for tomorrow and can do no more. Remember: things are never as bad as they seem.

It is Margie's last night with us—she cycled grandly yesterday, 100km—and we splash out at a seafood restaurant. The Maestro is there when we return. The car sticks out from the back of the truck, looking guilty, like a dog standing in a dug-up garden.

Our saviours, Derrick and Elaine, are the sort of matter-of-fact country folk for whom nothing is a problem. 'We sleep in the back of the van when we are on the road, and we find a shower when we begin to smell,' Derrick says as we drive to the auto-electrician the following morning. 'Eric told us what you're all trying to do, and we were only too happy to help.' They refuse payment for their troubles, and leave with a friendly wave. In the afternoon the auto-electrician tells me the alternator *is* the problem. He will order one from Perth but it won't arrive until Tuesday, in two days.

At least the Maestro is with us and we can fund-raise. We start at the dragon boat races on the Geraldton Harbour, Eric cutting a dashing figure on the golden beach among the revellers. He isn't as popular at the campground in the evening. One bloke gives me a dollar and whispers: 'It's the worst bloody noise in the world. Tell him to go away.' We raise $550.

Monday is frustrating. A big northerly wind blows through

Geraldton, sending leaves swirling and ladies' hats cartwheeling. Tomorrow, I feel sure, it will be a southerly again. Mid-morning we visit the garage and the car looks forlorn, hooked up to more wires than a bypass patient. The mechanic raises his eyebrows when I tell him we are heading to Sydney. 'We could replace every item under this bonnet, which would cost a lot of money, and it could still break down in the middle of the Nullarbor.'

Dad rings in the afternoon and tells me he is getting married early next year. I think of Mum and different emotions course through my head: happiness, sadness, confusion, even mild panic. I speak to my eldest sister, Caroline, in Melbourne about the news. We speak about Dad and about her 18-month son, David, now beginning to walk. Grandfather and grandson, 75 years apart, both moving ahead.

CHAPTER EIGHT

The Great Southern, WA
Hell West and Crooked

Damn the teamsters, damn the track,
Damn Coolgardie, there and back,
Damn the goldfields, damn the weather,
Damn the bloody country altogether!

Western Australian prospector's toast

Day 142: Tuesday 7 October,
Geraldton to Green Head
Distance: 170km
Distance so far: 9236km

I'm relieved to mount, as it were, Quasimodo. I was getting twitchy back in Geraldton and, I'm sure, difficult to live with. I have become a peripatetic pedaller and my home is the back of my bike not a hotel room.

We take a new road, the Brand Highway, and I hope it brings a change of luck—a new and more benign chapter in this crazy venture. Certainly the colours south of Geraldton point to a new start. The past five weeks have been browns and reds: today is green as new life.

Quasimodo, tuned in Geraldton, whirrs along the road as if re-born, and Emma, Nick and I cover 60km in under two hours. The road snakes along valleys next to the sand dunes

238

giving occasional glimpses of a sparkling ocean. Still, I cannot reconcile our position: no car, and a support driver twiddling his thumbs. I think of the Maestro and his unquestioning support. He came to play the bagpipes and raise money but has spent the past week getting us out of a mess that is entirely my doing. This afternoon he plans to drive the car back to Binnu, where our caravan remains, then meet us at Green Head—total distance 400km. 'These things happen,' he has said a thousand times. An approach borne of the war.

South of Geraldton is steeped in history. We pass ruined stone houses and two-storey mills with dark forbidding windows surrounded by tangled gorse. It is like something out of a Thomas Hardy novel and it would not surprise me to see Gabriel Oak wander past, pitchfork slung over one shoulder, wheat stalk between the teeth. The township of Greenough has been lovingly restored, with a nineteenth century school, nunnery, hall and two churches, all surrounded by closely cropped grass and trees blown parallel to the ground.

The Brand Highway peels away from the coast and heads inland towards the towns of Mingenew and Arrino. A new road tracks the coast south through Illawong and Coolimba. It is a relief to leave the highway for the first time since Broome and cycle three abreast, with no cars about. The wind is mild and I experience a feeling of relaxation for the first time since the car's unscheduled dunking.

The nearby Batavia Coastline is rugged in the extreme, and has a haunting past. In the seventeenth century, the Dutch East India Company sailed regularly from Europe to Java via the Cape of Good Hope, crossing the Indian Ocean and tracking the West Australian coast. Four wrecks have been discovered in the area, including the *Batavia* which went aground in 1629 on the Houtman Abrolhos Islands off Geraldton. A party was sent to Jakarta (formerly Batavia) to get help and by the time a rescue party returned three months later, mutineers had killed 120 of the survivors. The ringleaders were strung up and two others left to survive on the coast near today's Kalbarri, 150km north of Geraldton.

Eighty years later another Dutch ship, the *Zuytdorp*, ran aground beneath the Kalbarri cliffs. Wine bottles were discovered in the region decades later, as was the Ellis van Creveld syndrome among local Aboriginal children. The syndrome—which causes short limbs and small faces—was rife in Holland at the time of the wreck and the theory is *Zuytdorp* survivors passed it to the locals.

The ocean glitters like a string of Shark Bay pearls and we take a dirt track to the water's edge to admire the view. Four old shacks, cobbled together from bits of tin, driftwood and wire, sit low in the dunes and a handful of men fillet fish on the beach, as surprised to see us as we are to see them. They tell us they are crayfishermen and have been catching crays near Drummond Rock and Snag Island for years. This is about to change: the Department of Conservation and Land Management, they tell us, has given them until the end of the decade to vacate their shacks, which will be razed.

We battle a side-wind all afternoon and at the small hamlet of Green Head, hovering precariously over the Indian Ocean like an indecisive lemming, we have covered 170km. It has been an enormous day, separated neatly into three distinct sets of about 55km. It reinforces for me the notion that a large job becomes easier when broken up into bite-size chunks.

A message from Eric: the alternator did not arrive. I feel like a bit part in *Waiting for Godot* and ring the mechanic in Geraldton. 'It'll arrive tomorrow. Honest.'

Day 143: Wednesday 8 October, Green Head to Cataby
Distance: 123km
Distance so far: 9359km

The wind howls during the night and our cabin shakes like a feverish dog. I have nightmares that it is a southerly and am relieved at daybreak to find a northerly, a tail-wind. Northerlies bring bad weather, but give me a tail-wind and rain any day. I ring Custom Fleet, the owners of the vehicle, and my contact there says sternly the company will pick up the tab for *these* repairs. 'After that you're on your own.'

Bitumen is excellent to take frustrations out on. We hit 60km an hour on the way to Jurian and I feel like a Pacific gull in flight. It is a spanking new road, bisecting the Drovers Cave National Park, and about us are luxuriant native plants including vibrant bottlebrushes. We climb a giant sand dune on the side of the road, white as snow, and watch storm clouds gather in the north-west. The storm hits at the top of the Gairdner Range and we huddle under some shrubs, laughing. It is warm rain and the power of the storm is intoxicating. Back on the Brand Highway we enter paddocks of waving wheat and rows of gums planted by some forward-thinking farmer a century ago. Sheep huddle together in the wind.

The town of Cataby is three weatherboard homes and a roadhouse, where two nuns tuck into generous portions of cake and Coke. The owner frowns at us as we loiter like teenagers, waiting for Eric and becoming more agitated by the minute. I think of trying to explain the whole mess to the owner, but am sure he wouldn't believe it.

Eventually, at seven-thirty, a familiar stooping figure shuffles in, a small smile on his face as if returning from a Sunday drive. Maestro by name, Maestro by nature. I grab him in a bear-hug and order the biggest beer in the house. The car and caravan sit quietly outside, as if wondering what all the fuss is about. Rarely have I been happier to see anything, or anyone, anywhere.

The roadhouse is on a filthy plot of land next to the highway, and road trains clatter past all evening. At nine the heavens open and by nine-fifteen the caravan sits in a foot of water, rain cascading through a gap in the door. But I couldn't, as they are fond of saying in these parts, give a rat's.

Day 144: Thursday 9 October, Cataby to Gingin
Distance: 78km
Distance so far: 9437km

A week ago we were sweltering in 30 degree heat. Today frostbite is more likely. It rains for half the morning and we cycle in rain jackets, which flap maddeningly. Yesterday's tail-wind has become a strong cross-wind, screaming in from the west and up the ramparts of the Koodiwoodie and Darling ranges. The saving grace is that we are in danger only of being blown off the road, not into the path of oncoming traffic. The traffic builds up during the morning. In contrast to what we have become used to, there is no waving or friendly tooting, rather people with firm jaws hurrying to get somewhere. We make short work of the 80km, arriving in Gingin in the early afternoon. The owner of the campground gives us a free campsite and donates $50.

The media has shown interest, a reflection of the public's fascination with things weird. The endurance nature of the ride seems to strike a chord, coupled with the fund-raising and the school element. I do an interview with ABC radio, with three others lined up for tomorrow. It rains strongly all night. After months of hot weather we are suddenly, unmistakably, back in the cold.

Day 145: Friday 10 October, Gingin to Perth
Distance: 85km
Distance so far: 9522km

I wake with a start. It is only five-thirty and I drift back to sleep. Five minutes later the Maestro sounds reveille. 'Let's go!' he yells. We have to be on the outskirts of Perth at eleven.

It is the fiercest of winds and again, thankfully, a cross-wind. We struggle to make the deadline after I stop to do a radio interview from a hardware store in Bullsbrook. Hans, an enthusiastic German from the Northbridge Lions Club, meets us at Midland at the assigned time. He is hard to miss, looking like something from the Chicago Futures Exchange in his trademark orange Lions shirt. His colleague Diane Raymond, until now only a voice on the phone, is there too, looking nervous. 'Thought you weren't going to turn up,' she says. 'I would have been lynched.'

Forty cyclists, a range of colours and shapes, wait for us in a car park, mainly from Perth's Over-55s Cycling Club and the Western Australian Cycling Federation. We set off for the city, looking like a giant lycra python, accompanied by four Starsky and Hutch policemen. Our fellow cyclists grill us for information. How far have we come? Any health problems? One cycles alongside. 'Hi, I'm Frank Kelly, OBE. Know what that stands for?'

'Order of the British Empire?'

'No, Over Bloody Eighty!' he cackles before stepping on the gas and disappearing.

Several pedestrians heard yesterday's interview and clap from the pavement. Nick, Emma and I smile at each other with a crazy sense of fulfilment. The Maestro drives the car alongside, hand locked in a thumbs-up. I cycle in a dream, senses dazzled after two months on the road since Darwin. The department stores seem enormous and the advertising garish. After weeks of space and horizon Perth seems furious and cramped. 'Let's all keep together folks,' says one of the cops through a loud-hailer.

In his book *Cloudstreet* Western Australian author Tim Winton describes Perth as 'the most isolated country town in the world trying to be the most cut-off city in the world, trying desperately to hit the big time.' With a desert on one side and an ocean on the other the city is, Western Australians are fond of saying, as close to Jakarta as Adelaide. This isolation has bred a parochialism unmatched in the country, possibly the world. Perth residents can live with this reputation. Many are proud of it, and why not? When your city has a seaside location as beautiful as any in the world, sailing and seafood, world-famous vineyards and more than 300 sunny days a year—cooled by an afternoon breeze you could set your watch by—life is good.

In the city centre, bathed in sunshine for an enthusiastic lunch-time crowd, we are welcomed by Perth's Lord Mayor and members of the Cancer Foundation. Crowds hang from balconies though most seem more interested in a posse of models mincing in new summer swimwear on a nearby catwalk.

We are shown around the Lions Club Cancer Research Centre, where money raised this weekend will go. The head of the centre tells a far-from-unique story: 'We are acknowledged as a world-class research unit and always get knocked back by the Government for research grants. If it happens for much longer we will close.'

Next week's support crew, Dad and his fiancée Jean, arrive from Melbourne and treat the team, including Eric's wife June, to dinner at a Chinese restaurant. The Maestro, after three weeks of pasta and rice was, I know, looking forward to steak.

Days 146 and 147: Saturday 11 and Sunday 12 October
Rest days: Perth

A weekend of frenetic activity. We visit the local Lions con-
vention and thank them for their support, undertake more
fund-raising with the Cancer Foundation's head of publicity,
Fiona Paice, via a sausage-sizzle in the unfortunately named
Perth suburb of Dog Swamp, and attend a Lions ball in the
evening. It is fancy dress and we are persuaded to dress in lycra.
On Sunday morning I speak at a yacht club on the Swan River,
the function organised by the Northbridge Lions and attended
by 120 people.

Nick leaves for Melbourne after a heroic five weeks and Eric
calls it quits too, vowing to re-join me in Adelaide for the final
month. I present the Maestro with a pair of coloured underpants as close to Graham tartan as can be found in Perth, onto
which a red pom-pom has been sewn to match his piping hat.
Both have been stunning companions and I shall miss them.

Day 148: Monday 13 October, Perth to Pinjarra
Distance: 117km
Distance so far: 9639km

Fifteen members of the Rockingham Over-55s Cycling Club
have cycled 50km to Perth to accompany us south, and make
me feel like Samson after Delilah had taken to his thatch with
snippers. Mostly in their 60s and 70s the Over-55s set a
cracking pace through Spearwood, Coogee and Kwinana, and
I struggle to keep up. I tell myself that Quasimodo, with his
bulky touring frame and wide tyres, is the cause. Emma, on
the same kind of bike, looks as unflustered as ever.

The Over-55s are full of life, all sinew, washboard stomachs
and piston legs. 'It's because we love doing things,' one says

when I quiz him on their Peter Pan-ness. 'We are retired and none of us wants to sit around doing nothing. So we cycle three times a week. Two of the group just cycled to Sydney. Those Nullarbor head-winds were a bastard.' I quickly change the subject. They bid us goodbye on the edge of Rockingham, fizzing off into the distance, and Emma and I head to the camp-ground. Dad and Jean are there and I am relieved: I felt guilty leaving them in Perth with a car which, in the words of my friend, the Geraldton electrician, 'could conk out tomorrow.'

Tomorrow morning I speak at a Rockingham school then have a date at a school in Dwellingup, 100km away, in the early afternoon. The only way around the problem is to cycle to Pinjarra, midway between the two, this afternoon, return to Rockingham for the night, and then drive back to Pinjarra tomorrow.

The outskirts of Rockingham and Mandurah are full of retirement estates, villages with names like 'Meadow Springs' and 'Orchid Heights' surrounded by manicured lawns and waterfalls tumbling from mock sandstone piles. Emma and I cycle the last 20km in the gloom, aided by a stiff tail-wind, Dad and Jean lighting the way with the car.

Day 149: Tuesday 14 October, Pinjarra to Darling Range
Distance: 108km
Distance so far: 9747km

Two months ago, in Litchfield National Park south of Darwin, I struck up conversation with Rockingham residents Elaine and Michael McKeon, who had taken their kids from school to see Australia. Michael has cancer and they vowed to raise money upon their return and present the proceeds to me in Rock-ingham. We get a roof-raising reception at the Charthouse Primary School: a thousand students pack the open-air assembly. Concerted efforts at three schools have raised $1,000, a momentous achievement.

I get a sickly feeling that time is against us as we drive to Pinjarra, collect our bikes, wolf down lunch in the main street, and set off for Dwellingup. Dad and Jean drive the main road to Collie, where Emma and I will meet them this evening via a more direct logging road through the forest. Tom Atkinson, a 68-year-old who still races regularly and trains up to 400km a week, cycles with us to Dwellingup. While yesterday was on the flat, today we cycle into the hills that spawn the Murray River, passing through Swiss-style paddocks under a carpet of bright yellow and white flowers. Although we visit the school only for an instant we do not enter the forest until two in the afternoon, still 90km to cycle and only four hours of sunlight remaining. Tom, returning to Pinjarra, bids farewell with concern in his voice—says he thinks we may run out of daylight. 'Your call,' he says.

I bought a book in Sydney, *Cycling Australia*, and the road between Dwellingup and Collie received plaudits from the author. As we set off down the corrugated, dirt track I realise that what is attractive to the author, the road's remoteness, might count against us. Only two cars pass during the first two hours, and the thick gravel slows us. The road twists along the Darling mountain range, through forests of giant jarrah, their upper reaches blocking the sun and giving the place an eerie, forbidding feeling. The dull, thunking sound of a machine can be heard in the distance, a giant conveyor belt transporting bauxite from a mine near Boddington to a refinery in the valley.

At six o'clock, still deep in the forest and light fading, we come to a three-way junction in the road and take, at our guidebook's prompting, a road to the left. Ten kilometres later it is clear we are on the wrong road and we retrace our steps. A large dark shape leaps lithely across the road in front of us, disappearing into the undergrowth. 'What the hell was that?' says Emma urgently.

At the junction, still 40km from Collie, the light has gone. In the gloom we try another track and it peters out after 1km. Although the wind is nothing more than a gentle breath, the night sky is clear and it is very cold, especially when we are moving. Emma and I, already shivering in our thin cycling clothes, discuss the options and decide we have none but to wait for a car, then return tomorrow to complete the day's ride. Neither of us bothers to state the obvious: that we have not seen a car for hours.

It is freezing. Short of being totally naked we are as unsuitably dressed for a night in the open air as we could be, each wearing only a layer of damp lycra. We have no covering, no water, no food and no matches. Used to be a scout too, but prepared for this I am not.

A damp cold sets in and we entwine around each other in a desperate attempt to maintain body heat. When we retreat from the side of the road into a ditch at the base of a jarrah tree we admit to ourselves that no car will come through this evening. We are a pathetic sight, covered in dust, our bodies convulsing in the night chill, teeth chattering like castanets. Ants crawl around the base of the tree and I can feel them on my legs and arms. Too cold to brush them away. At midnight the conveyor belt, the sound of which has provided a small measure of comfort since our predicament began, is shut off. The silence is deafening and, somehow, our problems seem more manifold.

We take turns to hold each other. I have enough knowledge of exposure to realise that hypothermia is a real possibility in such a situation. Although our constant shivering is worrying I know that it is when you *stop* shivering that you are in the greatest trouble. I try to think of ways to make our predicament less dire but am stumped. Thank God there is no wind or rain.

Emma is in this because of me, and I apologise. 'That's OK,' she says through chattering teeth. 'At least we'll have a good story to tell people when we get out.' All I can think is that I hope we *do* get out.

If we sleep, it is fitfully. I dream of people with blankets, mugs of hot chocolate and kindly words. Our ears play tricks on us: sounds of approaching cars become silence. I have had many eventful experiences at night—nightmares as a kid, a car crash, even a night in a police cell at the tail-end of a good party—but this beats them all. It is, simply, the worst night of my life, daylight second.

Day 150: Wednesday 15 October, Darling Range to Collie
Distance: 40km
Distance so far: 9787km

The sun makes a feeble appearance through the trees, providing all the heat of a two-watt globe in the brittle air. We continue to shudder with cold in our dusty hollow, willing the sun higher. At five-thirty, before we have time to react, a car speeds past and disappears towards Boddington. Half an hour later we hear the grinding gears of a logging truck, and this time I make it to the road to wave it down. My legs are frozen through and refuse to function properly, a marionette controlled by a sadistic puppeteer.

'Excuse me, can you help? We've been here all night,' I squeeze the words out through chattering teeth.

The driver looks at me with disdain from his parapet.

'Quite a few idiots get caught out here overnight,' he says disinterestedly. 'You look OK.'

Bastard.

'Yeah, I think we're OK. You couldn't spare a box of matches, could you?'

'Nuh mate, haven't got any. Gave up the fags years ago.'

'Which way is it to Collie?'

'The turnoff is 200 metres down there,' indicating the way he has come.

'Right ... OK ... thankyou.'

'No worries.'

Bastard, again.

I watch in disbelief as he departs. There's no doubt our plight doesn't seem so bad now that daylight has arrived, but I expected at least *some* compassion. Another logging truck arrives and the driver reluctantly surrenders a lighter. 'Don't go burning the forest down,' he says, seriously.

Nice coming from a logger.

A fire flickers and we hover around it, life returning grudgingly to stiff limbs. We both fall asleep, curling around the crackling fire like a couple of hobos. Eventually, reluctantly, we start cycling, looking like swamp creatures, covered in dirt, sweat and grime, hungry beyond description. The overwhelming feelings are of relief.

The Collie campground owner, Gavin, produces mugs of boiling tea, 'Last night's temperature got to four degrees,' he says. Dad and Jean are at the police station organising a search plane. No-one knows anything of the logging road which is why no cars were despatched last night. Quite simply, no-one knew where we were.

Dad and Jean arrive and we hug—hard to know who is more relieved. We eat a mountainous breakfast, even by our impressive standards. They shake their heads in disbelief as our story unfolds. 'We were told there were huts in the forest and that you would be in one of them,' Jean says. Dad's first question is, as I knew it would be: 'Where were your matches?'

We were to cycle to Nannup today but agree to stay in Collie. A shower never felt so good. I reflect soberly on our

experience which reaffirms the dangers of exposure. Having no
option but to hunker down for the night in the dirt was a
primeval experience. We got lost because I felt honour-bound
to visit both schools as arranged. Had it been raining or windy,
last night could have had a different ending.

Day 151: Thursday 16 October, Collie to Manjimup
Distance: 180km
Distance so far: 9967km

We are now behind the itinerary and leave with firm intentions
to make up lost time. Perhaps my brain is addled by the events
of the past two days and confusion reigns about the best route
out of Collie. Towns in the district include Manjimup,
Munglinup, Muradup and Mullalyup, and we get lost again on
a thin dirt road. We consult roadworkers who know less than
us and eventually get a lift back to Collie to start again.

It is, I suppose, a good day to get geographically embarrassed; the temperature is cool and the countryside
breathtaking, although the wind is against us. Green fields roll
past, swathed in purple and yellow, a surreal sight under a
leaden sky. Farmers cut hay and the rich smell reminds me of
springtime lawns. A succession of cattle trucks rumble past on
their way to a market somewhere.

Back on track we arrive at Boyup Brook then follow bubbling Blackwood River to Bridgetown under forbidding clouds
which threaten rain, buffeted by a squally wind. It has been an
eventful three days since we last saw the highway. By the time
we reach Manjimup, after 180km, it is almost dark. Dad and
Jean, expecting us four hours ago, have been worried. They
must be wondering whether their time in the West will *ever*
be relaxing. I assure them that it has not *always* been like this,
though am sure they don't believe me.

Despite the long day Emma and I agree we feel strong. I am still amazed by how well I continue to recover from hard cycling, and am convinced that stretching—up to an hour on most days—and consistent food and water intake has sustained me. Over the months I have discovered reserves of resilience I never knew I possessed.

Day 152: Friday 17 October, Manjimup to Walpole
Distance: 126km
Distance so far: 10 093km

For a dry, barren state, the south-west of Western Australia, the Great Southern, is a contrary place. Mighty karri and jarrah forests link the boundless plains of the interior to the Southern Ocean, while green hills harbour sheep and fields of wheat, even the odd winery, and belie Western Australia's reputation for spinifex, sand and gold-bearing rock.

The giants of the Shannon and Mount Frankland national parks, trees 100 metres high and 400-years-old, line the South Western Highway, as Emma and I push south-east. Plans to reach Walpole by lunch-time are blown away by a head-wind ripping in from the south. It is like a boxer, jabbing and parrying, probing for a character weakness. I do my best to avoid the knock-out punch; can only set the jaw and churn the pedals. Tail-winds since Broome can be counted on one hand while head-winds have become a disturbingly constant companion. Today's wind seems particularly unsettled, perhaps because of the trees, which squeeze it into gusts and cause us to wobble precariously. We escape from the wind in a lay-by and an elderly couple offer us tea, in the finest bone china, and delicious moist fruitcake.

The Southern Ocean is a deep spectacular blue and the head-wind gathers strength as we approach the coast, arriving in Walpole after six hours of purgatory, buffeted, battered and short of patience. My odometer has ticked over 10 000km, but all I feel is lethargy. It has been a tough day, but we stuck to the task well. Perhaps tomorrow will give respite.

The clouds scudding over Foul Bay, where a group of fishermen wrapped in oilskins and footy beanies toss flathead innards to squawking gulls, foreshadow disappointment. 'The prevailing wind this time of year is from the east, mate. Sorry to disappoint you,' says one when I press him for information. 'Now if you'd come through six months ago, it'd be a different story. You could have set your spinnaker and been *blown* to Adelaide.' I have learned to treat weather predictions from the public with a dose of salt, but this dire meteorological morsel cannot be ignored. Fishermen know their knots.

Day 153: Saturday 18 October, Walpole to Albany
Distance: 127km
Distance so far: 10 220km

The treetops surrounding our camp are motionless and I hope that the God of Wind is showing some uncustomary benevolence. The hope has the half-life of a gnat. Our campground is in the lee of a hill and as soon as Emma and I leave the protection the wind hits us like an uppercut. It is another hellish morning: the wind stronger and more relentless even than yesterday, trees bending at crazy angles and flags snapping out like Nazi salutes.

I am cycling east for the first time and *should* feel like I am heading home, but the concept provides no contentment. Hills appear in front like an army of warriors, and the wind blasts unabated. Just when I feel at the lowest of ebbs, I am attacked by a magpie.

Past the turnoff to Peaceful Bay—a wildly inaccurate name

for this wretched piece of coastline—we take refuge in a crumbling hall in the shadow of Mount Shadforth. A plaque is dedicated to immigrants from Devon and Cornwall who settled here in the early 1920s, while inside a cobwebbed piano minus a few keys provides ghostly memories of Saturday dance nights.

Sixty kilometres east of Walpole is Denmark, established to supply timber for the development of the goldfields. Today Denmark is Western Australia's answer to Byron Bay and starry-eyed, tie-dyed hippies mingle in the town's square, humming to tunes strummed on beaten-up guitars. Emma and I perform intricate stretching exercises against two wheelie bins, watched intently by a youth in a technicolour dream coat. 'Great outfits guys,' he says, eyeing our lurid yellow jerseys.

All afternoon we struggle miserably, heads down. I now understand why the Mistral wind in southern France can be a mitigating circumstance in murder trials. I am overcome with ennui and fatigue, the ride suddenly seeming both pointless and futile. The purpose of the ride becomes shrouded in frustration as hour after hour passes, and we make little impression on the distance to be covered. We are lucky to raise 15km an hour on the flat, and 20 downhill. Forty kilometres to go we take a back road through Torbay and Elleker, where a fire rages out of control on Grasmere Hill, fanned by the gale. The fire's billowing smoke adds to the impression that we are, quite simply, on the road to hell. Sydney seems an eternity away.

Eventually Albany's whitewashed buildings appear. A former whaling port, Albany is the oldest settlement in Western Australia, settled by the English only to prevent the French doing it first. We limp to a hotel where Dad and Jean wait with hot drinks, marvelling at our persistence. A shower is liquid gold and the prospect of a bed transfixing.

Two new crew members from Perth, Josephine Vanderweide and Jenny Rayment, have made last-minute decisions to join the ride. Jenny, 33, is an overworked landscape gardener looking for time to 'chill out', and Josephine, 52, is a member of the Over-55s Cycling Club (work that out) in search of adventure. The fifth member of this week's team, Melbourne journalist Charlie Happell, arrives by plane tomorrow.

It is Dad and Jean's last night—tomorrow they return to Perth—and we celebrate their successful, patient week. I wonder what memories they will take home with them. They are both experienced campaigners and not easily concerned, though the past week must have tested even their resolve. They both agree that one week was not enough. Dad, 77, still has the energy of a person half his age. It is hard to believe they will be married in less than five months.

Day 154: Sunday 19 October
Rest day: Albany

Jenny and Josephine learn about the wind the hard way: cycling west for one hour and taking three hours to return with tales of hurricanes and precipitous terrain. I could have told them all this and saved them the trouble. I keep an eye on the wind all afternoon but it is clear nothing will change in a hurry. The flag of our hotel is no longer sticking out at right angles, pointing to Margaret River, only because it has been ripped from the flagpole.

Day 155: Monday 20 October, Albany to Borden
Distance: 118km
Distance so far: 10 338km

Another Monday, more administration. At the local super-market, staff have sausages cooking and a TV news crew films us handing them to passers-by and collecting donations.

255

Unrehearsed, a lady hands me a letter and a donation with a hug. Her husband died of cancer last year. It is a poignant moment—making up for all Saturday's windy ordeal—and the news crew captures it all. 'Great stuff,' says the reporter breathlessly. 'Can you do it again for cutaways?'

North of Albany are the Porongorup National Park and brooding Stirling Ranges. I convince myself that cycling through the yawning gap between Mount Trio and Yungermere Peak is entering a cycling Shangri-la which will herald better conditions. The secondary road carries light traffic but the wind is anything but light, howling in from the right quarter like a steam train. In the region are Toolbrunup, Peringillup, Nookanellup, even Ewlyamartup and Gnowangerup. No excuses for feeling down.

From above, the road would resemble a staircase, changing at right angles between north and east. When cycling east the wind is in our faces. North means a side-wind. The road torments me, pain and relief oscillating. Behind, over green fields of wheat, the imposing ramparts of the Stirling Ranges change to red, purple, blue and grey as the sun lowers and the shadows lengthen.

There is no campground in Borden. Charlie and Josephine find us accommodation in the tiny clubhouse at the Borden golf course, which includes showers and a kitchen. The club has only 33 members; four Milnes, and three each from Bungey, Sounness and Muir families, according to the membership board. Surely the smallest club in Australia. The course is strangely empty on this beautiful evening. 'In summer the ground is like concrete, and unless you drive your ball dead straight it will eventually run into the rough,' says the club president John, who arrives to see that we have made ourselves at home. 'If you find the ball you'll more than likely break your arm playing the next shot. We find it easier to simply close the course until the rains come.' There have only been five winners of the Club Championship in the past 34 years, with A O'Meehan and GF Sounness taking the honours 28 times between them.

Day 156: Tuesday 21 October, Borden to Jerramungup
Distance: 75km
Distance so far: 10 413km

A leisurely start. We don't have to be in Jerramungup, only 75km away, until one-thirty. John's wife Kerry drops by and writes a cheque for $100. To be hospitable to people they've never met is one thing: to be so generous another. It does nothing but underline the generosity of people I have met in the past five months.

The wind, mercifully, has switched to the north, which means another cross-wind cycling east towards Esperance. The wheat and barley fields sway like rows of dancers and wheat silos loom on the horizon. On the outskirts of Ongerup a sign advertises the Ongerup Hotel, 'Warm Beer and Cold Service'.

Forty kids from the Jerramungup High School wait 10km short of the town, doing wheelies, wrestling and generally creating havoc. Two cops and a handful of teachers try in vain to keep order. 'Glad to see you,' says a teacher. 'They're going nuts here.' We cycle into Jerramungup and gather in the school hall to speak about the ride and cancer prevention. The usual curly questions: Can you get cancer eating burnt toast? Sucking pencils? Mowing the lawn?

The school has raised $1,000 which they hand over proudly. Small schools in small communities can achieve giant things. One kid raised $150 alone during a shearing afternoon. 'It helped that the kid's Dad owned the farm,' says one of the teachers. 'All the shearers wanted work again next year.'

We have been bidden to dinner by the local Lions Club at the Jerramungup Hotel, and Emma and Josephine do a quick whip around among the locals, collecting $150. An offer for Emma's bike seat is politely refused. The Lions President, Joe, snorts that the wind of the past few weeks is a 'mild breeze'. 'Last year we had a gale for six months. Now *that* was a wind. Strong enough to blow a dog off a chain.'

Day 157: Wednesday 22 October, Jerramungup to Ravensthorpe
Distance: 120km
Distance so far: 10 533km

The traffic thickens back on a main road. Another ride with a school at Ravensthorpe at midday, which means an early start. The wind comes from the east and we average a painfully slow 20km an hour. I wonder, not for the first time, what we have done to deserve such a wretched run of head-winds. There is no rational answer; all research suggested we would get our fair share, but a few tail-winds too.

I am doing my best to remain upbeat about the ride, but at this stage it is becoming increasingly difficult. I seem to spend most of my time thinking about the comforts of home: cafés, a barbeque, the movies. My afternoons have become tangled with administrative demands—phone calls, updating the website, and keeping sponsors informed of progress. Moving camp each day has become a chore. This head-wind is slowly chipping away at my energy, and I am not getting enough sleep. Thank God the team is pulling strongly together—there are no passengers, and plenty of laughs.

Wheat fields give way to wildflowers. The agricultural land is behind us now, although peeling signs point to enduring hopes. We pass *Burt's Block* and *Fred's Place*.

Emma, single-minded as ever, powers strongly all morning

and we do four hours without a break. A group of 100 kids waits 10km from Ravensthorpe. Despite my urgings to cycle slowly they set off like demons, four abreast, mostly no hands. I am terrified that one will come a cropper and we will get the blame. After 5km we are joined by the school's primary kids, many no bigger than their bikes. They speed off, legs whirring, bikes wobbling. One gets a puncture and fights to hold back the tears as his bike is put on the car.

Again, the talk with the kids is a delight. 'Country kids are wonderful,' their teacher tells me afterwards. 'In the country, kids are not afraid to say hi when they meet you in the street. In the city they cross the road to avoid you.' The school presents us with a cheque for $650.

Day 158: Thursday 23 October, Ravensthorpe to Munglinup
Distance: 81km
Distance so far: 10 614km

My prayers have been answered; the wind has turned to the north. Could even be a hint of westerly about it. We revel in the new conditions, fizzing along at 40 through bushland that begins to have a barren, mining feel to it. I feel especially happy for Emma who maintains that she has only experienced two favourable winds since Broome six weeks ago, though I think she has miscounted by one. Charlie sets out to complete the entire day and succeeds, his face resembling a beetroot by lunch-time.

Early afternoon, I am nearly tossed from my bike. The easterly, like Freddy Krueger, is back. Nightmare on the South Western Highway.

There is no campground at the unprepossessing town of Munglinup and an officious lady at the town's service station points to a local lay-by, ten metres off the highway, with a dirty toilet block and no showers. We park the caravan and make ourselves as comfortable as possible. The phone booth crawls with red-back spiders. Phone calls are short.

Day 159: Friday 24 October, Munglinup to Esperance
Distance: 120km
Distance so far: 10 734km

Another early start, another favourable wind. Charlie shot his bolt yesterday and opts to drive while Josephine hammers out the entire day. For a 52-year-old she is fit as a trout, with formidable resolve. Jen cycles like a solid middle-order batsman. Nothing flashy, just get the job done.

A six-hour day through barren, dreary scrub, which eventually opens up to green pasture. Forty kilometres short of Esperance the heavens open and the rain descends in sheets for the rest of the afternoon. We battle it swathed in wet-weather gear, keeping enough distance from the cyclist in front to avoid the spray. Charlie drives behind, reminding us how warm the car is. I yearn for a quiet sunny day, a bottle of beer and a good book.

Esperance was once a booming gateway port to the gold-fields and since World War II has been a tourist haven. People come to lie on the golden beaches, walk along its Norfolk Pine-lined promenade or sail around the nearby Recherche Archipelago. It was discovered that the only thing stopping the area from becoming a rich agricultural producer was the deficiency of certain trace elements in the soil. Since then it has become an important farming region. For us, with a rest day tomorrow, it is paradise—time for a shower and relaxed media interviews. Emma even gets her legs waxed.

David Lowe, BP executive, arrives by bus from Perth having volunteered to do the Nullarbor. Charlie and Jen take us to dinner on the eve of their departure. Each has been a tower of strength and has demonstrated positive outlooks on even the blackest days. We are guests at a quiz night put on by the Esperance Lions and Rotary clubs, and come last. Cycling kills brain cells.

Day 160: Saturday 25 October
Rest day: Esperance

Glorious rest.

Day 161: Sunday 26 October, Esperance to Salmon Gums
Distance: 109km
Distance so far: 10 843km

What have we done to deserve such torment? None of us, as far as I know, is evil, nor cruel; we help old ladies cross roads; we pay our credit card bills, mostly, on time. Why then does this head-wind follow us around like a bad penny? The wind, which whipped off the Southern Ocean from the south all yesterday, and which would have blasted us northwards up the Coolgardie–Esperance highway today, has transmogrified over-night into a northerly, and we are cycling north by north-west.

Four riders from the local cycling club accompany us for the first 25km. One of them, Darren, loses control on the road out of Esperance and hits the bitumen with a sickening thud. As a passing motorist administers first aid to a bloody gash in his head I think about the good fortune we have enjoyed in the past five months. This is the first such incident we have seen. Must maintain vigilance.

We press north, heads down, saying little, following a lonely railway track linking the coast with the goldfields at Norseman and Kalgoorlie. The countryside becomes increasingly arid as agriculture makes way for land I know well: the arid, salty expanses of the Australian interior. At Grass Patch, David swaps duties with Josephine, whose face is swollen with hay fever. David has bought a racing bike for the Nullarbor and is quickly into rhythm, his bike purring along like a contented cat. He is a natural cyclist, with good wheel spin and a motionless upper body. Emma and I struggle to keep up, feeling ungainly and elephantine on our lumbering touring bikes.

From the distance, looking like two jello-men oscillating in the heat, appear two Japanese cyclists. 'You go wrong way,' one says, with a smile as big as the Great Australian Bight, when we stop to trade information. They are from Nagoya and are, naturally, in good spirits with their tail-wind. In broken English they tell us of their three-week ride across the Nullarbor. I don't understand much, but one thing is undeniable: their tail-wind is no stranger to them. We cycle off in silence—2000km of a head-wind is a frightening proposition. 'If we have this bloody head-wind all the way across the Nullarbor, I'm never speaking to you again,' says Emma.

Mid-afternoon we reach Salmon Gums, a one-horse town midway between Esperance and Norseman, so named because of the ghostly pink eucalypts lining its streets. The campground is a gravel siding next to the railway, a sign next to a rusty tin nailed to a tree suggesting that $7 would be a reasonable contribution. We eat outside in the mild evening air and the sky looks like opal. The owner of the nearby hotel, a New Zealander, looks like she could collapse with boredom. 'I've been here for 18 months and I've had enough of this miserable place,' she says. Throughout the evening a handful of kids peer through the pub's grimy windows, giving the finger to anyone who bothers to look at them, then run off sniggering.

Day 162: Monday 27 October, Salmon Gums to Norseman
Distance: 98km
Distance so far: 10 941km

Josephine, who planned to cycle to Ceduna in South Australia, announces she will call it quits at Kalgoorlie—where a rest day is planned tomorrow—and return to Perth with Eric and June, who are meeting us for a weekend of fund-raising in Australia's most famous gold town. Josephine remains a conundrum and I know her little more than I did when she arrived ten days ago. That she made the decision to come on the ride with two days' notice points to a life of little structure. That she can decide not to come across the Nullarbor after vowing a day ago that wild horses would not prevent her, points to a lack of resolve, something hitherto unseen. She says she wants to do more cycling and less driving. I suggest that this is unfair, given that she joined the ride recently on a whim while others signed up months ago. Her decision, I feel, contravenes a point of honour which, I also feel, is ridiculous. So be it.

She cycles strongly this morning and then swaps with David, who bolts ahead on his racing bike with his efficient, minimalist technique. The country between Salmon Gums and Norseman, near the edge of Lake Dundas, is nothing but small eucalypts and wildflowers struggling for life in the salty earth. Beyond the lake is good-for-nothing country, claypans and salt lakes as far as the eye can see.

The wind relents and I feel better than I have for some time. Emma says she feels *worse* than she has for some time. Perhaps, I suggest to her, she is a better rider *into* a head-wind than without one at all. 'That's sort of like being good at being punched up,' she replies. 'Not the sort of thing you aspire to.'

At the Norseman High School I get a bad feeling as soon as we walk in the front gate. Sure enough, where other students have been interested in the ride, these kids saunter into the room and are a study in listlessness. They are sullen, uncommunicative and smart-arsed. Most study the carpet during my talk, as if some new form of life has developed there. It is a relief to get away but not before they, for some odd reason, feel the need to take our photo for the school magazine.

Two hours' drive north of Norseman is Kalgoorlie, a prosperous, bustling metropolis which still oozes the excitement you associate with Western Australia's most enduring gold town. Stately buildings line 'Kal's' main streets, which are wide enough to accommodate a turning camel train. Miners, clad in dusty workboots and blue singlets revealing heavily tattooed arms, troop up and down Hannan Street, hands full of ready cash.

'Well come on,' says Eric, who has driven out for the weekend, as soon as we pull in. 'I've organised for us to collect at seven caravan parks and eight pubs, starting in ten minutes.' He has his kilt on, lovingly cradling his bagpipes, and looks worryingly enthusiastic. We groan.

We collect $1,000 during the evening, accompanied by a member of the Kalgoorlie Lions, David, and his daughter Lisa. Lisa's husband was killed underground five years ago at the Mount Charlotte mine. She has opted to stay on in the city. 'Kal's a little rough, but it's a good place,' she says as we follow the Maestro to another pub.

Kalgoorlie is not for the prudish. Harley Davidsons rumble their way down Hay Street, where prostitutes display their wares from corrugated iron bedrooms. Two-up is still played and central to the city's drinking culture are the famous skimpys, scantily clad female bar staff who give short strip shows for a couple of bucks. The law tried to ban the shows several years ago, but in vain. The skimpys, far from hindering our fund-raising cause, help it. 'I'll make more money than you,' says one in the Exchange Hotel, before grabbing a bucket and prodding the locals for donations. She's right; never argue with a professional. Eric, in his kilt, has had some tough assignments in recent weeks, Carnarvon springs to mind, but none have been more testing than Kalgoorlie's pubs. In some he is greeted with shouts of, 'Take off ya' skirt, sheila.'

'How are you coping with the heckling?' I ask him as we traipse along the footpath towards yet another watering hole. 'You keep forgetting I come from Fife,' he says, his back straightening noticeably, 'and men from Fife always win. A Fife man is the only person in the world who can enter a revolving door behind you and come out in front.'

Day 163: Tuesday 28 October
Rest day: Kalgoorlie

Gold was discovered in Kalgoorlie by three prospectors— Paddy Hannan, Tom Flanagan and Dan Shea—in 1893. Since then the area has been continually mined, producing 47 million ounces of gold from 200 million tonnes of ore. This represents 20 per cent of Australian gold production and one per cent of the world's.

The Superpit, a vast hole in the ground jointly owned by Normandy Mining and Homestake Gold, employs 1000 people. Fifty years ago it was a sea of headframes and wooden buildings owned by companies with romantic names like Golden Horseshoe Estates and Great Boulder Perseverance. The Superpit has swallowed the lot, and now covers three-and-a-half square kilometres. It will probably grow more: Kalgoorlie Consolidated Gold Mines holds 260 tenements, covering 22 000 hectares in the Kalgoorlie–Boulder area. Nothing stands in the way of a gold mine.

Day 164: Wednesday 29 October, Norseman to *Fraser Range* station
Distance: 85km
Distance so far: 11 026km

The distance between Perth and Adelaide, the best part of 3000km, is not much less than the distance between San Francisco and New York. As we stand beneath the road sign at the western reaches of the Eyre Highway, looking east towards the South Australian border, it is difficult to ignore the challenge ahead. We are, of course, not in Perth, but several hundred kilometres inland. 'More like San Francisco to Chicago,' says David, helpfully.

With Josephine gone we are a team of three setting out on one of the most isolated roads in the world, crossing a part of Australia known as The Paddock by the truckies who do it often. The road is home to outcasts and people on the run, or those simply heading west, or east, chasing a new beginning. The highway code and common decency are the only laws out here, and there's next to no-one to uphold either. The only cops between here and Ceduna, 1200km away, are at Eucla, roughly halfway.

Travelling the Eyre Highway today is still considered a major achievement for Australian motorists, who buy bumper stickers and T-shirts to mark the occasion. Although cars still break down on the highway, often requiring days to repair, travelling is certainly easier than it used to be. Large potholes are a thing of the past and no longer do people die of thirst out here. The distance, however, hasn't got any shorter.

Hopefully, we are prepared, topping up the caravan's gas bottle and buying another 50-litre water bottle, taking reserves to more than 200 litres. 'Hope you've got your brollies,' says the attendant at the Norseman service station. 'Storms expected this arvo.' Already clouds are muscling up in the west and electricity fizzes in the air. The wind is favourable and Emma and I yell like psychotics as we reach speeds of 50km an hour at the start of the Eyre Highway. My Kingdom for more of this.

Soon the road deteriorates to a pock-marked ribbon, lined by straggly eucalypts, but I couldn't care less about the surface, so long as we have this tail-wind. Emma and I cover the 85km in less than two-and-a-half hours, joined by David for the latter third, and arrive breathless and flushed at the camp-site near *Fraser Range* station, overlooking a lake amid ghostly gums. The owners of the only other caravan, a couple from the Gold Coast, insist on hooking our caravan up to their generator to provide electricity. 'Can't have you eating by gaslight,' he says.

The wind belts all night and both Emma and I choose the caravan over our swags for the first time in weeks. It is a good choice—at midnight the heavens open. I feel happy being back in isolation, amid the elements. All those people were beginning to get to me.

Day 165: Thursday 30 October, *Fraser Range* station to
Balladonia Roadhouse
Distance: 111km
Distance so far: 11 137km

Australian exploration in the mid-to-late 1800s produced some tough characters. Both John McDouall Stuart and the Burke and Wills team endured months of purgatory in their quests for the first south–north crossing, and no-one knows what Ludwig Leichhardt suffered after leaving Roma in 1848, bound for the Indian Ocean on the other side of the continent: he was never heard of again. Not that Leichhardt was new to the exploration game; in 1844–45 he walked 5000km from Brisbane to Port Essington, near Darwin.

In 1844, Charles Sturt left Adelaide searching for the inland sea. Not far from Cooper Creek, in the far north-east of South Australia where the temperatures regularly hit 40 degrees, he wrote of the hardships of his chosen profession:

The lead dropped out of our pencils, our signal rockets were entirely spoiled; our hair, as well as the wool on the sheep ceased to grow, and our nails had become as brittle as glass.

No list of brave and resilient explorers would be complete without the name of Edward John Eyre, the Yorkshireman who arrived in Australia in 1833 and who learned the ways of the inland as an overlander, driving stock from Sydney to Adelaide. In June, 1840 he set out to walk around the cliffs and the sandy wastelands of the Great Australian Bight, from Fowlers Bay, near today's Ceduna, South Australia, to Albany, a 2000km trek that took him not far from where we are today. His quest took five months, and included the death of his companion, John Baxter.

At one stage Eyre wrote of his horses:

It was, indeed, a fearful and heart-rending scene to behold the noble animals which had served us so long and so faithfully, suffering the extremity of thirst and hunger, without having it in our power to relieve them. Five days of misery had passed over their heads since the last water had been left, and one hundred and twelve miles of country had been traversed without the possibility of procuring food for them, other than the dry and sapless remains of last year's grass, and this but rarely to be met with. No rains had fallen to refresh them, and they were reduced to a most pitiable condition, still they travelled onwards with a spirit and endurance truly surprising. Whenever we halted, they followed us about like dogs wherever we went, appearing to look to us only for aid, and exhibiting that confidence in us which I trust we all reposed in the Almighty.

It took another 37 years before a telegraph line was laid across the Nullarbor, and later a dusty track followed the same route. Towards the end of the nineteenth century, after gold was discovered at Coolgardie in 1892, miners walked the track from the eastern states, often wheeling barrows of camping and mining equipment from Fowlers Bay to the goldfields, a distance of more than 1500km.

The first bicycle crossing was made in 1896 and the first car driven across in 1912. In the next 12 years only three more cars made the crossing. In the 1960s, after World War II had inspired the Government to upgrade the road, about 30 vehicles a day completed it, and when the road was totally sealed in 1976 the Eyre Highway was the obvious name.

Yesterday's tail-wind has changed to a north-easterly, a side-wind. I am confused by this because the temperature has dropped and my research says that hot air comes from the north, cold from the west. Although David has agreed to drive the car much of the way across the Nullarbor he will cycle today. We have agreed, on such occasions, to take turns hitching back to collect the car. The next driver meets us at the Nullarbor Roadhouse in a week.

The road from *Fraser Range* is surprisingly hilly and I cycle standing up—'out of the saddle' cycling aficionados would say—for much of the morning. This method not only gives good power and provides relief for my legs but, more importantly, it gives my long-suffering arse a rest. I am pleasantly surprised by how well the rear end has reacted to the workload. Generally it is delicate at the start of each day, but toughens as the morning wears on. Aside from the painful dose of jock-itch around Darwin—not technically the bottom and which cleared up before reaching Western Australia—it has had a dream run. David has whinged about *his* bum since he arrived, and I can only conclude that his bike seat, thin and angular, is built for speed not comfort. Then again, my arse might simply be tougher.

After 40km the wind shifts to the east, a head-wind, and the rain starts. We shelter under a tree and Emma tells David of our night in the open two weeks ago. A little rain seems nothing now. 'It's been raining, cats, dogs and the rest of the vet clinic, at Eucla,' says a passing motorist. If the easterly continues, we may get rain tomorrow.

The Balladonia Roadhouse, sitting at the end of a dusty track leading south to Cape Arid National Park on the coast, is nothing but a few sheds with not a blade of grass to be seen. Out the back is a dusty airstrip and an equally dusty ultra-light plane sitting disconsolately in a rusty hangar. Twenty wrecked cars line the airstrip like the aftermath of a smash-up derby. A fenceless tennis court sits alongside the main building—a few painted lines, and weeds pushing up through the cracked asphalt. I get a lift back to collect the car with a couple driving west for a niece's christening. 'Jeez, quite a road, eh?' says Julian, the driver, excitedly. His wife looks tired and turns to me. 'He's done nothing but rave about the road ever since we left Ceduna. Anyone'd think we were driving through the Taj Mahal. I think it's boring as batshit.' Julian continues to shake his head in wonder.

It might be pouring at Eucla but a *lack* of water could be more of a problem for us in these dusty parts. 'Absolutely No Water To Be Provided To Motorists', says a sign at the road-house. Emma convinces the owner that we deserve special dispensation because, although we have a car, we are not, strictly speaking, motorists. This perverse logic has the desired results—we are allowed to sneak around the back and fill the water containers—but it remains to be seen whether other roadhouse owners will be so benevolent.

Day 166: Friday 31 October, Balladonia Roadhouse to Baxter Cliffs
Distance: 116km
Distance so far: 11 253km

The Eyre Highway is mesmerically straight, mesmerically the
same as yesterday. Truckies rumble past driving rigs with names
like 'Mongrel', 'The Carringbush' and 'Cunning Stunt'. On
this still day they come through every five minutes, but on
windy days they drive one behind the other, as close as they
can, to reduce wind resistance.

What remains of *Balladonia* station appears after 40km,
sitting among the stringy saltbush, windows broken and walls
crumbling. The corrugated iron walls are peeling away and
25-year-old copies of the Melbourne *Truth*, discussing Dolly
Parton's knockers and Geoff Raymond's defection from
Channel Ten, are scattered throughout the rooms. I hope the
owners once had better days, dinner parties on the generous
verandah to celebrate a profitable wool clip, but it is hard to
imagine it. Today the house is home only to crows and spiders.

The longest, straightest stretch of road in Australia, 147km
ending in Caiguna, is described in the guidebook as 'the loneliest stretch of road across the Nullarbor'. A black blob on the
horizon becomes an overturned road train, the remnants of its
load, bottles of beer, scattered far and wide. A clean-up of sorts
has been attempted and a large pyramid of glass sits on the side
of the road. There is no-one about, and I wonder whether the
driver was OK. We pick our way gingerly through the shards.

From one obstacle to another, but this one is alive. Locusts
swarm in from the south, smashing into our faces as we cycle,
heads down. They splatter against our bikes and find their way
into our shirts and helmets and behind my glasses. Breaking
through them into the clear air is like emerging from a London
pea-souper. We call it a day 30km inland from Baxter Cliffs.

David gets a lift back to collect the car while Emma snoozes on the side of the road, curled up on a concrete picnic table like a question mark.

Tonight is the anniversary of Mum's death and I speak by satellite phone to Dad and my sisters. There could not be a lonelier place at such a time, but memories of a year ago renew my desire to finish the ride and hand over a sizeable cheque for cancer research. I feel contentment here at this dusty lay-by in the wilderness, as well as sadness. An eerie wind moans through the campsite. I walk after dinner, alone under a canopy of stars, which seem especially bright.

Day 167: Saturday 1 November, Baxter Cliffs to Caiguna Roadhouse
Distance: 68km
Distance so far: 11 321km

The road continues straight as a pool cue, the side of it littered with broken glass, plastic bags and rusted Coke cans. The wind is negligible. We reach Caiguna, a roadhouse undergoing badly needed repairs, mid-morning and debate briefly whether to press on while the wind is low. If the car was with us it would be an easier decision, but it remains at Baxter Cliffs and we decide to stick to the plan, stay here tonight and do 160km tomorrow. I spend the afternoon consumed with guilt as the wind comes from the west, then realise with horror at dusk that it has switched to the south-east.

At the roadhouse I meet Neil, a fast-talking Melburnian the size of a water tank, who is driving a warning vehicle for a trucking company. He and his mate, Vern, larger still, are delivering a tray for a tip truck to the goldfields and have stopped for refreshments: four packs of chips, three cans of Coke and a collection of chocolate bars. Neil has driven 70 000km since the start of July and has done The Paddock 'hundreds' of times.

'I know this bloody road better than I know me own mother,' he says, belting his truck's tyres with a piece of four-by-two to check for punctures. 'It's a bastard of a bit of bitumen but at least it's safe. It's certainly miles better than the Hume Highway which is full of pill-popping lunatic truckies.'

It is Emma's turn to collect the car. 'Would you mind giving me a lift to our car 70km down the road?' she asks.

'Be my pleasure darlin'. It's me twenty-second anniversary after all,' Neil chuckles, stomach wobbling.

The Caiguna Roadhouse is officially on Central West Time, three-quarters of an hour earlier than Perth time but still not on South Australian time. The owner tells us this betwixt-and-between time zone is 'all bullshit' and that she feels like a 'eunuch', aligned with neither Adelaide nor Perth. Inside the roadhouse are stickers saying, 'I've Been To Caiguna—Hub of the Universe' and 'Caiguna—Where The Fuck's That?' A makeshift cricket bat sits above the door next to a plaque: 'Caiguna versus Cocklebiddy Truckdrivers' Cricket Match. Cyclone Bobby Road Block. March '95. Won by Caiguna.'

Nearby, midway between here and the cliffs of the Southern Ocean, is a memorial to Eyre's white companion, John Baxter, killed on 29 April 1841 by two Aboriginal people, Joey and Yarry, from Eyre's party. The site is described as the loneliest grave on earth. Picture Eyre's misery as he discovered his companion's body during the night, then waited for daybreak on the edge of the cliffs. He wrote in his journal:

Suffering and distress had well nigh overwhelmed me, and life hardly seemed worth the effort to prolong it. Ages can never efface the horrors of this single night . . .

Australian writer Geoffrey Dutton captured the despair in his book *The Hero as Murderer.*

By eight o'clock they were ready to go, and there was nothing they could do but leave poor Baxter's body wrapped in a blanket, for it was impossible to dig a grave in the sheets of rock. The desolation of that scene, and the loneliness of the shrouded corpse left a few miles inland from the sheer cliffs of the Southern Ocean with twelve hundred unknown miles to the north, haunted Eyre for the rest of his life. The two living men walked silently westward, Wylie leading a horse and Eyre driving the rest after him, still more than five hundred walking miles from King George's Sound.

Walking stiffly across the Caiguna campground is 50-year-old cyclist David Sharpe, from Byron Bay in New South Wales. He has legs like chopsticks, a permanent smile, and is covered in bloodied bandages. Although it is 30 degrees he wears two jumpers. David tells us he has diabetes and takes drugs each day. 'I'm blind as a bat, and often I can't tell the difference between the road and the gravel. Cycling, for me, is very exciting,' he says.

His wounds are from a fall two days ago, not from his bike but when he was *running*. 'I forgot to take my insulin that day and began to hallucinate,' he says. 'I imagined I was in Saudi Arabia, running away from the Arabs. I really *was* running and I tripped over and gashed my face and knee on a rock. Luckily I was able to get back to camp for my insulin. If I had got lost I would have died.'

Diabetes and cycling are a hazardous mix. 'The symptoms for diabetes are poor visibility, sweating and loss of balance,' David says. 'My visibility is buggered anyway, I tend to sweat a lot when I ride, and I generally wobble around the road like a drunk at the best of times. I'm never quite sure whether I'm suffering from diabetes, or just generally incompetent.' His wounds are due for re-dressing and we offer him the contents of our medical kit.

David carries his gear in six panniers and has been hampered on the Nullarbor by extreme weather conditions. 'One day it was 36 degrees and the next it hailed on me. It was most confusing,' he says. During dinner we get a glimpse of a varied life. David is divorced with two children, and once drank four litres of wine at a single sitting. Australia and David, I realise, are good partners: he has decided to turn his back on society and Australia has the space to allow him to do it.

The conversation, of course, switches to wind. Because we are travelling in opposite directions we cannot both have a tail-wind. 'Hope you have the head-wind, David,' says Emma.

'We shall see tomorrow, Emma, shan't we,' he chuckles, stumbling into the gloom.

Day 168: Sunday 2 November, Caiguna Roadhouse to
Madura Roadhouse
Distance: 159km
Distance so far: 11 480km

David appears at six-thirty, poking his tongue out at us through the caravan door. *He* has the tail-wind and I hear him laughing like a jackass as he wheels his bike across the gravel. The caravan is buffeted by the wind as we pack up, and the feeling of foreboding is palpable, compounded by the fact that it is a Sunday, supposedly a day of rest. *Our* David has decided not to cycle today on account of earache and will drive the car. Although I feel for him there is no doubt that it will make things easier for us, especially me, whose turn it is to hitchhike next to collect the car.

We make good time, averaging 26km an hour into the wind, and reach Cocklebiddy, another windswept roadhouse near the remains of an Aboriginal mission, renowned for being the site of the world's deepest cave dive, in 1983. I am surprised by how well I am coping with today's wind—it is as if I have been given extra strength with such a long distance to cover.

The wind continues all afternoon and switches to a sou-easter. I feel my energy waning and fortify myself with memories of support received. If this were just a ride for no other reason I'm convinced I would pack today in. I derive strength and steel from the enthusiasm and keenness of others. The fact that so many people have supported this ride is an intangible source of strength to me. Simply, there is no way I *could* stop.

East of Cocklebiddy, the Hampton Tableland, once the bottom of an ocean, stretches away in an endless flatness. Nothing to show but scrub, rocks and salty unproductive soil. Eagles circle lazily overhead and a black snake slithers across the road ahead of me. The area has no redeeming features, although large piles of rocks off the road point to large plans and bold visions years ago. Growing something out here would require agricultural alchemy. Two stations in the region now lie abandoned, *Burnabbie* and *Noonaera*, and I see nothing for hours except a cattle grid, a couple of mangy fences, an overturned water tank and a telecommunications tower. The Eyre Highway is Australia's boulevard of broken dreams.

There are two hills on the Nullarbor, both of them dropping from the Hampton Tableland to the Roe Plains on the Great Australian Bight. We reach the first of these, Madura Pass, after 150km, with neither the strength nor the mood to admire the view. The scene ahead is one of desolation, which I observe through a shifting, shimmering haze, probably from surf breaking on the cliffs near Scorpion Bight. The Southern Ocean must be out there somewhere but I can see nothing through the mist, and am too tired to care. By the time we reach the Madura Roadhouse I have not a skerrick of energy left, and spend the rest of the day sitting around in the heat, swishing at flies.

Day 169: Monday 3 November, Madura Roadhouse to
Mundrabilla Roadhouse
Distance: 117km
Distance so far: 11 597km

The treacherous wind howls in from the east, mean as a dingo trap. David, still having trouble with his ears, drives to Eucla, 200km away, to track down the only nurse on the Nullarbor. He looks relieved to be in the car as Emma and I mount our bikes with heavy hearts. Nothing but saltbush and wretched, wizened trees. The road tracks the foot of the Hampton Table-land cliffs which act like a wind tunnel, the gusts tearing away at us, probing for vulnerability.

Peter Matthiessen, author of *The Snow Leopard*, an account of a journey in Nepal, perhaps has an explanation. He writes:

Tibetans says that obstacles in a hard journey, such as hail stones, wind, and unrelenting rains, are the work of demons, anxious to test the sincerity of pilgrims and eliminate the faint hearted among them.

Who could doubt our sincerity? What could I offer to make this infidel relent? My worldly possessions? The promise of my first-born? It already has my soul.

I dream of a Walkman, headphones and music. Although I have not categorically stated I would never use one, doing without has become almost a matter of principle, the implication being that relying on music to pass the time would somehow detract from the Australian experience, and demonstrate a character weakness. I would love one now. A hundred metres off the road is *Mundrabilla* station, nothing more than a house and a few sheds looking insignificant in the wasteland. It looks like someone lives there. How—why—would anyone choose to live in this wretched place?

We cover a meagre 80km in five hours. My energy is sapped and I continually seek refuge in the stash of food secreted in the back of my shirt—bananas, biscuits, sultanas, nuts. The wind is like a scheming older brother: pretending to relent then returning worse than ever. Emma screams at it, while I pretend it is a challenge—doesn't require much imagination—to be overcome. With still 30km to cycle a familiar sight appears on the horizon. 'The wind was so bad that I thought I'd better come back and see how you were going,' says David from the car, having received a jab for his earache from the Eucla nurse. We scoff sandwiches, fruit and chocolate bars, sheltering from the wind like Kalahari nomads, our teeth grinding on sand that blows around us in eddies.

Another three hours on the bikes, rarely reaching more than 12km an hour. I lick my lips in search of moisture, but taste only salt. We reach the nondescript Mundrabilla Roadhouse and collapse on the road, too tired even to stretch. The building is closed and lifeless, the wind moaning through the verandah struts, our door knocks echoing soullessly. The only signs of life are an officious goat and a camel, eyes half closed in the wind regarding us gloomily. Carmel the Camel has been at Mundrabilla for ten years, says the sign, having been rescued from beside her mother's decaying body on the east–west railway. Both animals look like they would prefer to be elsewhere, and who could blame them?

One other caravan occupies the bleak, gravel campground. Max and Wilma, a couple from Melbourne, have been on the road for 11 months and are presently enduring every traveller's nightmare, stuck here while their car is repaired in Kalgoorlie. 'The car's due back shortly,' says Max confidently. 'We've been doing a bit of cycling ourselves, though we've seen pretty much everything there is to see around here, and reading, though we've both read everything twice.' They take our proffered books with wide-eyed thanks. Wilma puts on a brave face about their predicament. 'I always try to see the bright side of things,' she says. I can see they are beyond the bright side, and slowly going bonkers.

Low Point on the Southern Ocean is 22km from the roadhouse along a twisting, potholed track. Among the sand dunes is a motley collection of cars and rusting caravans used by crayfishermen during summer. The beach is covered with drying seaweed. A wizened man in oversized clothes more hole than cloth drives up in a jalopy. That the car runs at all borders on the miraculous: its doors swing through 180 degrees and the chassis is held together with string and wire. The tray holds a collection of rusty tools, while a collection of cigarette butts on the dashboard threatens to obscure the view. The whole thing smells of fish.

Don, born in Adelaide and 'closer to 75 than 70', used to be a rabbit shooter on the Nullarbor. 'It was a good-enough life,' he says, hacking and gobbing on the sand. 'Used to pick up 80 cents a skin, but myxo and that calici-thing ripped the guts out of the business. Perhaps the rabbits will beat them both,' he says hopefully. 'They're tough little buggers.' Until then Don is the 'overseer' at Low Point, keeping an eye out for larcenous ne'er-do-wells until the crayfishermen return for the summer.

Day 170: Tuesday 4 November, Mundrabilla Roadhouse to Eucla
Distance: 68km
Distance so far: 11 665km

Plans to get away early to beat the wind are stymied—by six-thirty the caravan is already in danger of being blown back to Norseman. David's antibiotics have not yet kicked in and again

he opts to drive the car while Emma and I set off with resignation under a grey sky thick with foreboding. We are both
prickly and uncommunicative. I cannot exorcise a pleasant
though destructive vision: sitting at home on a green lawn,
sipping a beer on a balmy spring day, torn between spending
the afternoon in a hammock or at the beach.

The road could well be yesterday's as we inch along the
bottom of the escarpment, nothing to do but turn the pedals
and will the hours to pass. I think of my weeks organising the
ride, itching to get away from the city and the frustrations of
chasing sponsors. Heaven was to be on a bike in the Australian
wilderness. Today I have the opposite feeling. I would give
much to sit in an airconditioned office, dressed in clean clothes
instead of this filthy lycra. I have no doubt that my mind is
tougher than it was 170 days ago, but nothing has prepared me
for this wind. I calculate that I have pedalled two million
revolutions so far, with one million to go. I count up to two
thousand. I'm going nuts.

I look down at my speedo: 11km an hour. 'I reckon I can
run faster than this,' I gasp to Emma. I dismount and run alongside her, wheeling Quasimodo, for ten minutes. The weather
pattern seems gridlocked and we are caught in the middle. 'It's
Melbourne Cup Day today,' Emma moans. 'My friends will be
dressed up at Flemington, drinking champagne. And here am
I on this bloody ride.'

Pulsating white blobs hover on the eastern horizon. We are
mystified until they become giant sand dunes. The Eyre
Highway climbs the Eucla Pass to the township of Eucla, sitting
on the edge of the Hampton escarpment watching over the
Roe Plains like a guard dog. Emma and I trudge up the hill,
dispirited and upset, and collapse on the ground outside the
roadhouse underneath a concrete replica of a sperm whale
sporting an idiotic grin.

A man sits in the shade nearby, beard protecting a sunburnt face, his khaki shirt sporting a Bureau of Meteorology badge. From the moment I see him I know he will be the harbinger of bad tidings. He spends several seconds examining us. 'You're riding the wrong way,' he says, angling for a laugh. Doesn't get one.

'Is this wind going to let up?' I ask.

'Not for a couple of weeks, I'd say,' he chuckles, then launches into an explanation, which seems to be the way of weathermen. 'You see, at this time of year the high pressure systems centre themselves down in the bight, south of here. Because they are anti-cyclones the wind blows anti-clockwise, which means you get easterlies coming through. When it gets hotter, the high pressure systems move up to the middle of the country, north of here, and the anti-clockwise air-flow causes westerlies. Depends on the seasons you see. Now if you were cycling in the summer ...' Emma rolls her eyes and trudges off to buy a Coke.

Eucla is the largest town on the Nullarbor—the *only* town on the Nullarbor—populated largely by Government people: police and people from the weather bureau. I have no idea what they do all day. In the old days a telegraph line used to run along the coast until it was moved inland a hundred or so kilometres. Between the township and the sea, down on the flats, lie the ruins of the old telegraph station, now blown over with sand. High on the escarpment next to our campground is a cross, illuminated at night, dedicated to all journeying the Eyre Highway. A little dose of help from above wouldn't go astray right now.

CHAPTER NINE

South Australia *In Oppy's Tyretracks*

Who in the name of wonder are you?
I am King, Sir.

Conversation between member of rescue party, EJ Welch,
and John King, sole survivor of the Burke and Wills party,
Cooper Creek, 15 September 1861

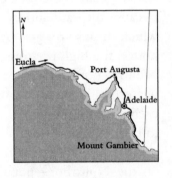

Day 171: Wednesday 5 November,
Eucla to Nullarbor Roadhouse
Distance: 205km
Distance so far: 11 870km

Throughout the night the wind is driven by demons—insistent, chaotic and brutal. The caravan rocks and things outside knock against its walls. Bins are blown over and bounced along the rocks, their contents ripped over the escarpment. We wake at four o'clock and decide it is pointless to start cycling, as planned. Why deprive ourselves of sleep if nothing can be gained from it?

At six-thirty we are confounded, and ecstatic. The wind is from the north, not the east. We reach speeds of 25km an hour cycling to Border Village, heads high and laughing. So must death-row prisoners feel when pardoned.

Border Village marks the end of Western Australia and the beginning of South Australia, or vice versa. In 1979, NASA's

Skylab hit the ground near here, putting the place on the map. Today a giant kitsch kangaroo toasts passers-by with a Coke can, while a sign perpetuates the space-traveller myth: 'Beware UFOs Next 111 Kilometres'. Intergalactic abductions are definitely rarer in Australia than, say, the USA, which is why many Australians sat up and listened ten years ago when a respectable east coast family claimed a UFO shunted their car off the road hereabouts. I cross the border with sadness. It is hard to reconcile the fact that 70 days have gone since I arrived in Kununurra. The Western Australians have been good to us and I calculate that we raised the best part of $20,000 here, mainly due to the Maestro. The total is now $210,000.

If Western Australia is big, then South Australia is dry. Although its capital, Adelaide, is called the City of Churches and most represents the country's ties with England, South Australia is the driest state in the world's driest continent. Two-thirds of it is near-desert and 83 per cent of it receives an annual rainfall of less than an inch. No arguments here: I see nothing but dusty plains and insubstantial trees reaching weakly to the sky, pleading for water.

East of Border Village I catch my first glimpse of the cliffs that run unbroken for 200km around the top of the Great Australian Bight. We gaze out over the sparkling expanse of the bight, a celebration of Australian wilderness—waves rumble on the cliffs 90 metres below, gulls wheel and turn on the updraught, and I can see the curve of the earth on the horizon. Thirty dolphins swim below, wending their way unhurriedly along the coast, jumping playfully through the waves. We watch in silence as they round the point and disappear.

One of the traditional banes of the Nullarbor, flies, have been kind so far but today they track our every move like miniature fighter squadrons. They buzz around our heads, get stuck between my face and sunglasses and sit on our clothes like resolute squatters. Our shirts might as well be made of flypaper. A stop for lunch and stretching is hurriedly curtailed as they drive us to distraction. We cover another 105km in the afternoon, past the road leading to the tiny township of Cook on the east–west railway line.

Past the famous signs marking the beginning of the Nullarbor Plain proper—a camel, a wombat and a kangaroo—we reach the Nullarbor Roadhouse as dusk falls, turning the sky into a palette of yellows and pinks. David, who drove the car, has been there several hours. It has been a hard and pleasing day. More than 200km is a formidable distance—second only to the 220km I cycled towards Tennant Creek—and, in a perverse way, I even enjoyed the pain of it. As Emma and I stretch on an old paling fence outside the roadhouse, speaking of flies and dolphins and airily tossing congratulations towards each other, a man approaches. 'Heard you were in the area a couple of days ago,' he says. 'You're heading to Sydney? How long will it take you to cycle there from Perth?'

I think for a bit, taking into account the sortie through Albany and Esperance. 'About six weeks.'

'You're slackin' a bit aren't ya? In the 1930s Oppy did it in 13 days on dirt roads. He would have covered the best part of 400 clicks with a wind like today's. You guys ought to be ashamed of yourselves.' He tramps back to his caravan, hitching up his shorts.

You can't cycle the Nullarbor without hearing about Sir Hubert Opperman, the cycling endurance machine born in Rochester, Victoria, and known affectionately around the world as Oppy. Pre-war he was as revered an Australian as any, at a time when cyclists rated alongside cricketers, runners and swimmers as the nation's idols. In 1931 he won the world's longest non-stop road race, the 730-mile Paris–Brest–Paris event, and the following year cycled 815 miles in 24 hours, breaking the world record by 44 miles. In 1937 he cycled from Perth to Sydney in 13 days, ten hours and 11 minutes, cheered on by thousands. I am mystified at this achievement: I calculate it would take us the best part of 20 days of today's distance to cover the route. By the time we arrived in Sydney, Oppy—and let's not forget he was on dirt roads—would have had his feet up for more than a week.

Oppy wrote in his book *Pedals, Politics & People*:

In 1937 the west-east road retained an aura of mystery and apprehension from the virtually unknown. Stories were common of rough, sandy roads marked only by dingo trappers and telegraph linesmen, aimlessly changing direction through vast deserted regions and of lost travellers snipping the overland wires in a last despairing bid for survival.

In my opinion ... the most magnificent achievement was that of Francis Birtles who pedalled his lonely way from Fremantle to Sydney in the early 1900s. He was unaccompanied by cyclists or vehicles. He was a wire and whipcord man ... carried his own water in a metal container, food, spare tyres and a rifle for protection ... Despite the excessive weight and not a smear of asphalt from Fremantle to Sydney, he averaged an incredible 100 miles a day.

Day 172: Thursday 6 November, Nullarbor Roadhouse to Yalata Roadhouse
Distance: 92km
Distance so far: 11 962km

Despite being shamed by Oppy's efforts half a century ago, we vote unanimously for a day's rest. Last night my second cousin, Richard Allen—who I last saw in Rockhampton three months ago—arrived in a bus from Adelaide which pulled in, belching fumes, air brakes sighing, at ten o'clock. He was, needless to say, the only one to get off. The bus company told him he was the first person who had *ever* bought a one-way ticket to the Nullarbor Roadhouse.

He has brought four boxes of fruit and vegetables and we gorge ourselves on peaches, pears and oranges. This is largely through want—I feel like we have single-handedly propped up the Heinz canning company in recent weeks—and partly through necessity: there is a fruit-fly zone near Ceduna, only four days away, and we cannot take fresh food beyond it.

Mid-morning David speaks.

'It's a tail-wind.'

Silence.

'So what?' says Emma, her head buried in a dog-eared copy of *New Idea*.

'Well, shouldn't we be cycling?'

'But it's a *rest* day, and we don't cycle on rest days. Can't we just sit here? We came so far yesterday,' Emma pleads.

The Eucla weatherman's prognostication from hell rings in my ears. A simple rule with long-distance cycling: always take advantage of a tail-wind. It is a form of insurance. If someone told you that you would *not* experience a large amount of pain tomorrow if you agreed to a small amount of pain today, how would you respond? We pack up and gingerly mount our bikes while Richard takes the wheel of the car. My arse feels like someone has taken a whip to it for several hours.

The Nullarbor Plain, a bastardisation of the Latin for 'No Trees', is one of the great fallacies of outback Australia. Although everyone refers to it as the space between Norseman and Port Augusta, 1700km, the vast majority of the Nullarbor is well to the north of the Eyre Highway, up near the railway line. Only a small finger reaches to the coast and we cross it in an instant, making a mockery of its fearsome reputation.

Past White Wells Cave is a road leading to the most northerly point of the Great Australian Bight. The gate across the road is bolted fast. We are later told that the road is only open during the whale-watching season, when Southern Right whales migrate across the waters of the bight, and is locked at other times to prevent vandalism. Quite how you vandalise cliffs is beyond me.

To the east of the head of the bight, on the western edge of the Yalata Aboriginal Reserve, the road swings noticeably to the south-east and the wind, which has helped for 60km, begins to work against us. Despite this, I am convinced we made the right decision to cycle. The terrain changes, from billiard-table plains to hills, and the trees seem somehow stronger and more upright. We have had a fortnight of nothing but flatness.

Several road trains line up for fuel at the Yalata Roadhouse, which is owned by the Nyangatja, Yalatanya, Nganampa and Manta Aboriginal tribes. We camp out the back, behind a permanent caravan housing a fisherman and his family, and alongside another camel, a baby, which munches on saltbush in a pitifully small enclosure, flashing its long eyelashes. 'Can we take it home?' says Emma.

'If you're willing to dink it.'

Dave manages the roadhouse for the community, which numbers around 200. 'That's just a rough guide,' he says. 'Sometimes numbers get as high as 2000. The Aboriginals here lead very nomadic lives. Friends and relatives often come here and can stay for weeks at a time.'

Max and Wilma arrive unexpectedly having been reunited happily with their car, and they join us for dinner, which consists largely of fruit and vegetables. 'Cripes,' says Max, holding an apple up reverently like it was the Dead Sea Scrolls. 'I haven't seen one of *these* for weeks.'

Day 173: Friday 7 November
Rest day: Yalata Roadhouse

It rains intermittently all morning, huge droplets spattering into the roadhouse dust, converting it to a quagmire. The camel stands in the rain, soaked and bleating plaintively, and we spend the morning huddled in the caravan. If yesterday was a good day to be on the bikes, today is not.

The Aboriginal community itself is located 5km north of the roadhouse, along a winding dirt track pockmarked with burnt-out cars and empty jerry cans. It seems a sorry place, rubbish blowing about and dogs panting in the heavy atmosphere. A couple of kids play with a flat basketball on an old asphalt tennis court. Aboriginal people have been treated dreadfully around here. One-hundred-and-fifty kilometres to the north, nothing in between but a couple of bores and the railway sidings of Watson and Ooldea, is Maralinga, scene of the British atomic tests in 1956–57. Ten years ago, with pomp and ceremony, the original owners, the Tjarutja Aborigines, were given back the land.

Day 174: Saturday 8 November, Yalata Roadhouse to Penong
Distance: 135km
Distance so far: 12 097km

The sound of steady rain wakes us and there is little to do but sit it out. Richard, who sails boats and understands matters meteorological, announces the weather will break mid-morning.

We are back in pastoral land, cycling past *Colona*, *Nundroo* and *Pintumba*. On our right is the turn-off to Fowlers Bay, where Eyre started his epic walk, now a ghost town. 'Best farming country in South Australia,' two Aboriginal people, Phil and Esme, tell us at the Nundroo Roadhouse, spreading their arms in gestures of munificence before posing for photos. 'You got good bikes here too,' Esme says, trying on my helmet.

The deserted houses between *Nundroo* and Penong suggest that Phil and Esme's claims are not altogether factual. As we pass Tallala Tank, Bookabie and Manandilla Wells, the shells of homesteads stand empty but for the ghosts of bold hopes and daring plans. Their paddocks are homes only to rusty cars, ploughs and Southern Cross windmills clinking aimlessly. The houses' windows are broken, with vines twisting through the wrought iron balconies, probing for chinks in the brickwork to complete the demolition job.

Our spirits soar as we see the whitewashed walls of the Penong Racing Club, the first town since Eucla, and we convince ourselves we deserve a night in the Penong Hotel. I am as fragile as glass after 140km and my knees ache fiercely. They are already scarred—20 years ago I tore cartilages in both of them. I feel they could snap off at any moment. Emma seems like she could turn around and cycle back to Yalata, and David too, seems unperturbed. He is to humans what Gibraltar is to rocks.

The main bar at the Penong Hotel is what you would expect in a place ... well ... in a place like the Penong Hotel. Ten blokes, each bigger than the other, sit in a row on stools ill-designed for the purpose. They swap yarns about a troubled past and an uncertain future. Phil, dressed in jeans covered in Cundilippy dust, introduces himself, his hands clasped lovingly around a VB can in a polystyrene Penong Pub cooler. For half an hour he cracks jokes like a stockwhip, the punchline of one dovetailing neatly into the opening line of the next—a repertoire which, I feel sure, has been followed before. They are about dogs, French sheilas, French letters, French bombs, the Pope and 'that bastard Paul Keating'. Phil is covered in blood.

'I'm a 'roo shooter,' he tells us. 'The most important thing about shootin' 'roos these days is to make a clean kill. This wasn't so important when we shot them as vermin years back. But these days 'roos end up on dinner plates—for some bloody reason—and you have to gut 'em within 20 minutes of shootin' 'em. I'm too old to be chasin' a 'roo through the undergrowth because I only winged it in the first place. Luckily, I'm a crack shot.' Phil takes aim with a forefinger at a framed photo of the Penong footy team. 'Pop,' he whispers, turning to us with a maniacal laugh, a mouth full of gaps.

Late in the evening Richard agrees to go fishing with Angus at nearby Point Sinclair. Angus—'call me Ang'—has done time in Adelaide for a 'small marital problem'. As they set off in our car, Richard driving—Ang lost his licence last year—and taking three rods and a bag of bait, Ang is singing and waving a six-pack of beer out the passenger's window.

Day 175: Sunday 9 November, Penong to Ceduna
Distance: 72km
Distance so far: 12 169km

Richard stalked in early this morning, not a minnow to his name. 'Ang was a better drinker than fisherman,' he tells us over breakfast. 'I had to bait his hook for him.'

Outside Penong 15 windmills crank over furiously in a vital breeze. Water is the staff of life out here and all possible avenues to collect and store it are covered—drawing it from the barren ground or collecting it from above. Catchment depressions, funnelling rainwater into giant tanks, line the road. Today they could be busy: above us the clouds present a symphony of greys, and it smells of rain.

The Eyre Highway has become busier. Thinner too. For the past week the road has had a generous shoulder but today we share the crumbling verge with potholes and smears of gravel. Although looking in our rear-view mirrors every ten seconds or so has become habit, we nearly come unstuck on the north side of Woolshed Hill, when two road trains meet alongside David and me in a cacophony of horns and swear words. We are forced off the road at speed, wobbling to a stop. Emma pulls up seconds later. 'Shit,' she says eloquently.

After the past week, today's short distance is welcome, and early afternoon we arrive in clean and prosperous Ceduna, passing the Big Oyster on the edge of town. The giant silos of Thevenard, 3km beyond Ceduna, hang in the air like a mirage. The silos represent the business end of local production, handling bulk grain, salt and gypsum. The ocean, absent for several days, greets us like a friend, swaying and twinkling as we gaze out across Murat Bay to the Nuyts Archipelago.

Day 176: Monday 10 November
Rest day: Ceduna

Ceduna means 'a place to sit down and rest'. So we do.

Day 177: Tuesday 11 November, Ceduna to Streaky Bay
Distance: 102km
Distance so far: 12 271km

The rest day has done nothing for my knees, which ache dully as soon as I begin to work them. I think of that newspaper article about the bodily dangers of long-distance cycling: although my knees are sore my hips and lower back seem to be holding out OK. Wonder how the sperm counts travelling.

We leave the Eyre Highway for the first time in a fortnight, heading south-west down the Flinders Highway, deep into the Eyre Peninsula, bypassing towns with captivating names like Mudamuckla, Nunjikompita, Wirrulla and Cungena. I always thought that New South Wales had the best names in Australia, places like Gundagai, Tumbarumba and Cootamundra. But the railway connecting Ceduna to Port Lincoln at the base of the Eyre Peninsula passes through sidings called Puntabie, Pimbaacla and Yantanabie. Further east is Karcultaby, Yaninee, Pygery and Cockaleechie.

Fields of waving wheat beckon to us as we leave the Wittelbee National Park. Mid-morning, storm clouds roll in from the west, bringing thunder, lightning and rain descending in sheets. We are soaked. A strong head-wind springs up beyond the turn-off to Haslam, and we inch along at a frustrating 12km an hour. David struggles, while Emma and I seem to be able to draw on a reserve of strength built up on the west coast. Still, Emma tries the screaming bit again, which she says gives her added strength.

Streaky Bay, named by explorer Matthew Flinders, is made up largely of statuesque sandstone houses, while photographs on the hotel walls show throngs of people watching white pointer sharks being winched onto the jetty from undersized fishing boats. The east coast of the Eyre Peninsula has obviously caused distress to people other than us over the years, hence names like Anxious Bay, Mount Misery and Avoid Bay. The ominous-sounding Coffin Bay, near Port Lincoln, was named by Flinders to honour Sir Isaac Coffin, whoever he was.

Day 178: Wednesday 12 November, Streaky Bay to Minnipa
Distance: 93km
Distance so far: 12 364km

The weather chart shows a high pressure system to the south of us turning anti-clockwise and a low pressure system to the north going clockwise. As far as I can make out we are riding right through the middle and as we set off, heading due east towards Chandada and Poochera, I feel like Odysseus sailing between Scylla and Charybdis. Or an old pair of jeans being stuffed backwards through a mangle.

Thirty kilometres east of Streaky Bay, on the rolling pastures of *Lupina Downs*, a bearded cyclist approaches looking like the giant from *Jack and the Beanstalk*, with a gaping, man-eating grin. Behind his sturdy bike he tows a trailer with crates, fishing rods, tackle, a radio—on—ten days of provisions and an esky the size of a fridge.

John Cunningham, 62, packed away his life three-and-a-half years ago and set off from Mackay in Queensland. Since then he has seen the 'best and the worst of the Territory, New South Wales and Victoria,' covering 23 000km. He arrived here via the east–west railway line, through the towns of Pimba, Woomera and Kingoonya. 'I'm heading to Streaky Bay to see a mate I haven't seen for years,' he says. 'Then I head off across the Nullarbor. After that it's up the Tanami Track between The Alice and Fitzroy Crossing, which should be a doozey. There's not a lot between the two places except the township of Tanami ... oh, and the Rabbit Flat Road-house a few hundred ks north-west of Alice. The only problem,' he says, kicking the tyres of his trolley, 'is that this thing only has a clearance of five inches, which could cause trouble in the bulldust.'

I like the cut of his jib. The Rabbit Flat Roadhouse on the Tanami is in the Guinness Book of Records as Australia's most remote pub, 460km from Halls Creek. It was established in 1969 by Bruce and Jacquie Farrand, who remained the only inhabitants for years. The population doubled when they had twins.

John has a belly like Pavarotti, strange, Emma points out, for someone who has cycled such prodigious distances. 'I work on it,' he says, cradling it like a delicate child. 'I love my beer. Normally I cycle 'til three or four, set up the tent on the side of the road, then hit the green cans 'til bedtime. There's a lot of goodness in beer, but it *has* caused me some trouble. I've had heart-bypass surgery twice since beginning the trip.' We watch as John continues on his way, a miniature road train. 'Now that's one hell of an Australian,' says Richard, shaking his head. John, if ever you read this, I hope the ticker survived the Tanami.

The township of Minnipa has been built on grain. Giant white silos sit like well-fed polar bears in the town centre, towering over a spaghetti junction of railway tracks. Sandstone cottages line the main street and trade seems slow on this lazy, hazy Wednesday afternoon. A man, angular and stilted, dressed in a dirty tanktop and faded jeans, eases himself out of an old Holden. A faded sticker on the rear window says: 'If it wasn't for guns we'd all be speaking Japanese'.

Day 179: Thursday 13 November, Minnipa to Kimba
Distance: 145km
Distance so far: 12 509km

Have to be on the outskirts of Kimba, 145km from here, at 12.30 and Emma raises the alarm at six. I drag myself out of bed, knees throbbing, hobbling like an old man in a nursery rhyme. Again, the wind is from the east and has the consistency of a brick wall. Nothing to do but put the head down, ignore the knees—not easy—and ride.

Should be getting used to this now, but I'm not. We make heavy weather of the first 40km to the Port Lincoln turn-off. I sip my water in a daze, wondering how I will get through the next 100. Gradually the countryside, fields of wheat and canola, gets hillier and I can clearly see the Gawler Ranges to the north and Weednanna and Wirrigenda hills beyond Buck-leboo to the east. The wind gives no respite and our planned meeting looks increasingly unlikely. It begins to rain.

David joins Richard in the sanctuary of the car, muttering

that he is a fair-weather cyclist. I feel a deep envy. Would that I could take that option. Mercifully the rain brings a change of wind, now a northerly, and we increase speed, passing a memorial to explorer John Charles Darke, speared on October 1844 on his way back from exploring the Gawler Ranges.

Twenty minutes late we come across a school bus, rain beating on the roof and 30 kids inside, their bikes in a jangled heap under a tree. 'They're still keen to ride,' says a teacher from under a wilting anorak. 'Aren't you kids? Come on!' They mooch out reluctantly, collars turned up, hats pulled down, grumbling. Can't blame them.

A few parents, mostly grain farmers, have also turned up. 'Bloody rain, always arrives too late,' mutters one in a blue singlet, looking heavenwards. My wheat'll end up cattle feed this year, and feed sells for $140 a tonne instead of $180.' On the edge of Kimba are more grain silos with their trademark lettering, SACBH, which stands for South Australian Consolidated Bulk Handling. 'My Dad always told me it stood for "Sack Bob Hawke",' says one of the kids, as we cycle towards Kimba.

That evening rain drums on the caravan like a hail of billiard balls, as we hoover down spaghetti to replace lost energy. At eight o'clock, in fading light, a bank of clouds tumbles in from the west, grumbling and cracking ominously. The wind becomes a gale and electricity fizzes in the air. Richard, drawing again on his seafaring experience, warns that the spare bicycle on the caravan's roof would be an excellent lightning conductor, and takes refuge in the nearby toilet block. We laugh at him until a bolt of lightening jangles nearby, then join him in the dunnies.

Day 180: Friday 14 November, Kimba to Port Augusta
Distance: 163km
Distance so far: 12 672km

At dawn I do a physical stocktake and decide that after yesterday's 145km into a head-wind, there is not a part of me that is not hurting. I feel like I have been run over by a train, which then reversed and ran over me again for good measure. And another 160km today. I am reminded of the Catholic definition of eternity: a granite rock a mile high, a mile wide and a mile deep sits above the ocean. Every hundred years a bird is blown off course onto the rock. Before it flies off it sharpens its beak on the granite. Eternity is the time taken for the rock to be worn to sea-level.

A Scotch mist hangs over Kimba, giving a surreal air to the place, not least to the town's main tourist attraction, the Big Galah, whose top third disappears into the fog. David vows to ride the entire day, a considerable pledge for a fair-weather cyclist. Fair weather is far from guaranteed.

East of Kimba the Eyre Highway sweeps in a wide arc to the north, past the Lake Gilles Conservation Park and through scaly scrub which has gained nothing from last night's rain. The cold front has brought with it a tail-wind, welcomed especially by my knees. It has also given life to the creeks. We cross bubbling Pine Creek, the first flowing water since Esperance on the other side of the country.

Australian mining began, it is claimed, at Iron Knob, at the turn-off to Whyalla. The knob, now a flat-topped hill and getting flatter by the day as graders tear away at the valuable earth, can be seen from 30km. Closer it gives off a sad and sorry air. The streets of the town are unkempt and the houses old and dirty, surrounded by fences of rusting corrugated iron and barbed wire. The oval has disappeared beneath strangling grass and the hotel is charred remains. It is hard to believe that the owner of the town, BHP, could have let the place fall into such disrepair. As we stretch in a park, an officious shopkeeper emerges from a pre-fab. 'Get your grubby feet off my table. It's a little unhygienic, don't you think, with your shoes up there.' I look down at the table, which is covered in a thick layer of birdshit.

Turning north-east to Port Augusta, the northern end of the Mount Lofty Ranges glowing over the tip of Spencer Gulf, we spin along at 60km an hour, aided by a stiff tail-wind. Just as the wind can be a conniving turnkey, it can also set you free, and we shriek like kids as we hammer along. A procession of trucks pass us heading in both directions, carrying goods between Port Augusta and Whyalla and I feel a huge sense of loss. The trucks represent the end of the Eyre Highway and the end of our glorious, if at times painful, isolation. I am not yet ready for civilisation.

Day 181: Saturday 15 November, Port Augusta to Gladstone
Distance: 123km
Distance so far: 12 795km

For the first time in weeks we share a road with traffic both heavy and dangerous. A side-wind buffets us as trucks, creating their own eddies of concern, fly past, gears grinding. Our new road, the Princes Highway, is pencil thin and cats-eye reflectors sticking up from the road present additional problems for us. On the Eyre Highway we were, for a while, Lords of the Plains. Now we are small fish in a very big pond of commerce and industry. And the trucks are the sharks, their speed and size mocking our humble task.

At Stirling North we escape the madness, peeling off the Princes Highway and cycling to Horrocks Pass. I glance back:

beyond the glistening waters of Spencer Gulf are the plains of the outback. Though they have tested me terribly over the past months they have been, by and large, good to me, and I will miss them.

David calls it quits after yesterday's herculean efforts and joins the support car. Emma and I turn to the south, along the aptly named Beautiful Valley. The dramatic outline of Mount Remarkable frames the tall eucalypts, and fields of Patterson's Curse carpet the valley in a brilliant purple hue. There is a sadder side to the valley: sandstone cottages, in varying states of decay, are overrun by sheep who peep through the broken windows like inquisitive landlords. Like the Eyre Peninsula this region has clearly been through difficult times.

Australia has long had the reputation of living off the sheep's back, yet the people who breed the sheep, or harvest the wheat, seem to be ill-rewarded for their labours. Research reported in *The Australian* newspaper shows that the 1990s has been a bad decade for the bush, with protracted drought, high interest rates and low commodity prices. In 1990 wheat prices fell to the lowest on record, in 1991 the same thing happened to wool, and in 1995 beef prices sank to a 20-year low. Cynicism is rife. Country folk say that cities get more than their fair share of Government spending and that NSW stands for Newcastle, Sydney and Wollongong. South Australia has been among the hardest hit: between 1991 and 1996 the provincial communities of Whyalla, Port Augusta, Port Pirie, Murray Bridge, Mount Gambier and Port Lincoln lost more than 2500 Government jobs.

The facts are indisputable: the bush accounts for 35 per cent of the Australian workforce but is home to 42 per cent of the unemployed. Country people die younger, get less medical attention and poorer education, and have inadequate telecommunication facilities. Factories, mines and banks continue to close. Suicide rates among young men in remote areas are more than twice those in the city. The sandstone shells of the houses we pass seem testament to all this, and yet Canberra seems unwilling to fix it. The result is that Australia, already the most urbanised country in the world, will become more so as people leave the land in search of better lives in crowded cities.

Emma and I cycle into the head-wind, through Melrose, Murray Town and Wirrabara, with wide tree-lined streets, stone pubs and antique stores. By the time we reach Gladstone we have cycled six hours, struggling to average more than 20km an hour. It has, we agree, been the best of days and the worst of days. It is pleasing to be back among paddocks and green grass, but six hours on the bike is a long time, especially following two days of 150km each.

Day 182: Sunday 16 November, Gladstone to Clare
Distance: 80km
Distance so far: 12 875km

Woken by whispers. Three kids want to ride with us this morning and have arrived at the campground, clearly non-plussed to find us in bed. 'Our folks said we should get here early because you would be leaving early,' one says as I emerge from my swag looking like a troll. 'Bugger,' says Emma under her breath, having looked forward to a sleep-in and a leisurely Sunday start.

One of the kids, a portly girl, is astride an equally portly pony. Another kid, Hugo, no higher than his bike seat and pedalling so fast his legs are in danger of breaking off at the hips, announces breathlessly he will be cycling with us to Clare, 80km away. His chum looks doubtful but, in the best tradition of Australian mateship, says nothing. The girl, who refuses to get her horse out of a slow walk, is left far behind.

A picture-perfect spring day, sun smiling from a blue sky, fields of pink and green, and birds singing like Te Kanawa. Fields bulge with wheat and barley and bees do their bit at the roadside hives. It seems everyone—except Emma, who still wants to throttle the kids—has been bitten by the happiness bug this morning: couples wave on their way from church and cars bank up behind us patiently, waiting for the road to clear, honking brightly as they pass. We leave the kids, collapsed on the side of the road, in Gulnare, after 25km. Hugo looks a little shamefaced. 'I think my bike's defective,' he announces, kicking the back wheel. 'Better have a word to Dad about it.' His friend nods sagely.

We are enveloped in the valleys of the North Mount Lofty Ranges, cycling through the plentiful vineyards of the Clare Valley. The region, named after the Irish county, was first settled by Europeans in 1842 and the first vines were planted by Jesuit priests at Sevenhill, south of the township, six years later. Today, having tinkered with copper and slate, the Clare Valley is ruled by vignerons. Stone cottages and stables have been converted to tasting rooms and tourists troop in and out of vineyards like ants, clutching boxes of wine with a care and reverence reserved only for things very special.

Day 183: Monday 17 November, Clare to Adelaide
Distance: 155km
Distance so far: 13 030km

A talk at the Clare High School rates second only to the Norseman High School for lack of pupil interest. It is like pulling teeth. Young kids are easier to speak to than older ones. Bike riding and cancer, for many older kids, are just not particularly cool subjects.

Cycling south the countryside reveals more grape vines,

plump cattle, and more fields of Patterson's Curse. Drivers are happy to tail us for hundreds of metres before passing. I can only put their contentedness down to the fact that they live in this beautiful place. It is the opposite of the attitude we met on the Princes Highway two days ago, where I am convinced the truckies had contracts out on us.

The wind swirls around in the valley, at times helping us, then hindering. At the top of a hill near Roseworthy, town of the famous winemaking college, Adelaide appears for the first time, spread out like a model below us, a sight after three weeks on the vacant Nullarbor. We have become good at adjusting speeds to make meetings but something goes wrong today. Due at Trinity College, Gawler, at one-thirty, we are still 15km short at the appointed time.

Organising the school visit is Susan Santella, a native of Adelaide who Roy Wiedemeyer and I met at Mataranka in the Territory. She said then she would organise a visit to a school and has produced the goods. We get a rousing reception at Trinity College: hundreds of kids line the street, cheering and waving banners and the principal presents us with $250. The contrast with the kids of this morning could not be more stark—here the feeling of goodwill, of kids mixing happily with each other and the teachers, is palpable. Anyone despairing of today's kids should pay a visit to Trinity College in Gawler.

Cities can be hell for cyclists. The road leading to Adelaide has no shoulder, brims with trucks, and the bike lane appears and disappears arbitrarily, without reason or warning. More than one driver voices frustration at us. On day 183, I have a hide like an armadillo. I wave at them all.

After 155km, feeling like I have been dragged through an assault course by my tongue, we arrive in the leafy suburb of North Adelaide, to stay with friend Brooke McLachlan. In the eighteenth century, English author Alexander Pope wrote: 'True friendship's laws are by this rule expressed. Welcome the coming, speed the parting guest.' Brooke follows Pope to the letter. We are offered cool drinks, warm beds, a shower and armchairs in which to recuperate.

The news from Richard and David, who drove on ahead to find a mechanic to overhaul the caravan, is mixed. Wear and tear on the caravan, including another broken winding cable, can be repaired, but at a cost of $400. The designers clearly had in mind elderly couples spending weeks in quiet, secluded caravan parks, meandering gently up a coast somewhere. Ours has been to hell and back.

Day 184: Tuesday 18 November
Rest day: Adelaide

I have become used to rest days being far from that. We visit two schools, Smithfield Primary School and Craigmore Secondary, and in the evening the McLachlans throw a fundraising party, raising $500. Half an hour before the guests arrive, dressed in trademark T-shirt and shorts and lugging his pipes, in shuffles the Maestro. At the party he plays like there is no tomorrow, as if standing on some blasted Scottish heath, railing the Fife forces against the Sassenachs.

Day 185: Wednesday 19 November, Adelaide to Wellington
Distance: 107km
Distance so far: 13 137km

Richard and David depart for eastern climes and it is sad to see them go after our shared Nullarbor experience. Both have been rocks, David since Esperance and Richard from the moment he arrived that fiery evening at the Nullarbor Roadhouse. He drove the car with care and consideration, propping up, mostly metaphorically and occasionally physically, cyclists overcome by the elements. Especially towards the end David cycled like a demon. 'Might even do a bit more of this cycling when I get home,' he says, matter-of-factly.

It is a morning for collecting the rebuilt caravan (cost $570), writing a press release (forgotten how to type) and doing an interview with *The Advertiser*. Emma and I finally get on the road by midday, the Maestro in his familiar place behind the wheel.

If heaven has a road it must be something like that which twists through the green hamlets of Bridgewater, Hahndorf and Mount Barker in the Adelaide Hills. The sun blazes merrily, the good folk of Hahndorf (descendents of German immigrants) wave, and the gardens vie for a prize. The elms and oaks, in springtime majesty, look over the scene like proud parents. I cannot remember a more enjoyable day on the bikes. It is far removed from the aridity of the Nullarbor.

We descend the Adelaide Hills, clocking up speeds of 60km an hour with the aid of a tail-wind, through the towns of Strathalbyn and Langhorne Creek. To the east the countryside opens up before us in a map of browns and yellows. The Orlando vineyard is a whirr of activity, teams of people in pointy Chinese hats, on their haunches, pruning vines. On the road someone has scrawled 'Deep Sea Turtle Crossing'.

The Maestro has driven on ahead and we catch him at a secluded cemetery, wandering dreamily among the gravestones. 'The first four gravestones I looked at were for people who died aged 94, 89, 87 and 93,' he says. 'They obviously live a long time in these parts. Might be quite a nice place to move.'

The mighty Murray River has its headwaters in the mountains of eastern Victoria, somewhere between the settlements of Tom Groggin and Suggan Buggan, where The Cobberas and Mount Misery mark some of Australia's most inaccessible land. It meanders westward for 2500km along the Victoria–New South Wales border, through Albury, Echuca, Swan Hill and Mildura, before taking a left turn after Renmark and heading south to the ocean, by way of Lake Alexandrina. The last town on the Murray is Wellington. We pull in there in the late afternoon, a busy sun setting over our left shoulders.

In 1866 Wellington was a bustling town, a population of 1000 servicing a thriving cattle industry that provided Adelaide with much of its meat. Eighty troopers also lived here, guarding the riches that passed through from the goldfields. In 1875 nearly 30 000 passengers crossed the river by ferry, en route to Adelaide or Victoria. The town died when the Government decided to build a bridge over the Murray 30km upstream. Now Wellington, population 180, is an outpost for tourists who want to get off the beaten track. The river is dazzling, 100 metres wide and lined by soulful willows. Stately pelicans drift up and down.

A cyclist at our campground, Zane, hails from Maleny in Queensland, and has been on his bike since May. We invite him for a feed. Like most people who have chosen a life on wheels, he seems to have had a varied life: spent years in communes, did some drugs in Nimbin, and makes ends meet on the road by collecting the dole. 'I plan to be back in Queensland by Christmas,' he says. He'll need to pedal like Oppy to get there.

Day 186: Thursday 20 November, Wellington to Salt Creek
Distance: 106km
Distance so far: 13 243km

'Reckon I'll make for Kingston today,' Zane says, squinting east into a blazing sun. Kingston is 200km away and I look down at his large load.

'Gee, Kingston's a long way Zane,' I say, doubtfully.

'Yeah, I'll just keep pedalling. Should get there around dinner time. It's a beautiful day. Thanks for dinner last night. See y'all again.'

As he disappears down the road to the ferry, I think of his words *I'll just keep pedalling*. In one simple sentence he has encapsulated an approach to life that has built Australia—one adopted by people facing diverse challenges: exploring the interior, battling drought on a South Australian sheep station, or building up a business from scratch. The approach is still alive today and it is a part of Australia I love. Put your head down and bum up, keep your mouth shut and keep working —ignoring the sceptics—and you will make it.

We share the Murray ferry with three cars, and set sail for Salt Creek. The wind comes from the north and Emma and I make good time down the eastern edge of Lake Alexandrina and Lake Albert to Meningie. The country around here is poor, largely due to the salt, a perennial bugbear for many Australian farmers. The land cannot support crops, only a sparse population of cattle and sheep. The houses, too, look to be struggling for life, rusty machinery lying about and gardens wilting. At 60km we stop to stretch and are attacked by mosquitos the size of spitfires.

South of Lake Albert is the Coorong, a 150km-long finger of water separating the Princess Highway and the ocean. The strip of land on the ocean side of the Coorong, the scrubby sand dunes of the Younghusband Peninsula, makes up the

Coorong National Park. Beyond the peninsula the waves of the Southern Ocean rumble. The Coorong was made famous by the film *Storm Boy*, about a boy's love for a pelican. Today it smells of salt, rotting seaweed and dead flathead.

The beauty of the mobile phone is that I can keep in touch with schools and supporters during the day. It fits neatly into the back pocket of my cycling shirt and I have become adept at answering it on the move. 'Are you cycling at the *moment*?' confused callers ask in the middle of conversations, especially if I am negotiating a hill at the time and breathing hard. This morning I receive a call from Neil Melville, who we met at *Boologooro* station near Carnarvon two months ago. He has organised a fund-raising party in Apollo Bay in a week's time.

The wind, at our backs for most of the early afternoon, becomes a head-wind. After one-and-a-half days of tail-winds we cannot complain. The small community of Salt Creek, on the edge of Messent National Park, is being entertained by the Maestro's pipes when we arrive. 'He's been at it all afternoon,' says the campground owner, head buried beneath his car bonnet, when we arrive. 'I'll give you a tenner for some peace and quiet.'

I cook roast lamb in the caravan's microwave and burn it. Couldn't care less. Burnt lamb tastes as good as unburnt lamb when you haven't had it for six months. I wonder what Zane is eating.

Day 187: Friday 21 November, Salt Creek to Kingston SE
Distance: 96km
Distance so far: 13 339km

The sort of wind that firemen despise blows us down the Princes Highway, past the stations of *Cortina*, *Tilley Swamp* and *Andmon Park*. The dog days of the Nullarbor seem long ago as

I revel in today's conditions, hunching over my aero bars, hammering along at 40km an hour. The 5km distance signs, which in recent weeks have passed with all the speed of an election campaign, fly by like a picket fence.

At midday, 25km short of Kingston SE, are 30 kids from the Kingston Community School. Their teacher, Mick, a keen cyclist, has organised the group which includes teachers, parents and a cop from Robe, Bob, who issues a kid with a ticket for bald tyres. Bob's lecture on road safety is largely ignored as we cycle towards Kingston: the kids undertake an array of jumps, skids and monos, mostly with no hands. Mick seems unperturbed, so I say nothing. Bob drives on ahead, his lights flashing. Like Trinity College in Gawler their school has a happy feel to it. Eric and I talk to the kids about the perils of smoking and the school presents a cheque for $800—another phenomenal effort by a modest community.

Australians' love affair with big things is alive and well at Kingston SE, where Larry The Big Lobster, 15 metres high, gazes over the town. A sign announcing that Larry is for sale looks weather-beaten, and has clearly been there some time. Not a great demand for giant lobsters.

Kingston SE is the lobster capital of South Australia and is currently suffering an infestation of seaweed which lies in stinking piles on its beaches. 'We get it every year, and it smells the joint out,' says a local. 'We put up with it for several weeks and then, when the wind changes and the tide is high, it all disappears as quickly as it came.'

Minor excitement in the early afternoon when Emma discovers maggots crawling in her half-eaten chicken sandwich (from our cool box, not a local shop). 'Ah they're good for you lass,' says the Maestro, who finishes *his* chicken sandwiches, also infested, then licks his fingers. Emma screams. 'I think I'm going to puke.'

The Maestro dons the kilt and we collect money in the two pubs, the green one and the white one, raising another $300. One owner insists on donating dinner, and the other puts us up for the night. Mick has invited us to a cocktail party with a beach theme, and we put in a tired appearance. A Grass-hopper and a Harvey Wallbanger later and I am ready for bed. The noise of the party carries on below, but I am not bothered. It is difficult to wake the dead.

Day 188: Saturday 22 November, Kingston SE to Mount Gambier
Distance: 202km
Distance so far: 13 541km

Mick joins us for this morning's ride and we are propelled by a demonic tail-wind which snaps at branches and sends hats and roadside billboards cartwheeling. We cover the 40km to Robe in an hour flat, at one stage hammering along at 65, hooting and hollering. Mick can't understand and we tell him horror stories of Eucla and Madura. '*Now* I get it,' he says.

Vineyards, pregnant with produce, flash by. 'The local wine industry started when a retired fisherman planted some vines several years ago and produced a respectable red,' Mick tells us. 'Eventually they reckon the region will rival the Coonawarra for the quality of its wine. Companies like Orlando and Southcorp are buying land here and planting vines. It could be the saviour of the area.' The Giant Wine Bottle can't be far away.

At Robe, overlooking Guichen Bay, ancient sandstone cot-tages sit by weather-beaten pubs. This is the summer hideaway of Adelaide's well-heeled and it has a colourful past as one of South Australia's first European settlements, dating from 1845. During the Victorian gold rush the citizens of Robe made their fortunes when the Victorian Government levied a ten pound tax on newly arriving Chinese goldminers. Ever resourceful, the Chinese evaded the tax by sailing here and slipping across the border on foot. In 1857 alone, 10 000 arrived.

Mick leaves to return to Kingston and Emma and I push the 100km to Beachport past Lake Eliza, Lake Saint Clair and Lake George on the west side of the Woakwine Range. The wind is furious and we make Beachport without raising a sweat. The Maestro, who has been asleep under a tree, urges us to try for Mount Gambier, another 100km. Pine plantations produce paper for the squeaky-clean Kimberly-Clark toilet paper plant at Millicent. The mature plantations look dark and forbidding while the recently cut ones look like they have been razed by a bomb. Beyond Snuggery—now *there's* a place to live—Mount Gambier sits on the slopes of an extinct volcano. We arrive late in the afternoon having covered 200km, and agree we could do another hundred without a problem.

Day 189: Sunday 23 November
Rest day: Mount Gambier

The Maestro is on a fund-raising roll and we find ourselves at the Mount Gambier speedway where locals have gathered in their hundreds to worship noise. 'I'll give them noise,' he says, licking his lips. What follows is a bizarre sight: Eric trooping around the speedway track with his pipes; on the other side of the fence, cars making a racket to wake the dead and spraying mud about. One kid follows Eric around for a lap, index fingers firmly planted in each ear. The result: $800.

CHAPTER TEN

Victoria *Getting There*

. . . instead of murders, rapes and robberies daily, lynch law and a Committee of Vigilance, there was less crime than in a large English town, and more order and civility than I have myself witnessed in my own native village of Hatfield.

Lord Robert Arthur Talbot Gascoyne Cecil
(Third Marquis of Salisbury): *Victorian Goldfields Diary 1852*

Day 190: Monday 24 November,
Mount Gambier to Portland
Distance: 114km
Distance so far: 13655km

A startlingly beautiful day to enter a new state, a crisp morning of roses and butterflies. Few places could better serve as a gateway to Victoria, Australia's 'Garden State'. The grass on the verge is a brilliant green as the Princes Highway twists through plantations of pine forest, dappled light diffusing through the branches. Sawmills dot the outskirts of Dartmoor on the Glenelg River, giant humps of felled trees stacked together in yards. I grew up in Victoria and, although I have been in these parts only a handful of times, it feels like home.

We are due at the South Portland Primary School at two o'clock, running late again. As we cross the border we lose half an hour owing to the state's time difference, so are running even later. We scoot through the towns of Lyons, Sinclair and Heywood, barely looking up, heads down and thighs aching, trying to recover lost time. The Maestro drives us the final 15km and we arrive in a flurry of dust and apologies. I do my stuff with the kids, a speech that now comes easily. The school kids have begun a disturbing habit of asking for autographs, on pieces of paper, hats, even shirts. What will Mum say when they get home?

The Portland members of the Anti-Cancer Council's volunteer unit produce an afternoon tea to sustain the French Tour de France team, and seem disappointed that *our* team consists only of three. Emma tackles the mountain of food with impressive commitment, consuming several plates of sandwiches, four lamingtons, a handful of cupcakes and a leaning tower of pikelets. 'My, you *can* eat, dear,' says one of the volunteers. 'Mmmpff,' Emma replies.

We return to our pick-up point and cycle the remaining 15km to Portland, joined in the evening by Sandy Fairthorne, who I last saw in Kakadu, and Heather Le Roy, manager of fund-raising at the Anti-Cancer Council of Victoria, who has been a formidable enthusiast and supporter of the ride. She joins the team until Melbourne and aims to do 'a little cycling'.

I have a cold.

Day 191: Tuesday 25 November, Portland to Port Fairy
Distance: 65km
Distance so far: 13 720km

The joy of a short day. After days of 200 and 150km during the past week 65km is a bagatelle. We follow the meandering Princes Highway, tracking the coast towards Port Fairy past the Crags and Yambuk, with light hearts. Off the coast lies Lady Julia Percy Island surrounded by a petticoat of sparkling sea, and Port Fairy's giant water tank peeks over the top of its own sea of Cyprus trees. The town has a rich cycling history, including the annual Murray To Moyne ride, more than 500km, completed in 24 hours.

Heather concedes that she is worried about the traffic, which reminds me that I may have become immune to the dangers of the road. For several months I have shared the bitumen with road trains and trucks of all description, and have had more close shaves than I care to remember. Perhaps it's time, as I approach more populated regions, to renew my commitment to safety. Heather seems to overcome *her* fears, a feat in many ways no different from us covering 200km in a day. It's about stepping out of the comfort zone.

The region around Port Fairy has been compared to Ireland, no surprise given its green hills and whitewashed houses. Port Fairy itself, a home once to sealers and whalers, used to be called Belfast and nearby is the hamlet of Killarney. After five months in a foreign Australia, suddenly I am back in an area I know well, travelling roads I have trodden before. It is most odd, and strangely uncomfortable, a feeling of disturbing *deja vu*—the ride is undoubtedly drawing to a close. I am a nomad now and have no desire to put down roots. Emma and Heather notice I have gone quiet and I try to provide an explanation, which is patently inadequate.

With familiar parts come familiar faces. After an interview with the *Warrnambool Standard*, we meet up with Kate Murray, a TV producer from Melbourne who will cycle to Sydney. Nick and David—two old faces—arrive for the remainder of the week, and Eric, Emma and I greet them like family. We are now a team of seven, pushing east to Melbourne. It is a large number, probably too many, but what the hell. Perhaps I should lighten up and start enjoying this a bit? My cold has reached epic proportions, head pounding and nose running like a tap, and demands a day off.

Day 192: Wednesday 26 November
Rest day: Port Fairy

The kids at today's two schools are sparky but the day reaches a low point at the Combined School when a small girl approaches after my talk and tells me her Mum died of cancer early this year, aged 37. 'How's Dad coping?' I ask her.

'He died when I was four. Me and my sister live with Granny.' Her name is Rebecca and I am at a loss for words.

A small crowd gathers for my talk in the local pub, including Rebecca, her sister and Grandmother.

Day 193: Thursday 27 November, Port Fairy to Peterborough
Distance: 115km
Distance so far: 13 835km

The coast between Port Fairy and Cape Otway, 120km to the east, has a grisly past. Known as The Shipwreck Coast, it was a notorious stretch of water when sailing ships were the major form of transport. Heavy fog and hidden reefs combined to wreck more than 80 ships around here in the space of 40 years. The most famous was the *Loch Ard*, driven onto rocks near Port Campbell, 48 passengers perishing. The two survivors, a man and a woman, both 18, were washed up. Although the papers tried to manufacture a romance the woman, the only survivor of a family of eight, returned to Ireland.

This history is hard to believe as we cycle towards Warrnambool: off the coast the ocean is mill-pond flat and seagulls cruise along the beach. For us the land has more perils, roadworks and plenty of cars. Kate, who broke her arm six weeks ago—fell off her bike actually—struggles. We collect money in Warrnambool's main street, the Maestro turning heads. Onlookers appear bemused as we follow Eric, in his kilt, around with buckets. The Pied Piper in drag.

East of Warrnambool we get lost on a maze of back roads which bear no resemblance to the map. 'Short-cuts always become long-cuts,' David mutters. We are supposed to be at the Timboon School north of Peterborough at two o'clock and I cycle alone through wooded hills, the others meandering to Peterborough. I enjoy the solitude, time to think about the future and what it holds. I had hoped to resolve issues of my life on this ride—in my mid-thirties, where am I heading? Do I wish to remain a writer? Where to live? But the past six months have swept by like spooled tape, a kaleidoscope of people and places. I am prepared for the inevitable let-down that accompanies the completion of a long and involved task. That aside, I resolve that I have resolved nothing.

Day 194: Friday 28 November, Peterborough to Apollo Bay
Distance: 112km
Distance so far: 13 947km

A freezing morning on the Great Ocean Road. We cycle in formation like a well-drilled cycling squad, not so much to decrease wind resistance but to keep *out* of the wind. We shed our layers of clothes as the sun rises, cycling with faces up, drinking in the warmth.

The expanses of the Nullarbor are well behind, but today is like going back in time. The country around Port Campbell, where the Twelve Apostles reach out like pleading hands to the sky, is arid and dry with low-slung bushes on the rocky ground. As suddenly as we enter it we leave, plunging into the verdant bushland of the Cape Otway National Park. I have been warned about Lavers Hill but the sun on my face makes me feel absurdly strong, and I power up it. I feel like I could cycle all day, all night, and still have room for more. Must be as fit as anyone about.

Short of Apollo Bay, at Glenaire, are Neil Melville and Bo Maslen, who I last saw near Carnarvon in the West. They are like old friends, plying us with food before sending us on through the Hordern Vale river flats and into Apollo Bay. I reach 65km an hour, an exhilarating end to an exhilarating ride.

In the evening Neil is disappointed that only 80 people come to my talk at the Apollo Bay football club, where $350 is raised. He has advertised the event on radio, contacted the local paper and placed notices in shop windows. How do you mobilise people? For me it does not matter; John Joyce, who I last saw in Exmouth, arrives for the night, as do sister Juliet and her boyfriend Kurt, on a motorbike. I have not seen them since Townsville. 'Gee, where are your legs,' Kurt says, looking down. 'They've disappeared.'

Day 195: Saturday 29 November, Apollo Bay to Barwon Heads
Distance: 120km
Distance so far: 14 067km

Eight people are cycling today, and we seem to take hours to get moving. Is a group merely as slow as the slowest person, or are there other factors at play?

Cyclists from the Apollo Bay Primary School, including the principal, meet us on the edge of town. Three are under eight, including one, Cliff, who has hearing aids and rides a bike too small for his sizeable frame. He oozes determination to Skenes Creek, before turning for home, proud of his achievement.

The Great Ocean Road east of Skenes Creek is as spectacular as any road I have seen. The Otway Ranges plunge vertically to the ocean, and the road switchbacks along the cliff edge in a road-builders' nightmare—hair-pin bends, passing places and blind corners. It feels precarious, as if the road itself could, at any moment, collapse into the swirling ocean. Above us patches of flat shiny rock indicate recent rockfalls and houses dot the hillsides. Occasionally the road cuts inland through small valleys, where a few lonely sheep mill around caravans and weatherboard shacks. The water below is a grey murkiness, and low, scudding clouds lick the hillsides. Cars creep along, giving us a wide berth. There is a head-wind and cycling is not easy. It is a good day to take our time.

Will Lester, who gave me such valuable advice when I was planning the trip a year ago, appears on his bike and flashes a familiar lopsided smile. 'How's it been?' he asks.

'Fabulous, Will.'

'Any problems.'

'Oh, a few.'

'Nothing that couldn't be overcome?'

'Sort of.'

Will's arrival from Melbourne sparks more realisations that the journey is drawing to a close. Although I am looking forward to *not* cycling I am aware that, a week after this is over, I will yearn to be back on a bike. Although the life of a nomad is painful at times, it is an intoxicating and heady brew and I am not relishing the thought of giving up the freedom. As usual, we want what we don't have; the crazy pendulum of the heart.

Will's arrival also brings the rain, which falls in sheets. Our rain jackets are useless as we spin through Aireys Inlet and the Angahook Forest Park towards Anglesea, where the Anglesea cancer volunteer unit—matronly ladies in wellies and sou'westers, looking like a group from a North Sea trawler—greet us by the side of the road with scones and tea. As we press through Torquay and Breamlea the sun breaks through. That's Victorian weather; if you don't like it wait a minute.

We arrive in the seaside village of Barwon Heads wet and happy. It has been a long day, 120km in testing conditions, and Kate especially has typified the 'head down and keep going' approach, covering the entire distance. Emma, also suffering a cold, has performed more heroics. Says she would beat Rip Van Winkle in a sleep-a-thon.

Day 196: Sunday 30 November, Barwon Heads to Melbourne
Distance: 100km
Distance so far: 14 167km

We're on a road I have travelled hundreds of times. Several years ago I cycled between Barwon Heads and Melbourne on Victoria's Bellarine Peninsula and thought it a momentous achievement. Never thought I would do it again at the business end of a seven-month ride.

Andy Mackinnon, from the Gibb River Road, joins the team to cycle to Melbourne. We stop for a photo shoot with the *Geelong Advertiser*, then enter the lottery of the busy Geelong Road. The cacophony and exhaust fumes of fast and furious traffic grind away at my senses. While I have been able to cope with most roads, today I feel a rising panic, as trucks scream past at top speed like lemmings. Little to do except stick to the outer edge of the gravel shoulder and hope they give a wide berth. Mostly they do, but I feel insignificant and vulnerable. It's hard to believe this is Sunday, traditionally a day of rest. I realise I have become totally out of touch with the get-there-at-all-costs aspect of city living.

The highway's exit ramps create more problems and we negotiate them with care. At Lara, Richard Smithers, a mate from Melbourne, cycles up. His job is lobbying local governments to install more bike tracks, and he lists by rote the recent cycling fatalities on this notorious stretch of road. 'One day hopefully all governments will recognise the importance of cyclists,' he says.

The Westgate Bridge is closed to cyclists and our small party takes the punt across the Yarra River from Williamstown. The fury experienced during today's ride has made me melancholic.

My mood improves as our team of eight cycles down Melbourne's wide streets to the Anti-Cancer Council's offices in Carlton. Seventy people have gathered, including relatives and friends. TV cameras run, champagne is produced, and Dad is choked up. Many people who have come on the trip are there: Juliet and Kurt, Caroline Walford and her kids, Steve Norris's family, Roy Wiedemeyer, John Joyce. Even Max and Wilma, who I last saw at the Yalata Roadhouse on the Nullarbor. My nieces and nephew have grown. Unable to ignore a crowd, the Maestro fires up the pipes and kids try to look up his kilt. 'Is that *music*?' my niece whispers in my ear. The afternoon is bedlam.

Days 197–204: Monday 1—Monday 8 December
Rest days: Melbourne

So is the week that follows. Speeches to make, schools to visit, interviews to do, and a fund-raising party for 300 which nets another $6,000. The total is now $230,000. At two in the morning after the party I get apprehended by the police for pissing on a tree in a city park, and they let me off with a warning. Old habits die hard.

There will be a team of six leaving Melbourne—the Maestro, me, Emma, Kate, and new recruits Tooey Morgan and Kurt Esser. Tooey, a Pom, has raised $1,000 back home, while Kurt, a barrister who is more used to horses than bikes, will come as far as Omeo, 400km. I drive to Dandenong to drop off the caravan. It is sad to see the back of what has been my home for six months. We now have only the car to carry supplies and must trim our luggage to one small bag per person.

The day before departure the team travels to Seymour to attend a function organised by Linda and Robert Brown, the helpful couple from the Gibb River Road. One-hundred-and-fifty people gather for dinner and a cheque is handed over for $7,000, the result of three months of fund-raising which saw Robert, six-foot-four, dancing down Seymour's main street in a pink tutu. One boy has raised $500 on his own, cycling 50km and door-knocking for donations. The total represents one dollar for every resident of Seymour. What a town.

Day 205: Tuesday 9 December, Melbourne to Warragul
Distance: 110km
Distance so far: 14 277km

I have difficulty persuading myself that the ride is not over. The remaining fortnight seems insignificant against the 200 days that have come and gone. I feel like a Marathon runner doing his final lap around the stadium.

The most direct route between Melbourne and Sydney is the notorious 900km Hume Highway, named after explorer Hamilton Hume, which tracks the middle of Victoria. It is nothing short of a bituminised war-zone and a road that, amazingly, still has stretches of single lane. We will travel the less direct and safer route through Gippsland, crossing the Great Dividing Range near Omeo and Tangambalanga, and entering Sydney via the nation's capital, Canberra.

The Princes Highway east of Melbourne is a carbon copy of the Princes Highway west of Melbourne. Motorists are irked that we should be sharing their precious road and their frustrations appear in many forms: some honk, others swear and occasionally we get the one-finger salute. I became immune to all this months ago and adopt the traditional greeting—a hearty wave and a lunatic smile.

Another head-wind. Through Dandenong, Berwick and Nar Nar Goon. As the trucks rumble past and the road's shoulder becomes ribbon thin, I feel especially for Tooey, who must endure these dreadful conditions on her first day. She, Kurt and Kate have gone on ahead, followed by the indefatigable Maestro, and when we catch them I expect tears and recriminations. She is, however, all smiles—a thick English epidermis borne of boarding school food and grim winters.

Warragul is a Victorian satellite city, its name coming from the Aboriginal for 'Wild Dog', which could explain some of the motorists about. We are met on its outskirts by seven members of the Warragul Cycling Club who put us up in their clubrooms and donate $200. The cycling club boasts famous names including former Coles Myer boss Peter Bartels, whose cherubic face appears on many photos alongside pictures of Miguel Induráin and other Tour de France winners. One club member is with the Australian Institute of Sport, road racing in Europe. 'He expects to cycle 40 000km this year,' says Ian, a club member. 'He is having the time of his life, and is treated like a King. He's fed, his bike is maintained and his clothes are washed.' You'd want *all* that cycling 40 000km.

Day 206: Wednesday 10 December, Warragul to Sale
Distance: 110km
Distance so far: 14 387km

To the local radio station at dawn. The two DJs are at their bubbly best and I can't keep up with them, brain gone and slurring. Sleep deprivation does that. A succession of 16-year-old girls ring in following the interview; my rising hopes are shattered—the station is running a Spice Girls CD giveaway.

Another head-wind makes me crotchety and on edge. Trucks belt past heading to the east Gippsland coalfields, a string of cars to the beaches of Mallacoota. The countryside is tinder-box dry, and there are bushfires in New South Wales. I lather on the sun-screen but feel the back of my neck bubbling.

Through Trafalgar, Moe and Morwell, inching our way to Sale. Emma and I pass Tooey, Kate and Kurt, struggling in the heat and the head-wind. Beetroot-red faces and Kate's knee is playing up. I hoped we would get tail-winds here, or at least still days, but nothing doing.

Our loyal sponsor, Coles, has been running a fund-raiser in Sale since noon but we don't arrive until mid-afternoon. 'It's good of you to turn up,' says a photographer. 'I've been here two hours and eaten 12 snags. Did you see the jail escapee near the pine plantation on the edge of town?'

'Too tired to see anything,' mumbles Emma.

The others struggle in at various stages throughout the afternoon, sunburnt and sore. Cycling into a head-wind is a tough initiation and they look like they could pack it in here and now. For Emma and me it has been more of the same. We look a sad and sorry bunch. British composer Sir Arnold Bax, who spent many years living on the wild coasts of Scotland and Ireland, once said, 'You should make a point of trying every experience once, excepting incest and folk-dancing.' Could easily have added head-winds.

Day 207: Thursday 11 December, Sale to Bruthen
Distance: 90km
Distance so far: 14 477km

No wind and a sparkling sun. Easy cycling north-east through Stratford on the Avon River and Bairnsdale on the sparkling Mitchell River. Together with the Macalister, Wonnangatta and Dargo these rivers have their beginnings in the Great Dividing Range, on the rugged slopes of Mount Skene and The Twins. It is true wilderness area with a history of exploration and goldmining and is, in its own way, as inaccessible as the outback. Amazingly, it is only three hours by car from Melbourne. Then, if you want to explore the inner reaches, it's by foot.

From Bairnsdale we cycle north along the Omeo Highway, nothing more than a secondary road, to Bruthen, a hamlet of wrought iron balconies and window-sill flower pots on the Tambo River. The Tambo is warm and Emma, the Maestro and I float in it waiting for the others to show, which they do several hours later. A thoroughly pleasant way to spend an afternoon.

Day 208: Friday 12 December, Bruthen to Omeo
Distance: 100km
Distance so far: 14 577km

A sluggish start, perhaps daunted by today's ride which, though no further than many in recent months, has the highest vertical climb of any. We track the Tambo River north—past Mount Little Dick, resulting in a raft of unfunny jokes aimed at people called Richard—over Haunted Stream and through Tambo Crossing and Ensay. For the first time we find ourselves in wooded wilderness. Eucalypts combine with giant ferns and thick undergrowth to produce impenetrable thickets. After yesterday's respite we resume the fight with our old sparring partner, the head-wind, which combines with the hills to create an even tougher opponent.

More hills after lunch. On the north side of Swifts Creek we reach the top of the Great Dividing Range. The range, one of the longest in the world, sweeps down the east coast of Australia from Queensland, and the last time I saw it was west of Townsville five months ago. Behind us, 100km away, the deep blue water of Bass Strait sparkles in the afternoon sun.

There is a feeling of the wild old days about Omeo—a gold-mining town nestled between the Dargo High Plains and the

Bowen Mountains—with hilly streets, inns with swinging doors, and shops set close to the street. The locals have not always had it easy here, enduring bushfires and two earthquakes. Today it looks gentle as a lamb and welcoming after a day of tough cycling. Eric, Emma and I swim in Livingstone Creek as a cool change sweeps through, lifting leaves high into the air. Three hours later the others arrive, shattered. 'Why I ever decided to come on this silly prick of a ride is beyond me,' says Tooey, before collapsing on the ground.

Kurt is due in court on Monday—defence counsel—and requires a lift to Melbourne. The Omeo Hotel owner announces Kurt's dilemma to the patrons and the local milkman saves the day. 'I'm leaving for Bairnsdale at six-thirty,' he says, swigging the dregs of his beer. 'You can sit in the back with the cream if you like mate, and I'll drop you at the train station. We'll wack your bike on the roof. See you at the dairy at six.'

'Thankyou sir,' says Kurt, doing his best Sandhurst salute.

Day 209: Saturday 13 December, Omeo to Tangambalanga
Distance: 170km
Distance so far: 14 747km

The thought of 170km through Victoria's high jagged mountains excites me, but it is clear the day will not be straightforward. Far from diluting the head-wind, yesterday's cool change seems to have given it new energy, and it charges down from the Snowy Mountains like a demented nephew. I am silent as we climb, heavy-hearted, the steep hill out of Omeo. If yesterday Tooey thought the ride was a 'silly prick' she will surely have a fruitier description by the end of today.

It is hard, hard, hard cycling. Why do people undertake endurance events when a necessary, inescapable by-product is pain? I think of the legendary running race, the *Marathon des*

Sables—The Marathon of the Sands—held every year in the Moroccan desert and billed as the world's toughest footrace. It involves, quite simply, running 230km in a week, through sand and in 50-degree heat, covering up to 80km a day. Amazingly, 500 people enter each year, but not before paying an up-front fee for 'corpse repatriation', just in case. Most interesting is not that they enter, but *why*. 'I am looking for myself,' responded one on last year's questionnaire. 'To fly my soul,' answered another. A Frenchman's reason was: 'Bread is the food of the body, adventure is the food of the mind.' An Englishman's reply strikes a chord: 'Because I am mad.'

The mountain ranges of eastern Victoria fold into the distance like the rippled edge of a cake, in successive shades of blue. Up close they are separated by verdant valleys, bubbling streams and mighty rivers. We follow the Omeo Highway alongside the Big River which flows down from the craggy flanks of Mount Bogong, through hamlets and pocket-handkerchief paddocks. The upper branches of the eucalypts reach over the road and join in a gesture of protection, their sweet smell evoking a strong sense of the Australian bush. Other names in the region—Snake Creek, Price's Downfall—evoke a different awareness of the dangers settling in this difficult area. The road turns to gravel and the wind strengthens. As if a great cover has been cast over the valley, black clouds roll in, the temperature drops by ten degrees in 30 seconds, and it hails. We huddle in the car on the side of the road, hail thrumming on the roof, Eric behind the wheel practising his piping on his chanter, a flute-like instrument which rarely leaves his side. It is a bizarre scene and I shake my head.

At the hamlet of Glen Wills, 70 white crosses mark the graves of the former inhabitants of the mining town of Sunnyside on the east side of Mount Wills. Life in Sunnyside last century was clearly tough. Many, according to a nearby notice, died in infancy—-

there were no doctors—and many women died in childbirth. A number were buried, it says ominously, 'at the policeman's direction'. There are graves of vagabonds, miners and pensioners, while one man died of 'too much of the evil drink'. Graveyard aside, Sunnyside, once home to 600 people, is now nothing but a few old fruit trees covered in vines.

The road descends from the mountains, an exhilarating ride through steam rising from the damp road. At Mitta Mitta we are starving, sating appetites with chocolate milk and muffins. The weather, though threatening, remains benevolent, the sun eventually creeping down between the clouds and the horizon, and bathing the valley in luminescence. We reach Tangambalanga in the early evening, having been on the bikes for more than eight hours. I feel surprisingly energetic.

Tangambalanga lies on the south side of Lake Hume and is surrounded by places with equally improbable names. It is, for instance, situated at the foot of Mount Murramurrangbong. To the north is Woomargama, to the south Mullindoolingong, to the east Tallangatta, to the west Yackandandah. Eric plays the pipes in the evening and a group of local nurses, celebrating something, dance around the hotel pool table. Whether the dances are reels, flings or some strange Tangambalanga hybrid is not clear. One thing *is* clear though: the nurses couldn't care either way. And when you come from a town called Tangambalanga, why would you?

CHAPTER ELEVEN

Southern New South Wales *Being There*

I became irritable, dogmatic and thankless. Two hours after midnight each pedal turn felt like the last; at 5 am impulses of power revived speed once more. I was a cycling apprentice in a new realm of physical and psychological reaction developed from prolonged sleepless effort separate from any previous form of cycling exertion.

Sir Hubert Opperman on his 1928 Sydney—Melbourne ride:
Pedals, Politics & People

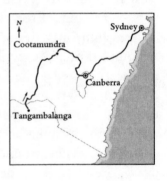

Day 210: Sunday 14 December,
Tangambalanga to Holbrook
Distance: 87km
Distance so far: 14 834km

The heavens open exactly 12 minutes after Kate and Tooey start cycling. It is as if Lake Hume, 30km away, is falling from the sky amid a chorus of thunder cracks and lightning. 'I could have had this bloody weather if I'd stayed at home,' Tooey says later.

We resort to the busy road to the west of Lake Hume, near Albury, over the more picturesque eastern route because the latter involves a ferry ride and no-one can tell us if the ferry is running this time of year. 'Pretty sure it is,' said the hotel owner last night. 'I think it's undergoing repairs,' opined the shopkeeper. For once the bush telegraph has failed.

Passing over the muddy waters of the Murray River and entering New South Wales is a significant moment. It is my sixth and last border crossing and indisputably represents the start of the last leg. Below the bridge the Murray gurgles in swirls and eddies, dwarfed by the giant concrete dam of Lake Hume. The end is now worryingly close; the vehicles passing us will be in Sydney by this evening.

The Hume Highway is the busiest highway in the country and does nothing but reinforce my belief that Gippsland was the best route for us. Seventy kilometres beyond Albury is Holbrook, a picturesque town bisected neatly by the highway. It was originally named Germanton, a name considered unfashionable during World War I, and was renamed after a British submarine Commander, Norman Holbrook, who won the Victoria Cross in 1914 for steering his submarine behind enemy lines to torpedo the Turkish battleship *Messudiya*. Today a full-size replica of the submarine emerges from the lawns of the local park, despite the fact that we are 300km from the ocean. I visit the Woolpack Inn Museum in the main street and glance through the visitors book. The last name in it, to my amazement, belongs to my sister Jenny, who travelled through here recently.

Fifty years ago my father's sister, Beverley, married a Scot, Ian Geddes, and they settled here, spawning a family that has infiltrated virtually every community in the region, including unlikely towns like Burrumbuttock and Book Book. In the evening many attend a gathering of the Holbrook business community in the local park where we let the Maestro loose. The Holbrookians are generous to a fault, and we raise $500.

Day 211: Monday 15 December, Holbrook to Wagga Wagga
Distance: 93km
Distance so far: 14 927km

'Grrrrrrrr.'

I am dragged from my campground slumber by the growls of Bev's dog, PJ. They are on their morning constitutional and thought they'd drop past. 'I wanted to take your pictures before you left, and didn't want to miss you,' Bev says. I stumble about in a paralysis of sleep, trying to assemble the troops into some sort of order for a photo that befits the final week of such an expedition.

We make pleasing headway along a secondary road towards Wagga Wagga. It is a relief to leave the Hume Highway—one afternoon was more than enough—and we spin along under a blazing sun through Cookardinia and Mangoplah, past verdant fields and hulking silos, stopping only to allow a mob of plump Herefords to cross the road. In a dusty utility a bloke sits behind them, like a movie extra, hat low, sucking on a piece of straw.

My phone rings constantly and, by this stage, it is almost a matter of pride that I answer it on the move. The calls are from journalists, sponsors and friends—expressions of disbelief that I am a week from finishing—and includes a call from a friend, Tim, in his New York high-rise.

After a TV news crew tracks us down—'can the old bloke play the pipes and cycle at the same time?' asks the journalist hopefully—we are joined on the outskirts of Wagga Wagga by two cyclists, Geoff and Brendan, aged 50 and 12 respectively. Geoff had open-heart surgery three years ago. 'Thought I ought to get out on the bike and do what I tell my kids they should be doing,' he says. My cousin Peter also joins us, on a bike one step from a penny-farthing.

Wagga Wagga, with its wide streets and rose-lined parks,

has a population of 57 000, which makes it one of the biggest cities in central New South Wales. At the Victory Memorial Park a group gathers to meet us, including another cousin, Mervyn, who presents us with the proceeds of the Book Book Tennis Club raffle. While lunching with Jan and Geoff Hamilton, two of their kids, aged seven and five, present a small packet wrapped up in a blue bow, with a scratchy letter:

Dear Richard. You would like you to know at a neighbourhood Christmas party we raised $27 and 60 cents. We raised it by selling ice-creams. It's very sad that your mother died of cancer. We hope that you can do a lot more research with the money. You have travelled a long way, so your legs must be very sore. From Lachlan and Claire Hamilton and Hannah and Edwina Reid.

The Maestro reads the letter. 'That's worth more than a $1,000 donation,' he says.

Day 212: Tuesday 16 December, Wagga Wagga to Cootamundra
Distance: 98km
Distance so far: 15 025km

My mobile phone has been cut off because of non-payment of the bill. Efforts to pay by credit card are hopeless: no credit left. Feeling like a petty criminal I visit the bank to pay off the card, then get the phone hooked back on. On the positive side we find ourselves on page five of the local paper and deposit $10,000 in the bank, the product of the Seymour night and subsequent fund-raising.

We cross the majestic Murrumbidgee River flowing west where it joins the Lachlan and the Murray, and pass through Junee, the walls of the Junee prison in the distance, stopping for fortification at the Jail Break Café. The wind comes from a furnace and the paddocks are golden brown and sirocco dry.

Many local firefighters have gone to fight the fires around Sydney. 'It'd be just our luck that a fire will start here while they're gone,' says the owner of the Jail Break. 'I'd have to go out and fight the bastard myself. Guess I've got a couple of buckets out the back.'

The Olympic Way tracks the Melbourne–Sydney railway line, through Illabo and Bethungra, the hulking Mount Ulandra jutting from the plains to the east. This morning we were told that the Olympic Way was a 'shocker of a road' and I am pleasantly surprised. Cyclists do not ask for much: a smooth road, wide shoulders and considerate drivers. Today we have all three.

At Cootamundra, birthplace of incomparable cricketer Don Bradman, one of Emma's teeth is causing her pain and she searches out a dentist. He extracts the offending incisor, pumping her full of pain-killers in the process, and she returns to our campground groggy and shaken, retreating to her tent.

Also at the campground is a contract harvester, his wife and their two kids. 'I've been here for two weeks and only worked five days,' he says mournfully. 'When the northerly wind blows we can't harvest because any spark can start a fire, and we're not covered by insurance. It's the worst weather possible for harvesters.' His wife is battling cancer, with a family history of it. Despite his harvesting woes they write out a cheque for $100.

Day 213: Wednesday 17 December, Cootamundra to Binalong
Distance: 85km
Distance so far: 15 110km

Today's distance, a minnow compared to past days, is monumental for Emma. Her mouth, she says, feels like it is harbouring the Kalgoorlie Superpit and she can't stop herself sticking her tongue—'my whole bloody tongue, can you believe?!'—in the hole that was, until yesterday, her tooth. 'Do you want to drive with Eric?' I ask.

'If you think I'm going to drive with bloody Eric having cycled all the way from bloody Broome you've got rocks in your head,' she says with no small measure of feeling, mounting her bike and grabbing her helmet.

'That's the spirit, lass,' says the Maestro, ignoring the 'bloody Eric' bit, as Emma spits another gob of blood onto the ground. We cycle to Wallendbeen and stop to stretch on a bench outside a shop. Above a sign proclaims, 'From henceforth there will be no credit given—Nev's New Year Resolution'.

East of Wallendbeen, a succession of hills leads to the twin towns of Murrumburrah and Harden. While you could shoot the proverbial cannon down the main streets of many country towns in South Australia and Victoria, New South Wales seems a different story. The shops are busy and the streets are full of utes, ladies wheeling prams, dogs sniffing each other, and kids belting each other.

The road climbs and falls like a roller-coaster and Emma toils with a headache. At Binalong we are met by Narelle Gibson, the mother of a Melbourne friend, who drapes wet towels over our necks and buys us drinks in the Binalong pub. Emma slumps in a corner, holding a towel to her chin and moaning, an Archibald Prize-winning portrait of local character, Charlie Cotter, peering down at her.

Narelle's family has lived at *Mylora*, a sheep station midway between Binalong and Bookham, since the 1840s. The region is steeped in history, its most famous son being bush poet Banjo Paterson, who used to compose his ballads while riding his horse between Illalong and Binalong. *Mylora's* gardens are an oasis of green grass and flowers in sun-drenched paddocks, but the drought has taken its toll—Narelle and her husband Ross are thinking of selling up. 'It will be a sad day for us,' she says. 'Don't know what we'll do without this place.'

Late in the evening she lets us in on a secret: a kettle of sovereigns is buried under a tree somewhere on the station. My ears prick up, sensing a quick and painless way of reaching the million that doesn't involve piping. 'Don't get your hopes up young lad,' says Ross. 'I've been casing the joint for years.'

It is revealed that Ross has talents beyond farming. He is Iceland's Honorary Consul-General in the Australian Capital Territory and can do important things like park wherever he likes and not get speeding tickets. 'Can't speak a word of Icelandic,' he says with a twinkle in his eye. 'And most of my diplomatic work involves bailing tipsy Icelanders out of jail.'

Day 214: Thursday 18 December
Rest day: Binalong

A fund-raising party at the property of Peter and Sandy Crisp, who own a glass-making and lavender business on the Hume Highway, nets $2,000. Eric plays the pipes with such zeal that he is asked to play at a society wedding in Yass on the weekend. 'You'll have to be prepared to be in the spotlight,' says the mother of the bride. 'A TV crew and the society mags will be there. Interested?' Does Dolly Parton sleep on her back? Pipers, by the very nature of their chosen mode of entertainment, revel in the spotlight. Eric accepts with a bow.

Day 215: Friday 19 December, Binalong to Wee Jasper
Distance: 80km
Distance so far: 15 190km

The back road to Wee Jasper, heading south and—extraordinarily—*away* from Sydney, is delightful, tracking jagged hills that resemble a heart monitor reading, and crossing an ancient iron bridge over the Murrumbidgee River flowing towards Lake Burrinjuck. Earlier, cycling through Yass, once the home of explorer Hamilton Hume, I witnessed the Maestro on the side of the road preparing mentally for tomorrow's nuptial performance, his fingers playing pretend bagpipes, brow furrowed in concentration.

Lake Burrinjuck, we are told, is as low as it's been for years, a consequence of El Niño, which produces warm air in the South Pacific Ocean and dry conditions on Australia's eastern seaboard. The annual rainfall is normally 50 centimetres in these parts—this year has produced less than 30. Aside from *Salt Box* which sports a new 'For Sale' sign, this part of New South Wales is far enough away from the city for Sydney developers to not buy sheep stations to slice up into 40-acre lots, a fate that has befallen areas around Bowral and Mittagong. Many stations here are up to 10 000 acres, and are owned, for the most part, by families that have been here for decades. 'Even Rupert Murdoch has owned a station here for 25 years, often flying in from Sydney by helicopter,' I was told at last night's party.

Narrengullen, a 17 000-acre station and one of the oldest in the district, is owned by the Reid family. George Reid, in his mid-thirties, was vaulted into the station's top job several years ago when his parents were killed in a plane accident. He married an English girl, Georgie, and they run the place with firm but fair hands, aided by half-a-dozen jackaroos.

The jackaroos are wild, twenty-something blokes learning the tricks of the farming trade before returning, mostly, to family properties of their own. According to George the past year has been 'a bastard', and tonight there's a party for local families and his workers. 'It gives the boys a chance to let their hair down after three months of 15 hour days, without a day off,' he says, rolling in a beer barrel. It is clear that the *Narrengullen* parties have legendary status, many of the ex-jackaroos travelling hours to attend. 'Could be a big night,' George tells us, winking.

The jackaroos arrive at sundown looking smart enough, ties and moleskins, but the respectability goes down as quickly as the beer. By the time most of the guests leave, around 11, the jackaroos have started their own party. One, Tim, broke his leg three months ago when a horse fell on him. Bob from Tennant Creek and Doug from Cootamundra relieve him of his crutches and use them to play air-guitar on the garden table. Bob, who is enormous and looks like he could *eat* Tennant Creek, then tosses Tim around on his shoulders while Scott sets about scaring the remaining guests by eating Christmas beetles. One of the guests, Lois, who runs an organic farm nearby, has brought along two South Korean students, who look horrified.

Day 216: Saturday 20 December, Wee Jasper to Canberra
Distance: 80km
Distance so far: 15 270km

The music has stopped by the time we get up, but the party has not. Tim, Bob, Doug and Scott are still drinking and carrying on. Tim's crutches are in a tree somewhere, and he has the mobility of a turtle on its back. They have not slept, but stopped drinking for an hour at dawn to load a few hundred sheep onto a truck.

Another short day, along the Mountain Creek Road, to Canberra. The city's outskirts are hills, giving views over the city, the Murrumbidgee and Lake Burley Griffin, Namadgi National Park and Black Mountain. I am morose, thinking about the prospect of finishing in three days, still no closer to working out what to do next year, or beyond.

Canberra was created in 1909 largely because the people of

the time could not decide whether Melbourne or Sydney should be Australia's capital. A competition held to design a new city produced, its detractors say, the result you would expect: a purpose-built place with no history, no soul, barren and featureless. The same people say the new Parliament House—a gigantic structure, all steel and concrete—perfectly reflects Canberra. It's grandiose, functional, but you wouldn't want to spend a lot of time there.

Emma and I get lost and end up cycling around Lake Burley Griffin, which *is* beautiful, willows and elms edging the lake and a startling view up Anzac Parade to the serene, green-domed war memorial. The other way, over the lake, is the old Parliament House, looking altogether more comfortable and homely than its replacement. Tooey and Kate struggle in late in the afternoon, after problems on the dirt road.

At Binalong, we spoke to a teacher whose student, Britte Cant, is in Canberra Hospital with leukaemia and we promised to visit her. Britte is only 19 and has had ten doses of chemotherapy in five weeks. Strands of hair lie on her pillow and her voice is shaky, but she manages a smile. Emma tells her of a friend, Karen, who had leukaemia 15 years ago and is now in remission. Britte says she gains strength from visitors. I tell her she gives *us* strength.

Day 217: Sunday 21 December, Canberra to Goulburn
Distance: 106km
Distance so far: 15 376km

Leaving Canberra by way of State Circle around Parliament House we are honked on an otherwise deserted double-laned road. 'Use the bike tracks,' the driver yells, accelerating past. Seconds later we draw alongside him at a red light. 'In a hurry?' I ask, in a butter-wouldn't-melt voice. He stares straight ahead, fingers strangling the wheel. I decide to give him the benefit of the doubt. It's seven-thirty and he's heading towards the Lodge. Perhaps he's late for brekky with the PM ...

The exchange worries me. I am, categorically, back in civilisation, with its deadlines, its short fuses, its prickliness. The feeling continues as we cycle along the Federal Highway and over a hill to Lake George. Cars speed past impatiently, tailgating. A sign announces 11 deaths on this stretch of the Federal Highway in the past five years. At present the highway consists of two insubstantial lanes—which explains the road toll—but a new highway is being built alongside. As good as finished but no cars allowed yet, it makes a sterling bike track and we hammer along it—50km of 20-metre-wide bitumen all to ourselves. Perhaps they should leave it this way.

The wind is like a blow-torch, a side-wind, and newspapers report fires still burning out of control around Sydney. Sweat drips from my face as we head north-east, guzzling water. Days like today are dangerous for cyclists: evaporating sweat cools you down, but you have no idea how much liquid you lose. We fill our bottles at Collector, where a lonely memorial to Constable Samuel Nelson, father of eight, sits on the edge of town. In 1865 Nelson single-handedly took on bushranger Ben Hall and his gang, before being shot.

We reach the Hume Highway, snarled with heavy trucks and cars driven by irascible drivers. Goulburn, or rather its 15-metre-high Giant Merino, appears on the horizon. For Emma it is not a moment too soon—her mouth aches, and the heat amplifies the pain. Cycling down the main street she hits a rut in the road and ends up, much to the amazement of both herself and the onlookers, upside down in a flower bed.

A Coles barbeque has not attracted much interest, hardly surprising in the heat. Emma collapses in the corner and the store manager, Wayne, plies her with soft drinks until colour returns to her face. She says pieces of tooth have been appearing over the past two days from the Superpit; the Cootamundra dentist did a shoddy job.

Wayne, fresh and angular-faced, has not been in Goulburn long. His last posting was in the central New South Wales town of Orange, where some people's behaviour belied, he says, the town's pristine appearance. 'A colleague at the supermarket was bashed twice and I'll never forget the all-in brawl we had there one summer's night,' he says, shuddering. 'Aisle five it was. Poultry. Pommy fruit pickers and some local boys. We locked them in until the cops came. What a mess.'

The heat drives us to the pool, where the whole of country New South Wales has gathered and water can't be seen for bobbing heads, rubber balls and other floating paraphernalia. In the evening the Maestro, inspired by the reception he received at yesterday's nuptials, kilts up, grabs two French kids who are standing about and goes collecting. Total: $7.55.

Tomorrow is my second-last day and I lie in my swag staring at the stars. The adventure is drawing to a close, far too quickly for my liking.

Day 218: Monday 22 December, Goulburn to Picton
Distance: 130km
Distance so far: 15 506km

The wind is with us, and strong. The traumas of the Eyre Highway still rankle and this is the least we deserve.

Kate, Tooey, Emma and I track the Hume all day and the riding is as good as it gets. Goulburn is 600 metres above sea-level and the road descends gently, bypassing Moss Vale, Mittagong and the Belanglo State Forest with its grisly history of backpacker murders. We cruise at 45km per hour for what seems like ages. At one stage I feel quite the daredevil, reaching

71, my fastest speed of the past seven months. As effortless as sailing with a spinnaker.

The Cancer Council's public relations unit has gone into overdrive. The phone rings constantly and I do radio interviews or confirm them for tomorrow. Up ahead Kate has a flat tyre, the first for many weeks. Nearby sits a group of trucks. 'The road authorities have installed electronic devices above the roads to monitor our speed between Brisbane and Melbourne and we're killing time before going under the next one,' says one of the truckies when we stop to stretch. I think of Neil the truckie at Caiguna and his comment about 'pill-popping lunatics on the Hume'.

There is a haze in the air and I smell smoke. In Picton, after 130km, a group of firemen lie exhausted on the grass outside the fire station, steam coming from their sweat-soaked clothes. 'There's a fire 20km away and it flares up whenever the big westerly gets up,' a local says, donating $20. 'These guys have been fighting it for days.'

Sydney artist Richo Allen and his wife Lisa have offered to put up the team for the last night at Berrima. Several years ago they turned their backs on the big smoke and bought a plot of land in the Southern Highlands, built a house and turned creative. Richo is currently working on two giant canvases for the Hong Kong Jockey Club, while Lisa sells a line of leather goods. Somehow they find time to bring up two boys. 'Best thing we ever did moving out here,' he says as we gaze at his house, corrugated iron, wood and old sheds. 'We were losing our minds in Sydney. There's nothing like the bush to give you a new perspective on life.'

In the evening there is a happy frisson, laughter, joking. We have all achieved milestones in recent months: Emma has cycled 8000km, Kate the best part of 2000 and Tooey more than 1000. The Maestro has played to more people than Elvis.

While they reminisce about their best and the worst bits, I pace the floor like a cat on speed.

'Nervous?' Kate asks.

'Terrified,' I reply.

I have been prepared for the sense of let-down—the feeling of 'so that's over, now what?'—but I was not ready for fear: of the unknown, of *not* having 120km to cycle each day, of being static, of urbanisation with its dubious benefits.

'You could always do it again,' says Tooey, straight-faced.

'Now *there's* an idea.'

The night is a warm one and we persuade Tooey to sleep under the stars for the first time: to experience a night with the bats and dingoes and the strange bush noises. She makes a song and dance about setting up a swag and dossing down, looking forward to a 'true Aussie nocturnal experience'. In the morning we discover she snuck inside and slept on the couch.

Day 219: Tuesday 23 December, Picton to Sydney
Distance: 90km
Distance so far: 15 596km

'So Richard, tell us about your ride.'

It is six a.m. and an enthusiastic interviewer wants to know about commitment, flies and cycling the Nullarbor. With the last day upon me, it's hard to think straight enough to give sensible answers. They all seem trite and hollow. I find myself saying inanities like, 'Well, it's a big country' and 'Yes, there's a lot of emptiness out there'.

Ending the ride in Sydney necessarily means cycling through the city's suburbs, and there are few places in Australia less conducive to safe, enjoyable cycling on the day before Christmas Eve than the Hume Highway as it ploughs through the enveloping suburbs of Liverpool, Bankstown and Ashfield.

Pity we couldn't finish in a leafy country lane somewhere, in a quiet field with a picnic and Pimm's. Probably could have. Instead there are trucks belching fumes and mad, mad Christmas traffic, grim-faced drivers running desperately short of Yuletide cheer, klaxon horns, noises of grinding gears and protesting brakes, the whole catastrophe steaming in a hot-pot of Sydney summer build-up.

I do my best to internalise my thoughts, gaining solace from the memories of the last seven peripatetic months: of Jo at *Boologooro* waking us at sparrow's fart probably having already rounded up half her sheep; of dunking the car at Denham and wondering whether it would ever see bitumen again; of the Maestro being heckled about his kilt in Kalgoorlie, and taking it on the chin; of the kid at the Jambin School near Biloela donating his birthday money; of Gwenda driving the Gibb River Road bus like Alain Prost, yelling at the kids to, 'sit down and shut up or we'll run into a tree and all be mincemeat, mark my words'; of the kids not taking any notice; of weeks on end in the Never-Never; of my realisation in Beaudesert, having struggled over the Border Ranges, that this ride *was* possible. Even the Eyre Highway head-winds don't seem quite so bad now. I always knew it would be a fun seven months, but I had no idea it would be so bloody *different*.

Near Warwick Farm, 25km from the Opera House, is a sign showing the image of a bike with a firm red line through it. No cyclists allowed on the highway. 'Bugger it,' I say, cycling on. 'What can they do, send us back?'

The phone rings—more interviews drowned out by the traffic. Eventually the phone's battery runs out. Blessed silence. Eric follows in the car, having cleaned the fund-raising sign for the first time since Kalgoorlie. Congratulatory honks.

We see the Harbour Bridge an hour before reaching it. Up crazy Parramatta Road, through Ultimo, into George Street.

Circular Quay is bustling with tourists, ferries pulling out into a sparkling harbour. The nautilus outlines of the Opera House. 'Welcome back,' says the man on the Opera House boomgate. 'Good ride?'

There's a crowd on the Opera House steps. Friends, kids running up and down, babies in prams, and seven people from the Cancer Council holding a banner, 'Welcome Home Richard. Thankyou'. Champagne corks pop, clapping, and Japanese tourists wondering—just as they did seven months ago in the same place—what the fuss is about. An emotional kaleidoscope: relief and happiness, sadness, and those twinges of fear lurking behind it all, like a bad reputation. The ride has consumed my life. What the hell will I do now?

I hug Emma, and Kate and Tooey, all of whom seem mighty relieved, and happy. 'Where'd the harem come from?' shouts someone. I hug, too, the Maestro. A moist eye? Could be mistaken. 'Well done son,' he says, reaching for his pipes for one last blast. 'You've done a bloody good job.'

A bloody good job. It has been too. A bloody good job by a team who kept faith when it would have been easy to toss it in and say, 'Well, we tried.' Who, given an itinerary drawn up by a bloke who didn't know a spoke from a sprocket, made it with a few sore knees and tender arses, but unbroken spirits. Who, although live in Australia, didn't *really* know what to expect but a big country, and lots of space. Who kept their heads down when things were tough, and met hundreds of people out there doing exactly the same. Pulling together, working as a team, and helping each other.

There, too, is Margie, last seen boarding a bus in Geraldton. 'Where have you been?' she yells. 'You're ten minutes late!'

Epilogue

Buddhist prayer flags flutter in a brisk Nepalese breeze. Beyond them is the Kanchenjunga Massif, well-defined against a pale blue morning sky, its foothills obscured by the smoky haze drifting from the valley. All around are the sounds of a Nepalese village coming to life: cocks crowing insistently; men hacking and coughing; wide-eyed children at the town tap—where a stream of water explodes in sun-drenched diamonds—waiting patiently to fill copper urns clearly far too big for them to carry home; porters washing before setting off on another day's toil, lugging 70-kilo loads up the valley; women carrying their own loads, babies or wicker baskets via a strap over the forehead, rolling through town in slow, rhythmical steps that will take them far up the valley by nightfall. This is the fourth-poorest country on earth and things have changed little here in recent centuries. No electricity, no machines, no roads. No welfare, no hospitals. If you get sick here, you walk to a doctor, or someone carries you. But everywhere is laughter and chatter.

Englishman Lord John Hunt, who died a week ago aged 88 and who led the 1953 Mount Everest expedition in which Sir Edmund Hillary and Tenzing Norgay climbed the peak for the first time, says of rural life in Nepal:

There we can see the meaning of community, free of the drive of competition. We see human happiness despite—or because of—the absence of amenities furnished by our Western civilisation . . . it behoves travellers from the modernised countries to understand and respect the values and virtues of life today in rural Nepal. They have much to teach us about how to live.

The 11 months following the completion of the ride have passed in a blur. I have spent many weeks writing this book, done some freelance writing to earn a few dollars, and given many talks about the ride. I have not, I hope, become morose or introspective, and have enjoyed many of the things I missed while on the ride. Having seen so much of Australia I now look at Melbourne from a different perspective. I see her parks and gardens, beautiful tree-lined boulevards, history and cultural diversity.

But no day goes by without me thinking of some aspect of the ride. Coming to Nepal is, in many ways, to revisit it. Things I learned on the ride have definite parallels here in a remote Nepalese village on a mountainside, crystallised in a morning scene around the village tap.

Life's journey is not easy, but much can be achieved by persistence. I discovered a steeliness, a reservoir of emotional and physical endurance that I never knew I had. Some days were harder than others, and were not necessarily a function of distance or wind. It is as if, occasionally, everything conspires to make a journey difficult; and the only way to tackle this is to get moving, and to keep going. Complaining will not bring a target closer, and procrastination will not make it go away. A long journey becomes possible by dividing it into achievable bits. Keep putting one step after the other and logic says you *must* eventually arrive. Provided, of course, you are heading in the right direction.

I learned that Western society is increasingly being strangled by greed. Here in Nepal the villagers live simple lives, singing folk songs around a fire, children spinning hoops with a stick or kicking around a rolled-up sock. Equally, Nepali nomads live, by definition, on what they can carry, and must jettison the surplus. It is a rule-of-travel which acts as a natural disposal unit and keeps their lives uncluttered. Small things become treasured, a book, a view, a thought. I returned to an environment where material possessions are coveted more and more—the latest cars, new homes, cable television, updated computer packages with e-mail, gizmos of all description. Fast food is served in throw-away polystyrene packaging, promoted by catchy advertising jingles and television campaigns. Plastic bags choke our waterways. The important things—friendship and family—are in danger of being smothered.

I learned that it is a privilege to experience a nomadic existence, if only for seven months. I miss the feeling of covering distance each day and setting up camp. Of cooking dinner with minimal utensils and sitting under the stars, then setting up the mosquito net under an old gum tree. I miss the *simplicity* of the ride, the friendships forged and maintained in the face of a common goal and a shared purpose. It was certainly a privilege to see Australia by bike. Cycling is a beautiful way to travel. Something about self-propulsion, and about being closer to terra firma.

I learned that the road less travelled *is* often the best. It is often more scenic, usually more fun, certainly more challenging (if you like that sort of thing), generally slower, and more likely to bring you into contact with like-minded people.

I learned that Australians are, by and large, good people and will help others, especially if they see them having an honest dip. The country was built on mateship, on a fair go and on helping those in need. From what I saw this is still the case, especially in places where social services are minimal. I met many people: farmers and truckies, travellers, miners and hotel owners, 'roo shooters and drunks, larrikins and God-botherers. People took us into their homes and opened hearts as big as the country we were cycling through.

Cycle Against Cancer has been adopted as an annual fund-raising event by the Anti-Cancer Council of Victoria; schools are completing endurance events and raising money for cancer research via sponsorship. Money has continued to come in. The total raised is now over $300,000, and that money has been distributed to the states in which it was raised. The greatest amount, raised in Victoria, has been allocated to the Baker Medical Research Institute. I remain hopeful that a cure for cancer is not far away.

The other members of the ride have, by and large, returned to their jobs. Emma went back to spaying cats and disconnecting dogs' vitals. My father married Jean in March, and they are happy. David returned to BP and Nick to the ANZ Bank, where he continues to write computer programs which no-one can understand. Steve returned to teaching and Andy now markets water filters. Kate tossed in her job and went back to university and Tooey returned to London after a year in Australia, where she learned to ride a horse, crack a whip and rig up a tent. Catherine married the head of fund-raising at the Anti-Cancer Council, and is now employed there part-time as a fund-raiser. All together, 36 people joined the ride for different legs. They have no concept of how invaluable their support was. Without them there would have been no ride and no money raised.

The Maestro and his wife, June, are living contentedly in Perth. In many ways he typifies the Australian spirit, volunteering on a chance meeting to drive the support car for three months. He ended up contributing more than anyone. He wrote recently to say that he has converted to plastic reeds in his pipes, which play as sweetly as ever. He recently went to the doctor for a routine prostate check-up. His letter read:

The diagnosis was a bit like those good news, bad news jokes. The bad news was that I had it [cancer], the good news was that I could be cured. I was put on hormones for about six weeks then onto radiation. At the start of radiation the quack said I would have a dose of the trots and prescribed two tablets a day of Sucrafate. I am sure one of the ingredients was super glue. When I saw the quack yesterday he told me that when I started my PSA [Prostate Specific Antigen] was 22 and it is now down to 0.03 which he was very pleased about. Enough of that. I am not a great believer in fate, but stranger things have happened.

They certainly have, Maestro, they certainly have.

Suketar, Nepal, November 1998.